HERBCRAFT

HERBCRAFT

THE CULTIVATION AND USE OF HERBS

by Nerys Purchon

illustrations by Dhenu Jennifer Clary

Hodder & Stoughton

SYDNEY AUCKLAND LONDON TORONTO

DEDICATION
To Nirala and Prakash
with love

ACKNOWLEDGEMENTS

There are many people who have been an invaluable help to me during the writing of this book. I have received information, advice, support and tolerance (the last very important during my many 'nervous' days). I give my love and thanks to Prakash, my husband, for all the years together; Dhenu, my friend and colleague, who lovingly and painstakingly produced the beautiful paintings and drawings; Nirala, someone very special, who was with me during all the farm adventures and who can always be relied upon; Fred Kraeter, a fount of knowledge, willingly shared, of all things pharmaceutical; Priya and Tony Martin, dear friends who carefully, and with humour, proofread my manuscript; Norm, my son-in-law, who produced a meticulous drawing and description of compost bins, compiled lists of gardening equipment and listened to my moans; Jane, my lovely daughter, who tested a lot of the skin care formulae even when she didn't have much time; Satyamo, a sensitive photographer and a good friend; my children who have survived my whims and grown into wonderful people; and to all herbalists throughout the ages without whose courage and persistence none of us would have the knowledge we have today.

First published in 1990
by Hodder & Stoughton (Australia) Pty Limited,
10-16 South Street, Rydalmere, NSW, 2116.

National Library of Australia Cataloguing-in-Publication entry

Purchon, Nerys.
Herbcraft.

Includes index.
ISBN 0 340 54194 6

1. Herb gardening - Australia. 2. Herbs - Australia - Therapeutic use. 3. Cookery (Herbs). I. Clary, Jennifer. II. Title.

635'. 7'0994

Designed by Christie & Eckermann, Art and Design Studio, Sydney
Edited by Jo Rudd
Typeset by Aaron Paul's Typesetting
Printed by Colorcraft, Hong Kong.

CONTENTS

INTRODUCTION

This book is the result of a lifetime of involvement with herbs. In my childhood it was an unconscious involvement as it was so much a part of my life that I didn't question it. Herbs were not plants which grew in gardens but were gathered from (and often used in) the wild as the need for them arose. I have realised that, quite accidentally, the chapters in this book have followed the pattern of my life so far:

Chapter 1 Learning about the herbs in my childhood and using meadows and hillsides as my pharmacy.

Chapter 2 Moving to a beautiful valley in west Australia and establishing terraced herb gardens which flourished in the chocolate loam, pure air and river water.

Chapter 3 Using the herbs as medicines for people who came to the farm looking for natural remedies.

Chapter 4 Beginning a skin and hair care cosmetic business using herbs and natural oils.

Chapter 5 Opening 'The Prancing Pony' restaurant where the emphasis was on herbs and fresh produce from the orchard and vegetable gardens.

We now live in a quiet street in a small city. We have three cats and two dachshunds who dig holes, fall in the pond and bask in the sun in the large herb garden. Shading the house from the fierce west Australian summer sun is the biggest Liquidambar tree I have ever seen.

I still make herbal mixtures and potions for healing, beautifying and cooking, run meditation, cooking and herb classes, take care of my garden and write. My five children are all grown up and away from home — this book has taken nine months to write and feels like my sixth child! All my life I have been supported and helped by family, friends and many talented people who have shared their knowledge so generously with me.

My husband has always been an enthusiastic partner in every venture, allowing packs to be spread on his face, building workshops, and going out on the road as a cosmetic salesman. As 'head waiter' in the restaurant he kept everything flowing smoothly and now helps me to use a computer as well as fulfilling a host of other roles. This book is a result of the support and generosity of all these people.

Note: The format of the recipes in this book may be unfamiliar to you. I devised this method many years ago and it has proved very popular. In the example below you will see that the recipe is read from left to right across the page instead of the conventional layout which reads down the page. The lines divide the process into easily understood sections. Each section is to be completed before moving on to the next. This method makes it almost impossible to miss an ingredient or to become confused over the instructions.

Tomato sauce

Onions, chopped	*2*	
Garlic cloves, crushed	*2*	Sauté together until soft.
Olive oil	*2 tablespoons*	
Tomatoes, canned	*440g (16oz)*	
Stock (see p220)	*1 cup*	Add, cook until thickened.
Tomato paste	*2 tablespoons*	

CHAPTER ONE

GETTING TO KNOW THE HERBS

The wholesome sage, and lavender still gray,
Ranke smelling rue, and cummin good for eyes,
The roses, reigning in the pride of May,
Sharp hishop, good for green woundes remedies.
Fair marigolds, and bee alluring thyme,
Sweet marjoram, and daysies in their prime,
Cool violets, and Alpine growing still,
Embalmed balm, and cheerful galingale,
Dull popie, and drink quickning setual,
Veyne-healing verven, and head purging dill,
Sound savorie, and basil harti-hale,
Fat coleworts, and comforting parsline,
Colde lettuce, and refreshing rosemarie,
And whatso else of vertue, good or ill,
Grew in this garden, fetched from far away,
Of everyone, he takes and tastes at will.

The Fate of the Butterfly **by Edmund Spenser**

The herbs described in the following pages have been chosen for several reasons.

1. Unlike many herb books, I have only included herbs which can be grown in most gardens. For reasons discussed below, I have restricted the herbs to just over sixty. This may not seem many when you consider the hundreds of different herbs available on this earth, but you will discover that there is, in fact, a herb included for everything you need. As with other things, quantity doesn't always mean quality. I have found it better to use fewer herbs with which you are totally familiar, than to get confused by using a large number which you never get to know and love. My grandmother used herbs which grew in the meadows, by the river and at the roadside. I doubt that she used even as many as I have included in this book but she was never at a loss when asked for help or advice. She would have been scornful and incredulous at the idea of buying herbs.

2. I have tried to use herbs which are reasonably available for you to grow yourself. It is sometimes quite a treasure hunt but, once you have established a connection with other herb growers by placing an advertisement in your local paper or by looking in the *Yellow Pages* or alternative lifestyle magazines, you will find it becomes easier to track down those elusive plants. The benefits to be derived from growing your own plants include knowing exactly how they were grown, dried and stored, and how old they are. Dried herbs exported from Europe are now likely to be contaminated with radioactive fallout.

This book provides an easy way for you to learn about every aspect of herbs. You can begin your collection in a small way, enlarging it as you become more confident. I have been teaching herbal medicine and the general use of herbs for many years and I find that students feel more confident with herbs they've grown themselves, and use them more efficiently.

There is something magical about planting a seed, then several weeks or months later using the plant to make a skin cream, a healing ointment or as a flavour in Mexican beans. You also have the satisfaction of knowing the whole life history of that plant and being sure that you are using the best, better than any shop-bought herb can be.

3. They are all basically very safe herbs. Where care needs to be exercised there is a caution at the end of the description. Herbs such as foxglove, aconite, arnica and many more have been omitted as they contain principles called 'alkaloids' and can cause death if not used in correct dosages by trained professionals. All herbs, however, need to be treated with respect. If a recipe or formula calls for one gram, two grams will *not* be better.

Record keeping

It's a good idea to have a loose-leaf folder separated into sections for 'Growing', 'Medicinal', 'Cosmetic' and 'Culinary'. These can have sub-sections; 'Culinary' for instance, might have 'Vitamins and Minerals', 'Teas' and 'Cooking' as separate parts. Every time you experiment, make careful notes about quantities, methods and results. This avoids those devastating times when you make something superb and can't remember what you used. I speak from bitter experience here. I have often cooked something which was enjoyed by everyone but which I was never able to repeat.

How plants are named

Some explanation is needed about the naming of plants. In the herb descriptions which follow, the layout is:

Common name	**Genus**	**Species**	**Family**
Borage	Borago	Officinalis	Boraginaceae
Parsley	Petroselinum	Crispum	Umbelliferae

Common Name

This is the name by which most people know a plant. It's also the name that I have used first in the headings so that you may find the herbs more easily. If you intend to make a serious study of herbs or use them in any of the many ways suggested in this book, you will need to learn the genus and the species names, as these are the only accurate way of identifying plants.

I don't know how many plants there are bearing the common name of 'All Heal'. Mrs Grieve (see Booklist) mentions three and I have heard of a couple more. Bruisewort and Colic Root are other examples of widely used names. I recently saw a punnet of plants in the nursery labelled 'Queen Anne's Lace', but when I looked at the Latin name it was something quite different from the herb used medicinally. Had I not known the Latin name I could have grown and used the plant with possible serious consequences.

Buy your plants or seeds from reputable sources and only if the label carries the Latin name.

Genus and Species

The genus and species names are usually used together, e.g. *Borago officinalis.* This system of naming is called the 'binomial system'. A genus is a group of lower rank than a family, and species are the different varieties within the genus. There are sometimes disagreements among botanists about these relationships. You will often see the name, shortened name or initial of the botanist who classified the plant added to the genus and species name, e.g. *Borago officinalis* (Linnaeus). The species name 'officinalis' means that the plant is recognised in the pharmacopoeia as having medicinal value.

Family

This is a group of plants having the same characteristics e.g.

Umbelliferae: With hollow stems.
Leaves: Alternate, deeply divided.
Flowers: Compound terminal or lateral umbels.
Stamens: Five alternating with petals.
Examples: Parsley, angelica, anise, caraway.

Labiatae: Having quadrangular stems.
Leaves: Opposite.
Flowers: Axillary cymes. Calyx five-toothed. Corolla usually forms two lips.
Ovary: Four-lobed, each containing one seed.
Examples: Catnep, marjoram, oregano.

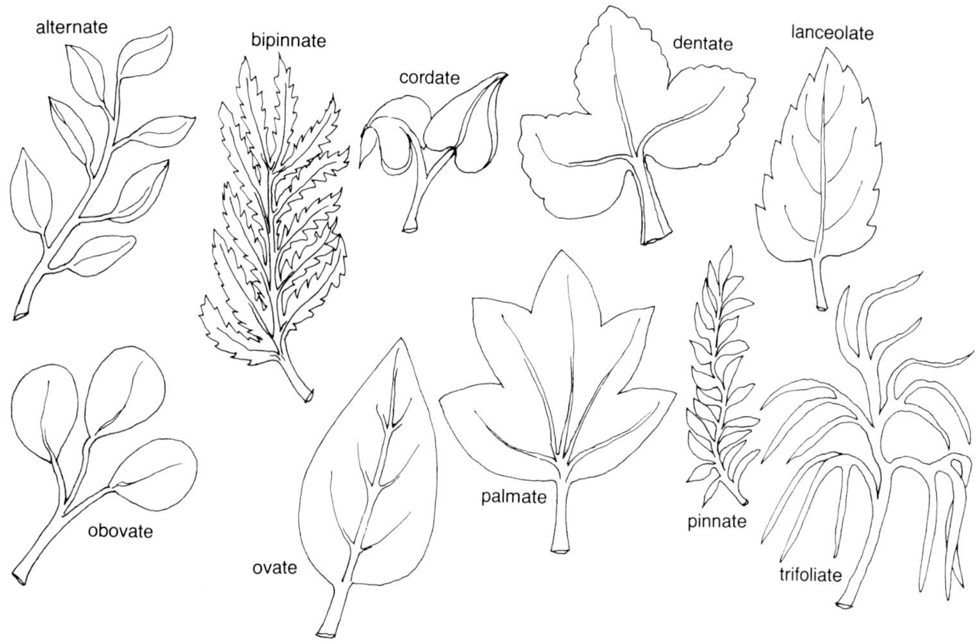

Leaf types

Glossary of botanic terms

Acid Soil, water etc, with a pH level below 7.0, indicating the absence of lime.
Acuminate Coming gradually to a point.
Acute Coming sharply to a point.
Alkaline Soil, water etc, with a pH above 7.0; can indicate the presence of lime.
Alternate Leaves coming one after the other by turns, alternating.
Annual Lasting or living for one year.
Anther Part of the flower that produces pollen.
Apex Tip or point.
Axil The angle between leaf or branch and stem.
Axillary Growing from an axil.
Axis The main stem or root, or the main line of growth.
Biennial A plant that fruits in its second year and then dies.
Bilabiate Having two lips.
Bipinnate Leaves which are doubly pinnate.
Blade The flat or expanded part of a leaf or petal.
Bract A small leaf that bears a flower in its axil.
Bulbil A small bud which may grow into an independent plant.
Calyx The outer covering of a flower; its separate petals are called sepals.
Cordate Heart-shaped.
Corolla The inner circle of petals.
Corymb A flat-topped cluster of flowers where the stalks are different lengths. The outer flowers are the first to open.
Cotyledon The first leaves produced by a seed, often different from the adult leaves.
Crenate Having rounded teeth between sharp notches.
Deciduous Plants which lose their leaves at the end of the growing season.
Dentate Sharply toothed or notched.
Dissected Cut in fine segments.
Dormancy The state of a plant which rests for a season; the growth above ground usually withers.
Entire A petal or leaf with no teeth or indentations.
Evergreen Plants that retain their leaves all year.
Filament The slender and threadlike stalk of a stamen.
Filiform Threadlike.
Floret A tiny flower, usually part of an inflorescence.
Glabrous Smooth and hairless.
Hardy A plant which can survive frosts; the opposite of tender.
Heel A small twig or branch, carefully torn away from the main stem. This will root very readily.
Inflorescence The flowering part of a plant; most generally used to describe a cluster of florets.
Lanceolate Wide at the base, tapering to a point.
Linear Long and very narrow with parallel sides.
Node The part of a stem from where leaves and side shoots grow. Sometimes nodes are slightly thicker than the rest of the stem.
Obovate Egg-shaped with the narrow end next to the base.
Obtuse Petals or leaves which are rounded or blunt.

Opposite Two leaves growing opposite to each other on a node.
Ovate Egg-shaped with the narrow end at the apex.
Palmate Hand-shaped.
Panicle A raceme whose branches are themselves racemes.
Pedicel The stalk of a single flower in a cluster.
Peduncle The stalk of an inflorescence or of a single flower.
Perennial A plant which lives for more than two years.
Petiole A stalk.
Pinna Single segment of a pinnate leaf.
Pinnate Shaped like a feather; two or more pinnae arranged on opposite sides of the petiole.
Pinnatifid Divided in a feathery fashion about halfway to the midrib.
Pistil The female reproductive organ of a flower.
Prostrate Growing along the ground.
Raceme A lengthened cluster of flowers growing in pedicels along part of the peduncle.
Rhizome A fleshy stem, usually underground, which grows both roots and shoots (e.g. couch grass).
Rosette A circular arrangement of leaves growing from a centre.
Runner Similar to rhizome, but growing above the ground horizontally.
Sepal A leaf of the calyx.
Sessile Having no stalk.
Spur A long, hollow, tubular projection from a sepal, containing nectar.
Stamen The male, pollen-bearing organ of a flower.
Stigma The tip of the pistil.
Stipules Small leaf-like appendages at the base of leafstalks.
Taproot A strong, single main root growing vertically downwards.
Trifoliate Having three leaves.
Tuber The fleshy storage part of a rootstock.
Umbel A semi flat-topped cluster of florets where the pedicels grow from a common point (e.g. fennel).

The herbs

Before you begin to read about the herbs, I would like to point out that any description of height and colour can only be general. There are many factors which determine the size and colour of a plant: the position in which it grows, the amount of water and fertiliser it gets and how happy it is. I have just measured a dandelion leaf in my garden and it is 37 cm (15 in) long. I also measured one from a dry piece of waste ground and it was 7 cm (3 in) long. The colours were different as well; mine was a softer green and had a much more tender leaf. I'm not saying that the wild one is inferior, only that it makes identification much more difficult if you are not aware of these potential differences.

ALFALFA *Medicago sativa* Family: Papilionaceae

Synonyms: Lucerne, purple medick.

Description: A perennial legume growing 30-90 cm (1-3 ft) in height. The leaves are bright green, succulent and trifoliate, the leaflets dentate and oblong, about 1 cm long. The flowers are violet and are borne in an inflorescence followed by hairy, spirally twisted pods.

Parts used: Whole herb.

Uses: Charts 1, 5, 6, 7, 13, 14, 15, 16.

Interest: This is a most nutritious herb for man and beast, a valuable source of complete protein and vitamin A. Each 100 grams of alfalfa contains about 8000 IU of vitamin A. This is more than apricots and about the same as beef. This vitamin is not affected to any great extent when the plant is dried. Alfalfa contains many other minerals and vitamins (see Chart 13), but has only recently been recognised as a valuable food for humans. Farmers have been feeding it to their stock for centuries without being aware that the animals were possibly eating better food than they were themselves. It's available in health food shops as seeds and in the supermarket as sprouts. As this is usually a field crop it's not really practical to grow it in your garden so I have included instructions on sprouting in the growing section in Chapter Two. It is a herb of great antiquity — I have heard that viable seed has been found in the pyramids.

Caution: Alfalfa contains 20,000-40,000 units per 100 grams of vitamin K1, which is a blood-clotting agent. This is normally a desirable vitamin as it reduces the risk of haemorrhage and seems to reduce blood pressure. However, if you are on medication to prevent blood clots forming, you should possibly avoid the use of this herb.

ALOE A. *Aloe vera* Family: Liliaceae
B. *Aloe arborescens*

Synonyms: A. Barbados aloe, Curacao aloe
B. Tree aloe

Description: A. *Aloe vera* reaches a height of about 60 cm (2 ft), growing straight from the soil with no stem as a rosette of thick, fleshy leaves, sometimes having pale creamy spots. The leaves are edged with spines, but they are not very sharp. The tall, annual flower head is a stalk bearing reddish-orange flowers.

B. *Aloe arborescens* grows tall. I have seen bushes as high as 3 m (10 ft) in the South West of Australia where I live. The leaves are narrower and have sharper spines than *Aloe vera*. I have never found much difference in the medicinal properties of the two aloes and use either or both depending on availability.

Part used: Pulp inside the leaves.

Uses: Charts 1, 5, 6, 8, 12.

ALFALFA

ALOE

Interest: This plant is amazingly drought resistant. I have seen aloe plants survive a long, hot Australian summer with no water at all. They look a bit sad and 'thin' by the end of the season but, as soon as the rains break, they become plump and juicy again. I am told that the aloe is planted on graves near Mecca. The Arabic name *saber* means patience, and patient this plant certainly is, as it waits on the graves of the faithful for resurrection day. It also waits in a dry corner of my garden for the autumn rain to fall.

ANGELICA *Angelica archangelica* Family: Umbelliferac

Synonyms: Garden angelica.

Description: A large, handsome, biennial plant growing to over 2 m (6 ft) in its second year. The stalk is round, grooved and hollow with a bluish cast. The lower leaves are very large and have serrated edges. The upper leaves are smaller. Large round flower heads are borne in umbels in the second year. The florets are greenish-white and the seeds which follow are pale brown. The seeds are viable for a very short time, maybe as little as two weeks. The whole of this plant has a most delicious flavour.

Parts used: The whole plant.

Uses: Charts 1, 5, 6, 7, 13, 14, 15, 16.

Interest: Angelica was (and maybe still is!) considered one of the most important herbs for witches' brews. A well known story tells of an old monk who dreamt that an angel visited him at a time when plague was sweeping through Europe. The angel told him to use the herb to cure the plague-smitten people, hence the name angelica.

Caution: Angelica must not be used by pregnant women as it is an emmenagogue. It should also be avoided by diabetics as it has been known to raise blood sugar levels.

ANISE *Pimpinella anisum* Family: Umbelliferae

Synonyms: Anise plant, aniseed, common anise.

Description: A dainty annual growing to about 60 cm (2 ft) high. The stem is ribbed and contains pith. The lower leaves are kidney-shaped, the upper are twice pinnate, feathery leaflets of bright green. The flowers are umbels of creamy white followed by grey-green, hairy, aromatic seeds. Care needs to be taken when identifying this plant as it is very similar to caraway in appearance. The seeds need a warm climate to ripen.

Parts used: Seeds.

Uses: Charts 1, 2, 3, 5, 6, 7, 12, 13, 14, 15, 16.

Interest: Aniseed is the main flavouring for pernod, anisette and ouzo. This plant has the reputation of being able to avert the evil eye. There appears to be confusion about the aniseed mentioned in the Bible — some authorities feel the plant in question was dill and not aniseed.

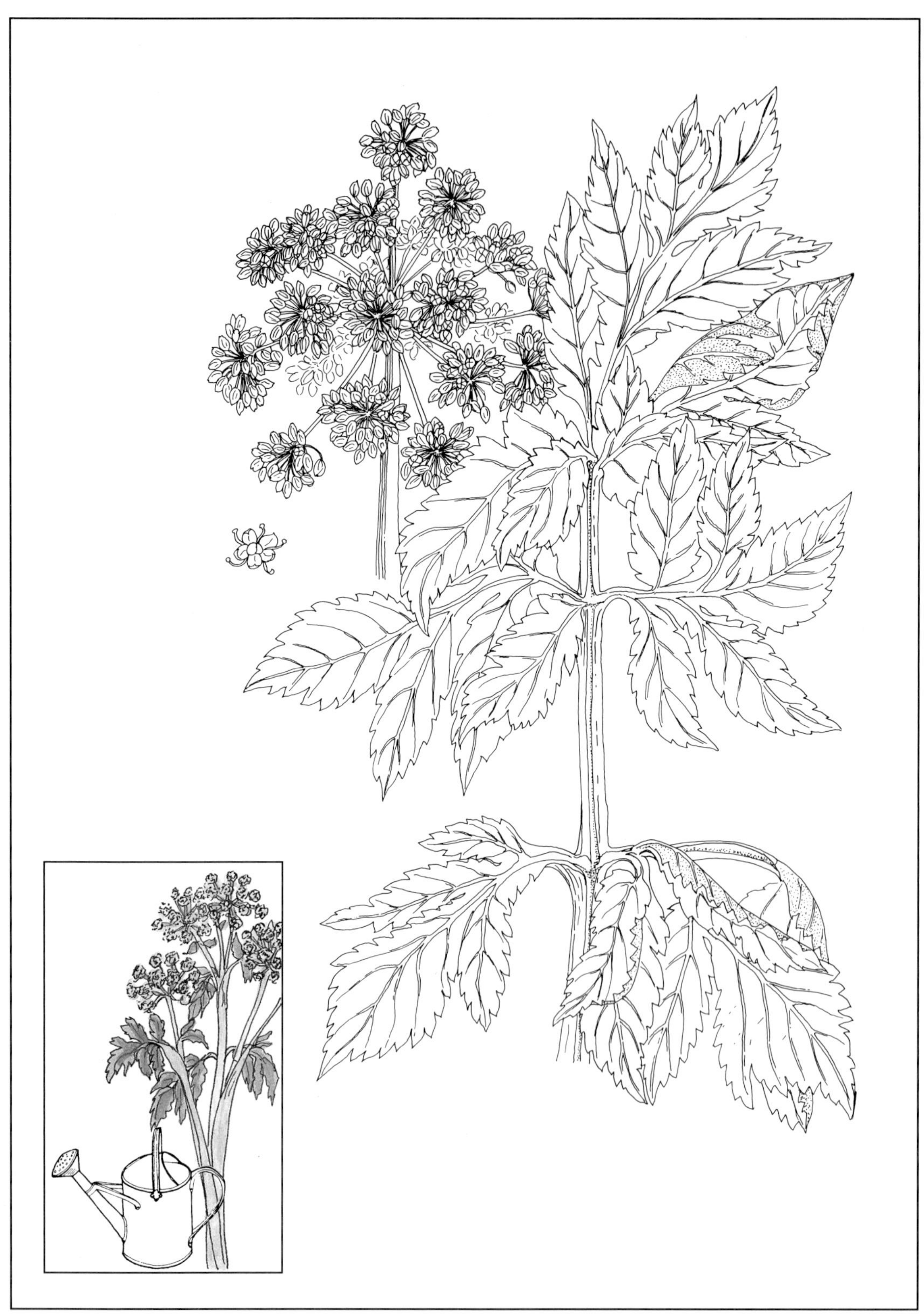

ANGELICA

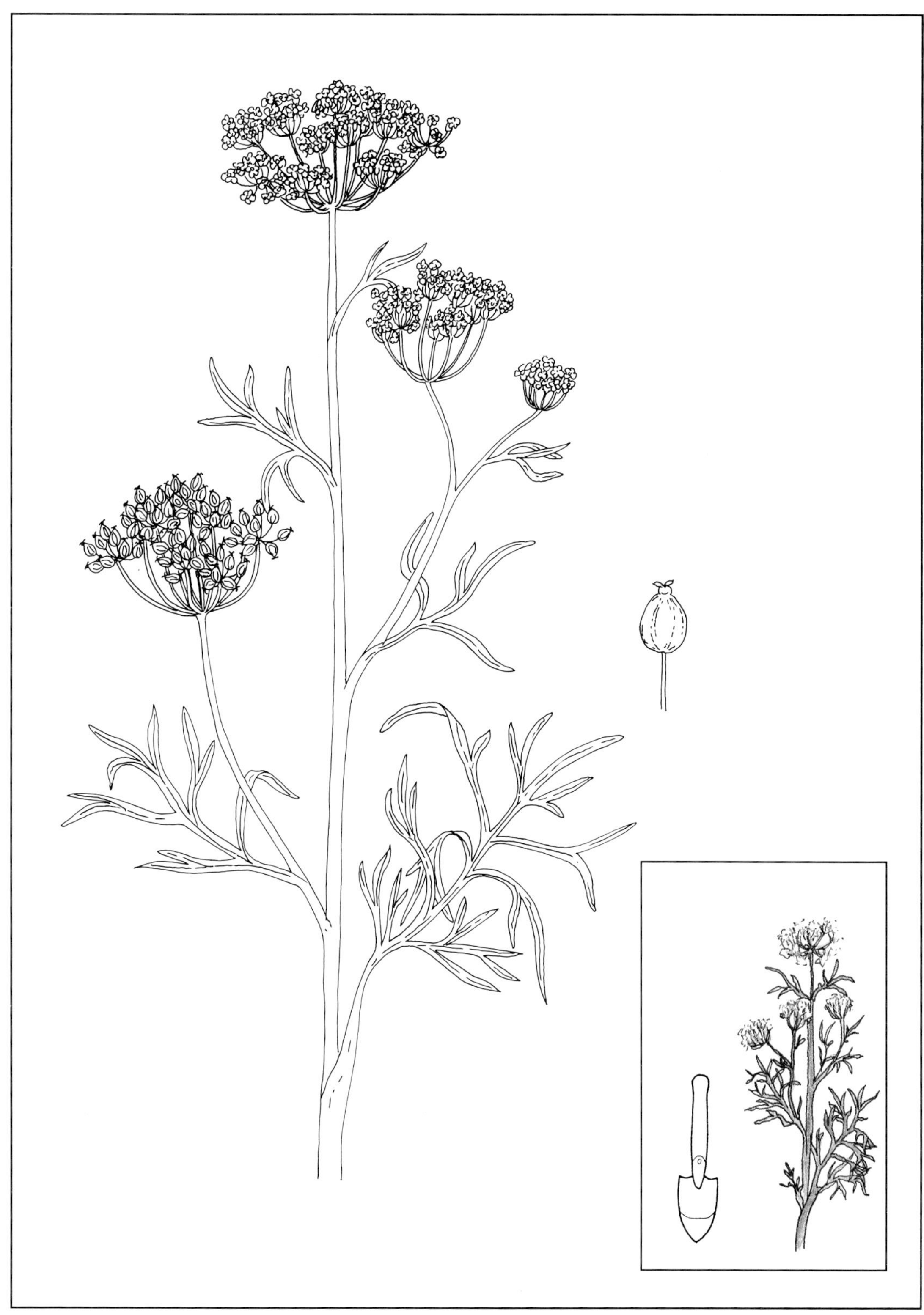

ANISE

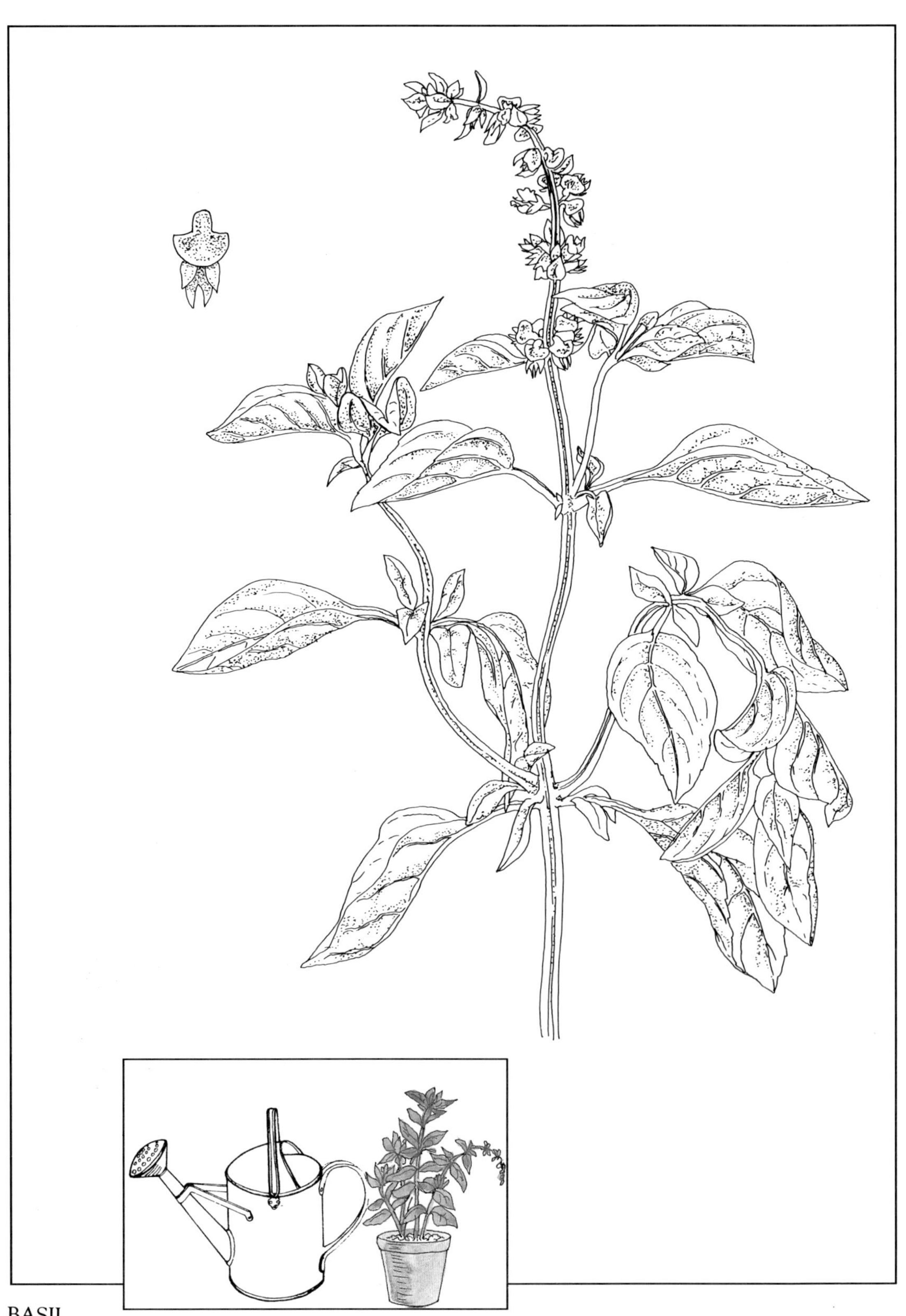

BASIL

BASIL *Ocimum basilicum* Family: Labiatae

Synonyms: Sweet basil, garden basil.

Description: A bushy annual plant growing to about 30 cm (12 in) high. The leaves vary from dark to light green, are smooth, opposite and can be entire or toothed. The flowers are white or pale lilac and labiate, occurring in whorls in the axils of the leaves. The scent of the plant when bruised is very strong and clove-like.

Parts used: Leaves.

Uses: Charts 1, 2, 3, 5, 6, 9, 11, 14, 15, 16.

Interest: This plant has often been called the king of all the herbs and the name could be derived from the Greek *basileus*, meaning king. Basil must surely be one of the most popular and familiar herbs. Even the most ignorant (herbwise, that is!) visitors to my garden will rush to the basil with cries of relief that at last there is something they have used and can identify. In India, from where it originated, basil is revered as a herb sacred to Vishnu and Krishna. The perfume of crushed basil certainly helps to sweeten and possibly disinfect germ-laden air. Another good reason for being fond of basil is the belief that by carrying it in your pocket you will always attract money!

BAY *Laurus nobilis* Family: Lauraceae

Synonyms: Sweet bay tree, true laurel, Roman laurel.

Description: In warm climates the bay tree can grow to a height of about 18 m (60 ft) but in cold regions is much smaller, looking more like a big shrub. The bark is smooth with an olive-green colour. The leaves are dark green, leathery and glossy. They are opposite and lanceolate, about 5 cm (2 in) long on a short stalk. The flowers are highly perfumed, creamy yellow clusters and are visited by lots of bees.

Parts used: Leaves.

Uses: Charts 1, 3, 5, 11, 12, 15.

Interest: A tree which carries many traditions in many cultures. The Greeks and Romans dedicated the bay to their gods of medicine, and in ancient times the leaves were made into wreaths to crown victors in sport and literature and on the battle field. The bay was grown to protect households against witches, warlocks and lightning strikes — woe betide the family if the bay tree died!

BERGAMOT *Monarda didyma* Family: Rustaceae

Synonyms: Bee balm, Oswego tea.

Description: A most attractive perennial growing to medium height, about 60 cm (2 ft). The stem is square, stiff and hairy, bearing opposite, ovate, serrate leaves which are greyish-green and rather rough. The whorled, bilabiate,

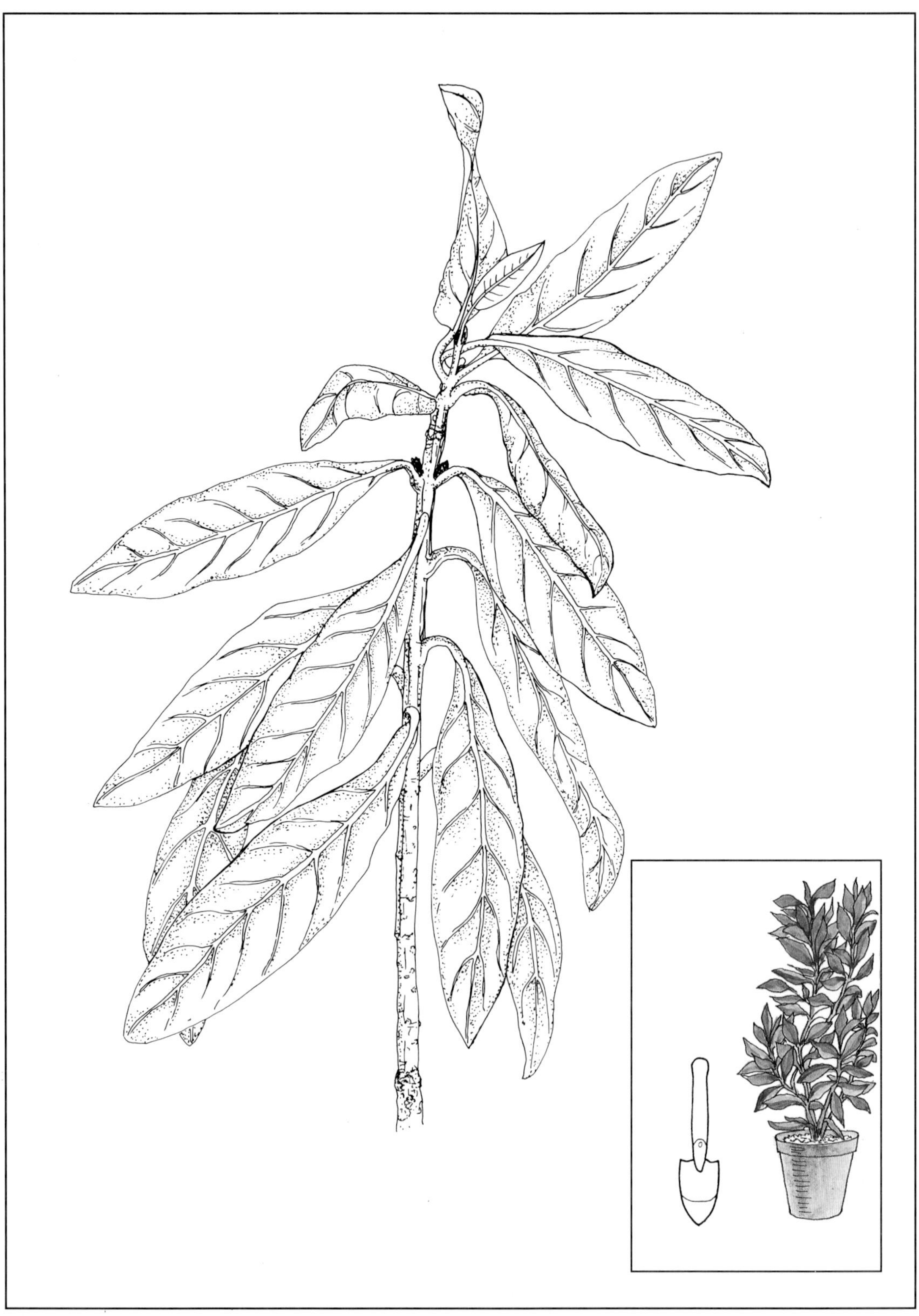

BAY

BERGAMOT

	scarlet flower heads are borne singly at the end of the stem and are supported by pale green leafy bracts. The whole plant has a delicious fragrance and is loved by bees.
Parts used:	Flowers, leaves.
Uses:	Charts 1, 5, 9, 12, 14, 15, 16.
Interest:	The Oswego Indians of North America are said to have used this plant as a tea — hence the synonym. Another story tells of the time in America when British tea was subject to a boycott and bergamot tea was drunk as a very acceptable substitute.

BORAGE	*Borago officinalis*	Family: Boraginaceae
Synonym:	Burrage.	
Description:	An annual which self-seeds so readily that it can take over the entire garden unless kept under control. Borage grows to about 60 cm (2 ft) high. The whole plant is very hairy, stems many-branched and hollow. The leaves are large, grey-green, oval and pointed. The borage flower is exquisite, bright blue and starlike, with very prominent black anthers growing from the centre. The flowers hang down, so to see them at their best plant them on a bank or wall where you can look up at them.	
Parts used:	Leaves and flowers.	
Uses:	Charts 1, 2, 3, 5, 6, 10, 12, 14, 15, 16.	
Interest:	The flowers and leaves have a reputation for cooling any liquid in which they are steeped. I have never tested this in any scientific way, but I frequently float the flowers in a jug of water or lemonade because they look so lovely and add a delicate cucumber flavour to the drink. This plant has always been known as the 'herb of courage'; ladies would embroider the dainty blue flowers on the jerkins of knights about to embark upon the crusades.	
Caution:	The sharp hairs on the leaves and stems can cause throat and stomach problems. Any preparation used internally needs to be carefully strained.	

CALENDULA	*Calendula officinalis*	Family: Compositae
Synonyms:	Marigold, pot marigold.	
Description:	An annual familiar to everyone with its bright flowers ranging from yellow to vivid orange. The pale green leaves are alternate, slightly hairy and entire or dentate with very widely spaced teeth.	
Parts used:	Leaves and flowers.	
Uses:	Charts 1, 2, 3, 4, 5, 6, 8, 10, 11, 12, 13, 14, 15, 16.	
Interest:	This is *the* herb to take as an ointment or tincture in your car or on expeditions of any sort. It is a fine healer for burns, cuts and lacerations. We had frequent dramas when we lived on the farm — axes slipping when chopping wood, blisters raised from over-enthusiastic gardening, rocks falling on feet and leaving bad grazes. The immediate treatment for	

BORAGE

CALENDULA

these and many other injuries was to apply calendula tincture if there was haemorrhage, and ointment if it was a graze. On every occasion the wound healed quickly, with no sepsis and no scarring. It has been said that the hybridised calendula can't be used in the same way but I would dispute this. I have used both the single and the new double varieties and find them to be equally efficient.

Caution: There is a plant called African marigold which mustn't be confused with the calendula. The African marigold is quite different in appearance and is used as a companion plant.

CARAWAY *Carum carvi* Family: Umbelliferae

Synonym: Caraway seed.

Description: A medium-sized biennial growing 40-60 cm (1½-2 ft) high. The stem is furrowed and hollow. It bears finely cut, feathery, bi- or tri-pinnate leaves and summer-borne umbels of white flowers. The seeds are crescent-shaped, dark brown and have five distinct ridges.

Parts used: Seeds.

Uses: Charts 1, 3, 5, 6, 12, 14, 15, 16.

Interest: There are records of caraway having been in use for more than 5000 years. It is one of the most ancient of all herbs and one of the best known today. Legend would have us believe that if caraway seeds were made into a potion and fed to straying husbands, they would mend their ways and become faithful. I have heard that pigeon fanciers use the seed in the mash of homing pigeons, so maybe there is some truth in the old legend!

CATNEP *Nepeta cataria* Family: Labiatae

Synonyms: Catnip, catrup, field balm.

Description: A perennial, medium-sized, shrubby plant growing to about 60 cm (2 ft) in height. The branching stems are square, erect and hairy. The leaves are cordate and pointed, with scalloped edges. The whole plant is covered in a fine, soft whitish down, particularly on the underside of the leaves. The bilabiate flowers are whitish with lilac spots and grow in whorls on spikes. They bloom from midsummer until winter.

Parts used: The whole herb.

Uses: Charts 1, 3, 5, 6, 7, 11, 12, 13, 14.

Interest: Even the most docile, aged and dignified cat goes quite silly when it smells bruised catnep. I have seen very superior cats lying on their backs, flapping their paws in the air in ecstasy as they roll on the newly transplanted herb, usually destroying it in the process. Catnep self-seeds so readily that you very rarely need to transplant it. "If you set it, the cats will eat it. If you sow it, the cats won't know it."

Caution: In large doses this herb is an emetic. However, it is one of the best herbs for children if used as directed.

CARAWAY

CATNEP

CAYENNE.

CAYENNE *Capsicum minimum* Family: Solanaceae

Synonyms: Bird pepper, capsicum, chilli pepper, red pepper.

Description: A perennial reaching 60-90 cm (2-3 ft) tall. It is best treated as an annual in order to grow the best fruit. It has a smooth, glabrous stem which branches out towards the top. The leaves are bright green, shiny, ovate, entire and petioled. The flowers, which are small and white, have a drooping habit and grow either in groups of three or singly. The many-seeded fruit, which is ovate and long, changes from green to red as it ripens.

Parts used: Fresh or dried fruit.

Uses: Charts 1, 4, 5, 6, 8, 15, 16.

Interest: The name is derived from the Greek word *kapto,* meaning 'I bite', and is well named as it is pungent and fiery. Cayenne is a valuable source of vitamin C.

Caution: Overuse can cause gastroenteritis and damage to the digestive tract. Be very careful when handling fresh chillies as the oil can create severe burns or blisters. I wear rubber gloves if I'm preparing a large quantity or use a fork to hold the chilli if I'm just doing one or two.

CHAMOMILES A. *Anthemis nobilis* Family: Compositae
B. *Matricaria chamomilla*

Synonyms: A. True chamomile, maythen, manzanilla, Roman chamomile.
B. Wild chamomile, German chamomile.

Description: A. True chamomile is a low-growing creeping perennial. The leaves are alternate, bipinnate and feathery in appearance. The flower heads grow singly on stalks which are erect and up to 30 cm (12 in) tall. The flowers are similar to small daisies with solid, cushion-like centres. The whole plant smells of apples when bruised.

B. Wild chamomile is an annual with foliage similar in appearance to true chamomile but coarser. The flowers have hollow centres, only one row of florets and are smaller than those of true chamomile. The plant is rather straggly and untidy-looking; it grows to a height of about 60 cm (2 ft). It has a less intense but still distinctive apple aroma.

Parts used: Flowers (both varieties).

Uses: Charts 1, 2, 3, 4, 5, 6, 7, 8, 9, 10, 11, 12, 13, 14.

Interest: To the Anglo Saxons of England, chamomile was one of their 'nine sacred herbs'. The others were mugwort, plantain, watercress, nettle, crabapple, fennel, chervil and a ninth herb which has never been identified. A country name for chamomile is 'herb of humility' as it seems to like being walked on. There is a variety of chamomile used for making lawns, the most famous of which is at Buckingham Palace. There is an old English saying: "The chamomile shall teach the patience that rises best when trodden most upon." Another name is 'herb doctor', as it benefits sick or ailing plants growing near to it. If you water your seedlings with weak chamomile tea the anti-fungal properties will prevent 'damping off' (see p122).

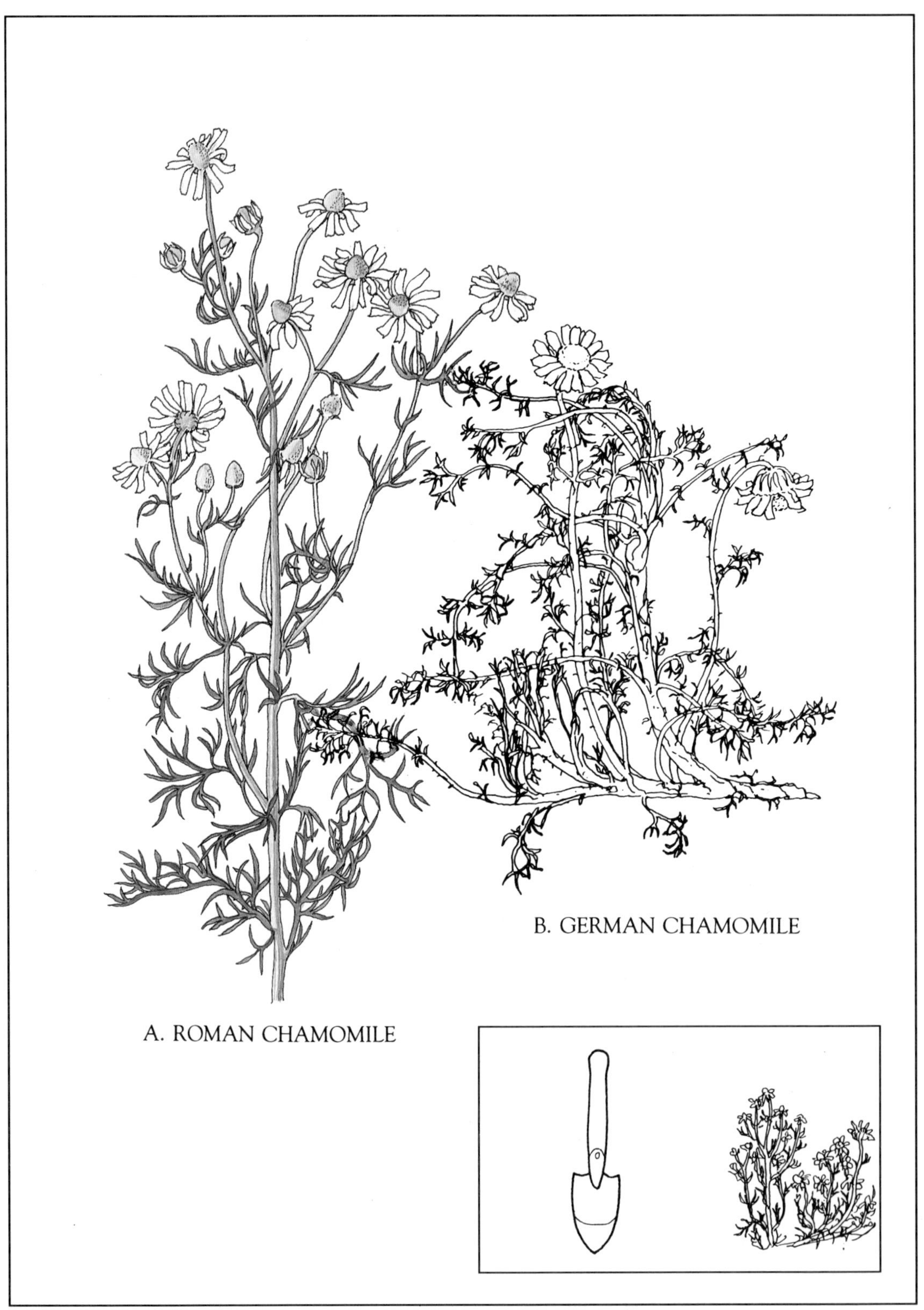
B. GERMAN CHAMOMILE
A. ROMAN CHAMOMILE

Caution: Chamomiles are members of the ragwort family, and ragwort has been known to produce severe allergic reaction in some individuals. Treat this plant with care at first, especially if you know that you suffer from plant-related allergies.

CHIVES *Allium schoenoprasum* Family: Liliaceae

Synonym: Cives.

Description: A hardy perennial growing as a cluster of bulbs. The leaves are hollow, cylindrical, green and spearlike. A lavender cluster of florets grows like a pompom on a single stem. The whole plant rarely exceeds 20-30 cm (8-12 in) in height. If the flower head is nipped off the leaves grow much more luxuriously.

Parts used: Leaves.

Uses: Charts 1, 2, 3, 5, 15, 16.

Interest: Chives is another very ancient herb — there are records of its use by the Chinese dating back 5000 years. They are most satisfactory plants as they grow easily both in and out of doors, have very pretty flowers and would be ideal as one of the plants your children could grow to begin their own herb gardens. Unless you are growing chives for their floral display, cut the flower stalks off as they appear or the plant becomes weakened.

COMFREY *Symphytum officinale* Family: Boraginaceae

Synonyms: Knitbone, knitback, boneset, bruisewort, gum plant.

Description: A leafy perennial growing as tall as 90 cm (3 ft) under good conditions. The rootstock is very brittle, blackish on the outside, white and fleshy on the inside. The juice in the root is sticky. The stem is hollow, angular and very hairy. The leaves are hairy, oblong and lanceolate, some petioled and some sessile. They are very large at the base of the plant and decrease in size further up the stem. The stem is terminated by clusters of pale pink, pale yellow or pale mauve flowers which are drooping in habit. Comfrey is the only plant I know that will tolerate fresh manure and thrive.

Parts used: Root and leaves.

Uses: Charts 1, 4, 5, 6, 8, 10, 11, 12, 13.

Interest: There is so much written about comfrey that it seems an insult to devote only a few lines to this herb. Those interested in knowing more should get hold of a book called *Comfrey Report* by Lawrence Hills. The myths and legends surrounding comfrey are many. I like the following extract very much but don't know how much credence I can place on it!

CHIVES

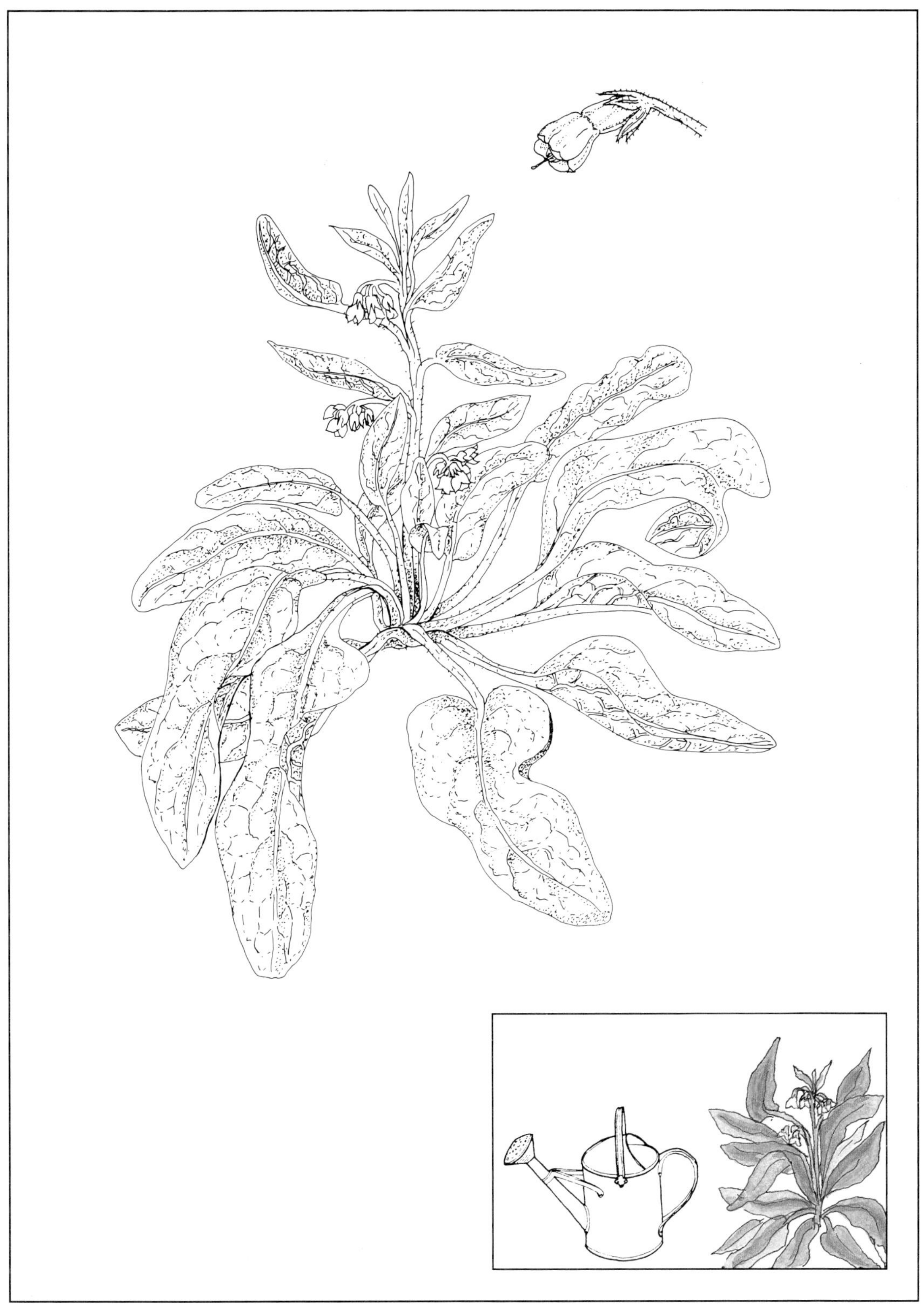

COMFREY

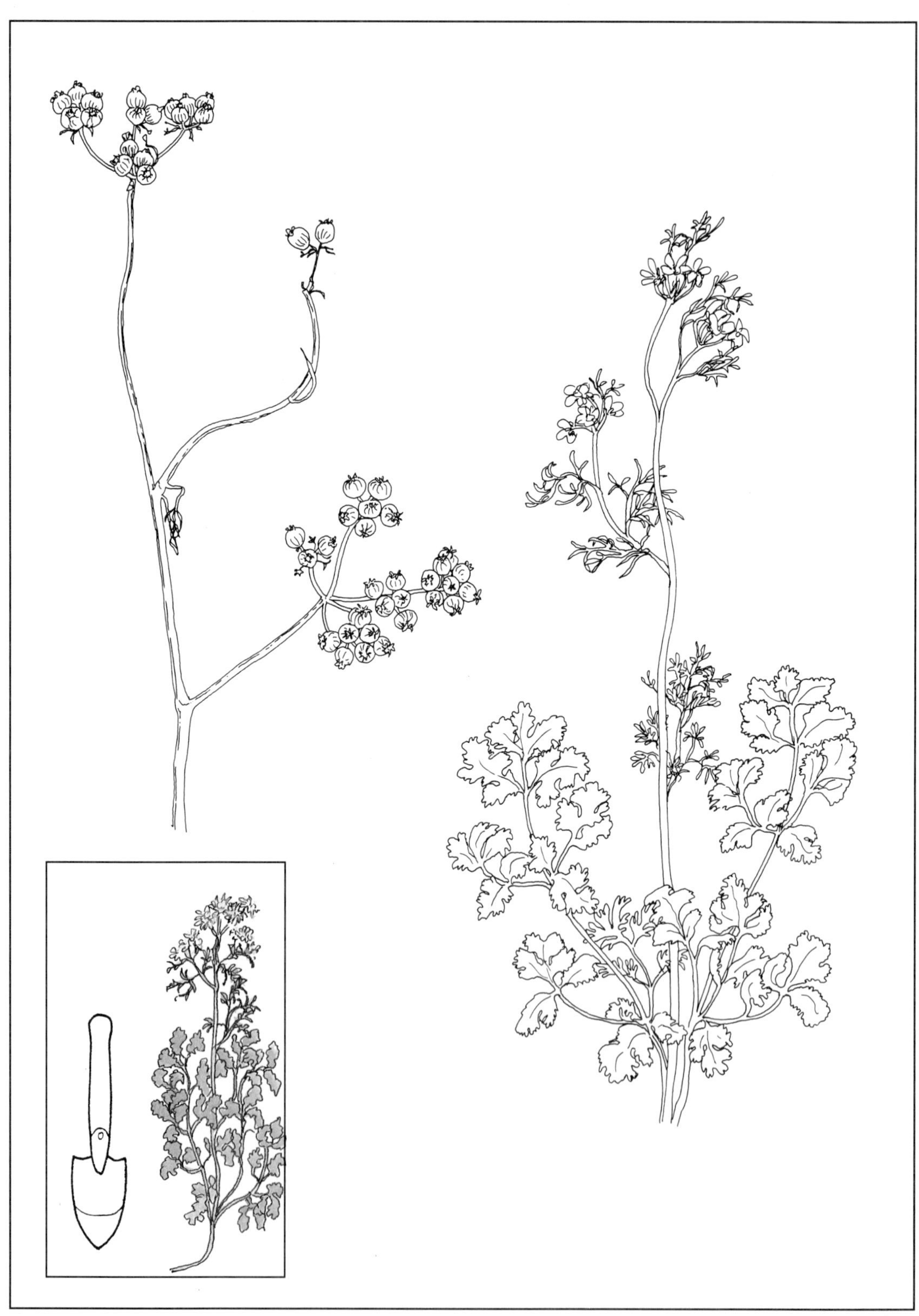

CORIANDER

The rootes of comfrey, stamped, and the juice drunke with wine, helpeth those that spit bloud, and healeth all inward wounds and bruising. The same bruised and laide to in a manner of a plaister, doth heale all fresh and greene wounds, and are so glutinative, that it will sodder or glew togither meate that is chopt in peeces seething in a pot, and make it in one lumpe.

John Gerard, *The Herball,* 1597

Caution: The advisability of using comfrey internally has been questioned by some researchers in the past few years. The research is by no means conclusive and is ongoing, but until further reports are released it may be wise to restrict internal use of this plant. One of the findings was based on tests of dried comfrey leaves fed to rats in large quantities: perforation of the stomach wall was reported. However, perforation of any body lining will take place with threads of a certain length (such as those found in comfrey). Asbestosis is another example of perforation caused by threads.

Further study is being conducted into the possibility of the constituent, symphytine, being a carcinogen. It's not clear from the report whether the symphytine was isolated before tests were conducted. Active constituents often appear to behave differently or become more dangerous when isolated.

CORIANDER *Coriandrum sativum* Family: Umbelliferae

Synonyms: Dizzicorn, Chinese parsley, cilantro.

Description: An annual, growing 30-60 cm (1-2 ft) high. The stem is many-branched and erect, bearing bright green leaves which are stalked and pinnate, and upper leaves which are finely dissected. The flowers are delicate umbels in shades ranging from pink to mauve. The seeds turn from green to a pale beige colour as they ripen, and the rather rancid smell of the underipe seed changes to a warm, aromatic, spicy odour.

Parts used: Leaves and seeds.

Uses: Charts 1, 2, 3, 5, 9, 14, 15.

Interest: Coriander seems to have originated in the East, but when I smell that wonderfully warm, spicy aroma from either the leaves or the seed my mouth begins to water and I have visions of Mexican food. I disliked the taste and smell of the leaves intensely until Dhenu (the illustrator of this book) came back from Texas bringing with her lots of genuine Mexican recipes. She persuaded me to persevere with coriander leaves as they were a vital ingredient in the food. Sure enough, my resistance dropped and now this is one of my favourite culinary herbs.

In the Arabian story, *The Thousand and One Nights,* coriander is said to have aphrodisiac qualities. It is also documented as having been used in love potions during the Middle Ages.

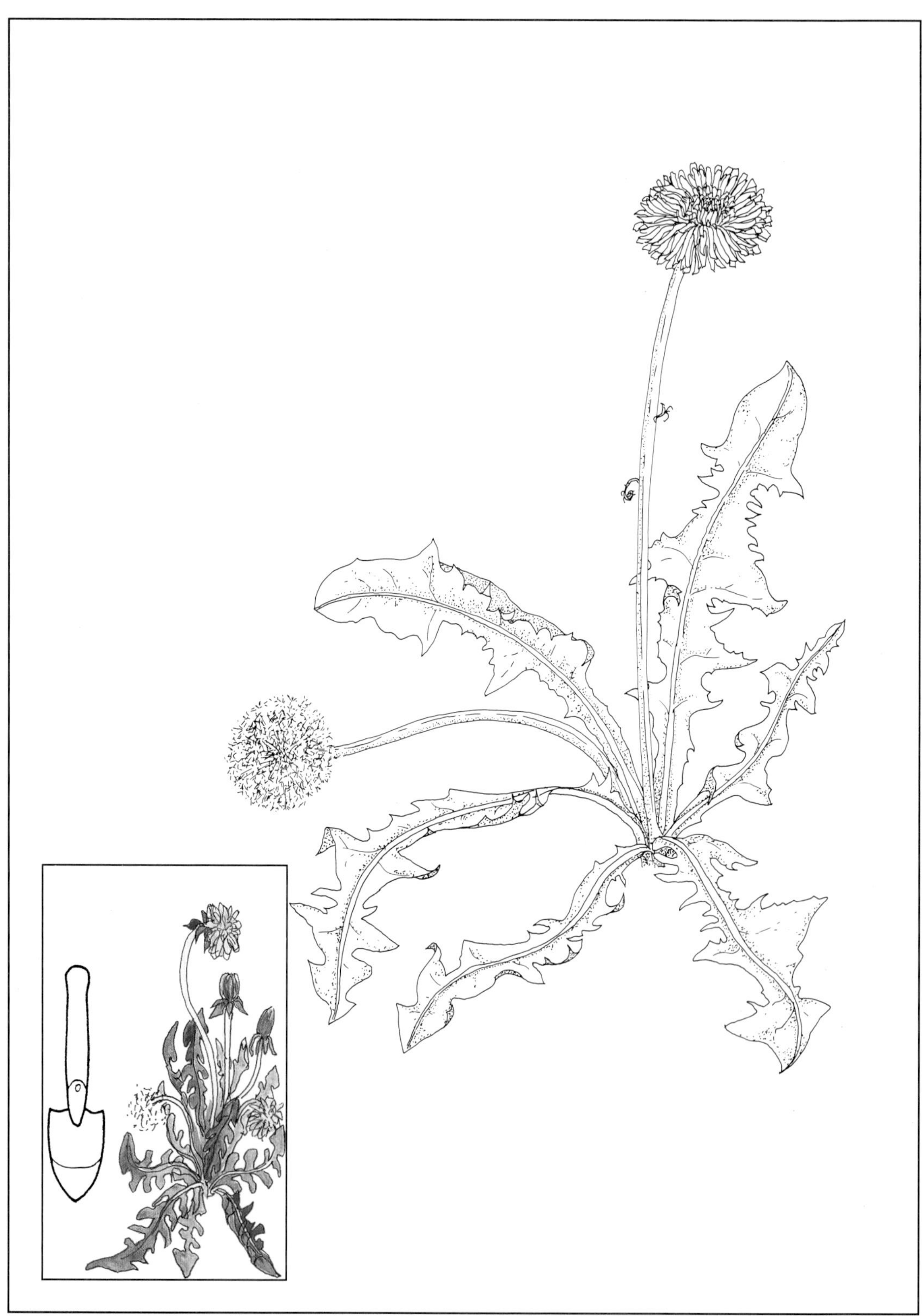

DANDELION

DANDELION *Taraxacum officinale* Family: Compositae

Synonyms: Blowball, swine's snout, priest's crown, timetable.

Description: A perennial with a thick, juicy root, black on the outside and white inside. The pale green, hairless leaves are oblong, irregularly dentate and rise directly out of the root. A single smooth flower stem also rises from the root. It is hollow and ends in a single flower head. Each flower is a collection of golden petals which turn into a white, downy, 'puffball' head of seeds. The stem, when snapped, exudes a white 'milk'.

I find that people have more trouble identifying the dandelion than any other herb. One of the first things I do in my herb classes is to ask my students to bring in a dandelion. They very rarely deliver the right herb. I usually end up with a mixed bunch of catsear *(Hypochoeris radicata)* and capeweed *(Arctotheca calendula)*. So don't forget to look for the hollow stem and single flower on each stem.

Parts used: Root and leaves.

Uses: Charts 1, 5, 6, 12, 13, 16.

Interest: Dandelion is often called a Royal Herb and is one of my most used herbs. It is a powerhouse of goodness. All down the ages, the dandelion has been revered as a 'cure all', so think twice before you weed it out of your garden. As a child I looked forward to the spring with mixed feelings. The best which would happen was dandelion and burdock wine, fizzy and delicious — I well remember the stone bottles standing to cool on the slate floor of the larder. The worst was the daily dose of sulphur and molasses — yuk! The idea of both these was a 'spring clean' for our insides after a long Welsh winter. They certainly seemed to work as I was a very healthy child.

DILL *Anethum graveolens* Family: Umbelliferae

Synonyms: Dill seed, benth, fructus anethi, dill weed.

Description: An annual, growing to a height of 30-60 cm (1-2 ft). The stem is smooth and upright. The leaves are similar in appearance to fennel, being bipinnate, but are a darker green and much smaller. The flowers are small and yellow, borne on flat umbels from midsummer onwards. The seeds which succeed the flowers are oval, flat, ribbed and light brown in colour.

Parts used: Leaves and seeds.

Uses: Charts 1, 2, 3, 5, 7, 14, 15, 16.

Interest: Dill water must surely be known to every mother who has had a 'colicky' baby. Its properties of being able to 'bring up the wind' are such a blessing to sore tummies. Dill is often confused with fennel. The main differences between these two plants are the shape of the seed and the fact that fennel usually grows several stems from one root, while I have never seen more than one stem rising from a dill root. It wouldn't be

DILL

such a disaster if you mistakenly used one plant instead of the other as they are both very mild and have a similar action.

Dill was once considered to be a protection against witches. Michael Drayton, a sixteenth century poet, wrote in his poem *Nymphidia:*

Therewith her Vervain and Dill
That hindereth Witches of their will.

ELDER — *Sambucus nigra* — Family: Caprifoliaceae

Synonyms: Black elder, European elder, German elder.

Description: A large bush which can grow to about 6 m (20 ft) given the right conditions. The leaves are borne on rough grey stems and are large, opposite and pinnate. The flower heads are large, creamy white umbels of sweet-smelling flowers, followed (if you're lucky) by drooping bunches of purple berries. The fruiting doesn't seem as reliable in Australia as it is in Britain.

Parts used: Leaves, flowers, berries, bark.

Uses: Charts 1, 3, 5, 6, 7, 11, 12, 14.

Interest: It would be possible to fill a small book with folklore about the elder. My children and grandchildren are always impressed when told they need to ask permission from the Elder Mother before taking any part of her tree or she will punish them severely! Another story is that if you make a cradle from elder wood, the fairies will steal your baby and leave a fairy baby in its place. I have never seen a fairy baby but I understand they are exceptionally ugly and very bad-tempered, so it really doesn't seem worth taking the risk.

FENNEL — *Foeniculum vulgare* — Family: Umbelliferae

Synonyms: Sweet fennel, wild fennel.

Description: A most handsome perennial, graceful and feathery. Fennel is an ornament to any garden. The stems are strong, tubular and bright green and grow to a height of about 1-2 m (3-6 ft). The leaves grow from sheaths which surround the stem; they are filiform and similar to dill but much larger. The flower heads are flat umbels of bright yellow florets blooming from late spring onwards. The seeds are slightly curved and greyish-green in colour, becoming brown when dried.

Parts used: Leaves, seeds, roots.

Uses: Charts 1, 2, 3, 5, 6, 7, 9, 12, 13, 14, 15, 16.

Interest: Many of the ancient writers mention the slimming properties of fennel as it seems to be an appetite depressant. I have chewed the seeds to keep

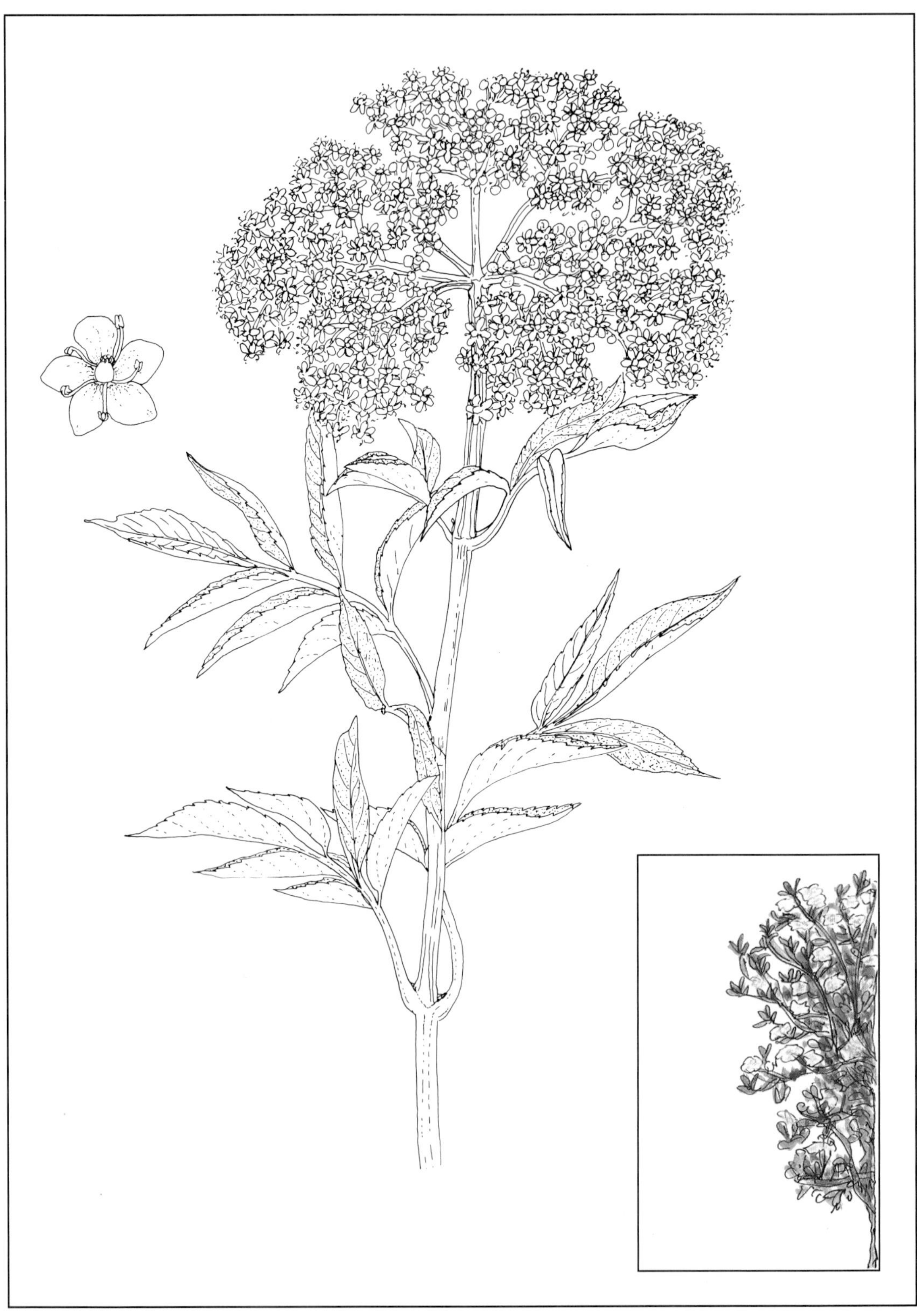

ELDER

FENNEL

hunger pangs at bay and it works very well. Fennel is one of the 'nine sacred herbs' (see chamomile).

Above the lower plants it towers,
The Fennel with its golden flowers;
And in an earlier age than ours
Was gifted with the wondrous powers
Lost vision to restore.

Longfellow

FEVERFEW *Pyrethrum parthenium* Family: Compositae

Synonyms: Featherfew, featherfoil, flirtwort.

Description: A hardy perennial growing 60-80 cm (24-32 in) tall. The leaves are a light golden green, alternate, bipinnate and borne on a leafy, many-branched stem. The flowers are daisy-like with yellow centres and white rays with toothed edges. The plant self-seeds very easily and is an attractive addition to any garden.

Parts used: Whole herb.

Uses: Charts 1, 3, 5, 6.

Interest: Here's a beauty! According to some old herbals, feverfew heals best if gathered with the *left* hand while speaking the name of the sick person, but under no circumstances must you look behind you while performing this ritual.

The name 'feverfew' seems to have been derived from the word *febrifuge*, which is descriptive of the herb's properties. It is an old 'cottage' herb which served as an ornament in the garden and appears to have been used as a whole pharmacy on its own. It was bound to the wrist to protect the wearer from plague, and used for bites of mad dogs, opium addiction and 'young women inclined to hysteria'. These are a few uses from a formidable list.

Caution: The dose must not be exceeded as excessive use can cause vomiting and diarrhoea. In rare cases, chewing the leaf can cause mouth ulcers.

GARLIC *Allium sativum* Family: Liliaceae

Synonyms: Poor man's treacle, clove garlic.

Description: A hardy perennial which grows to about 30 cm (12 in) high. It has long, green, straplike leaves growing from leaf sheaths up the unbranched stem. The flower head topping the stem is a globular umbel comprising small white florets and bulbils, held together by a leaf-shaped skin. The bulb is the most important part of the plant, both for cooking and medicinally. This is at the base of the plant with the stem growing from

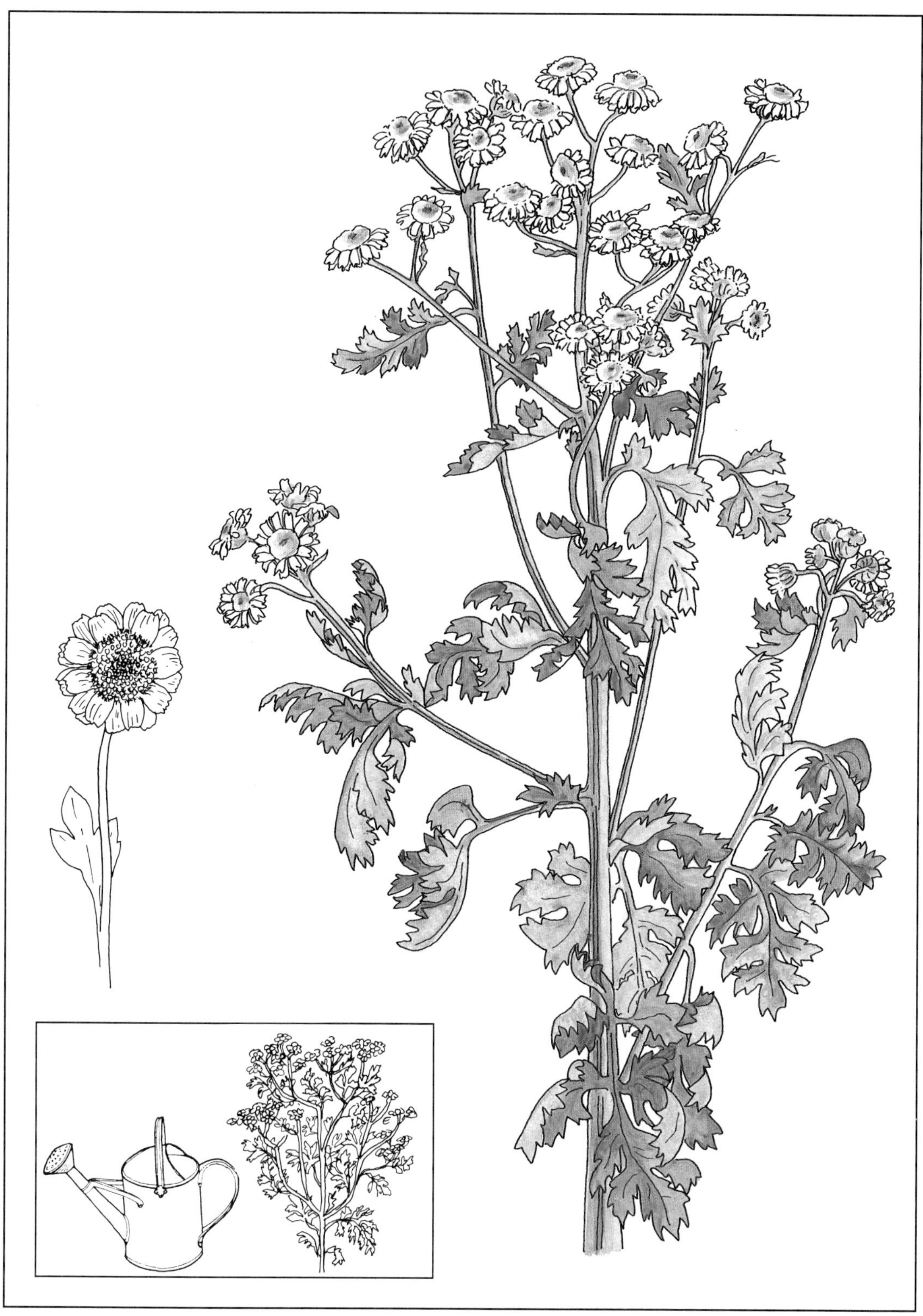

FEVERFEW

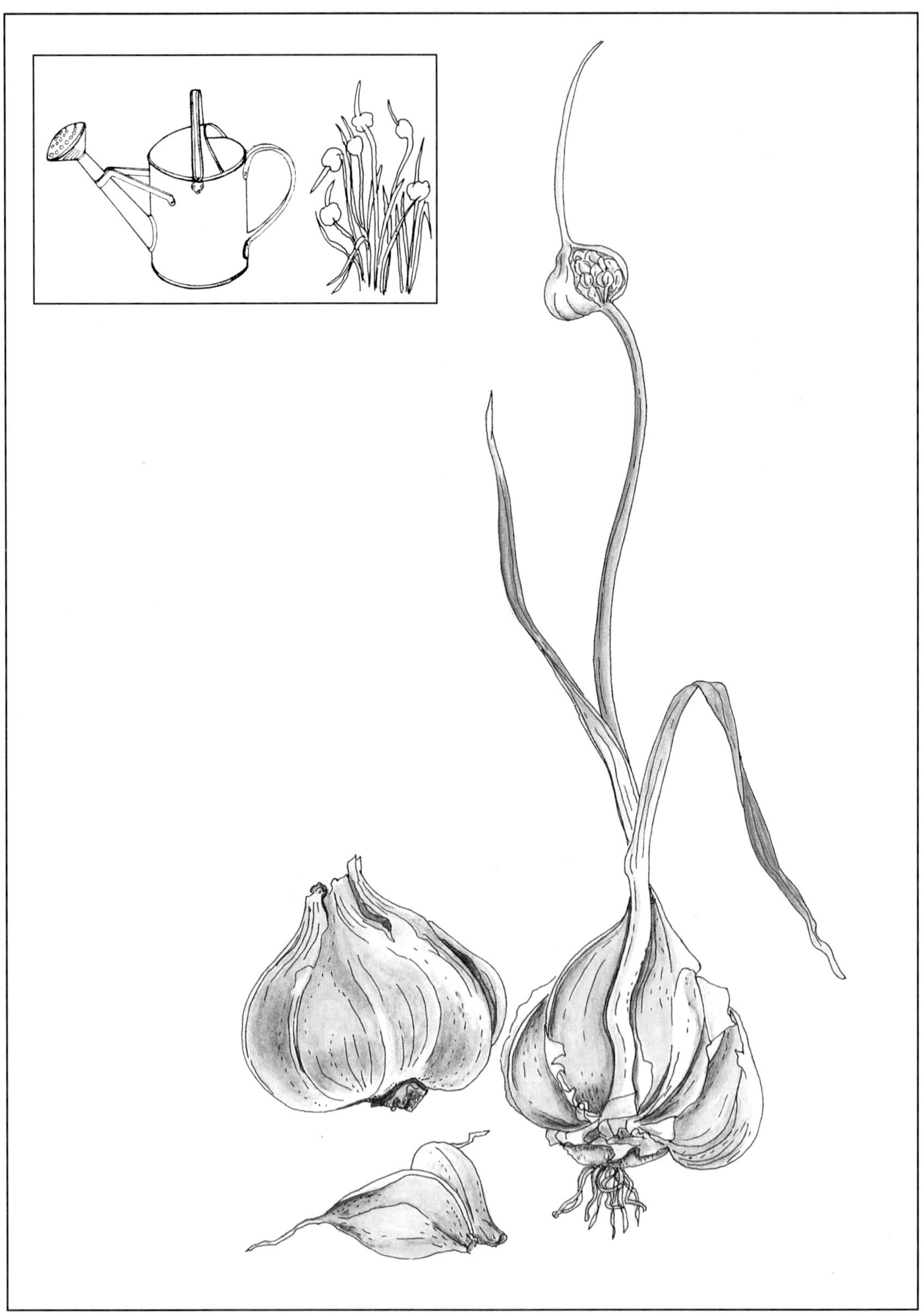

GARLIC

its centre, and is made up of a number of cloves or bulblets enclosed in a paperlike skin.

Parts used: Bulb.

Uses: Charts 1, 2, 3, 4, 5, 6, 7, 8, 13, 15, 16.

Interest: There are many references to the protective qualities of garlic, one suggesting that a clove worn on a string around the neck will protect you from harm, especially by vampires. My theory is that you would smell so bad nobody would want to get close enough to damage you! I would hasten to add, however, that garlic is one of my most trusted herbs and I certainly wouldn't let the smell stop me using it. I think the myth came into being because of the great number of ailments which can be cured or alleviated by the use of garlic. Used on a daily basis it becomes a first-rate prophylactic.

Caution: Children need to be introduced very slowly to garlic. It's much better to use it in their food than to give extracts, which may cause problems in the young.

GINGER *Zingiber officinalis* Family: Zingiberaceae

Synonyms: Race ginger, African ginger.

Description: A perennial plant with a fibrous, knotted root which is thick and highly aromatic. The simple, reed-like stem grows to about 1 m (3 ft) high. The leaves are narrow and lanceolate, 15-30 cm (6-12 in) in length, and grow from sheaths on the stem. The yellowish-white flowers grow on spikes coming straight from the root. The root needs to be 12 months old before use. Unless you are living in the tropics or sub-tropics you won't be able to grow this plant without the use of a heated greenhouse or conservatory.

Parts used: Root.

Uses: Charts 1, 4, 5, 6, 7, 8, 14, 15, 16.

Interest: Ginger has been a favourite for many centuries as a culinary and medicinal herb. It was mentioned by Confucius 500 years before Christ, and is still used widely today in both Chinese and Western herbal medicine. It was one of the expensive and valuable trading spices. You will find a recipe for preserving ginger root on p244.

HORSERADISH Armoracia rusticana Family: Cruciferae

Synonyms: Spoonwort, red cole, mountain radish.

Description: A hardy perennial, very robust with a large, fleshy, pungent root. The basal leaves are green to yellowish-green, very large and shiny, lanceolate with

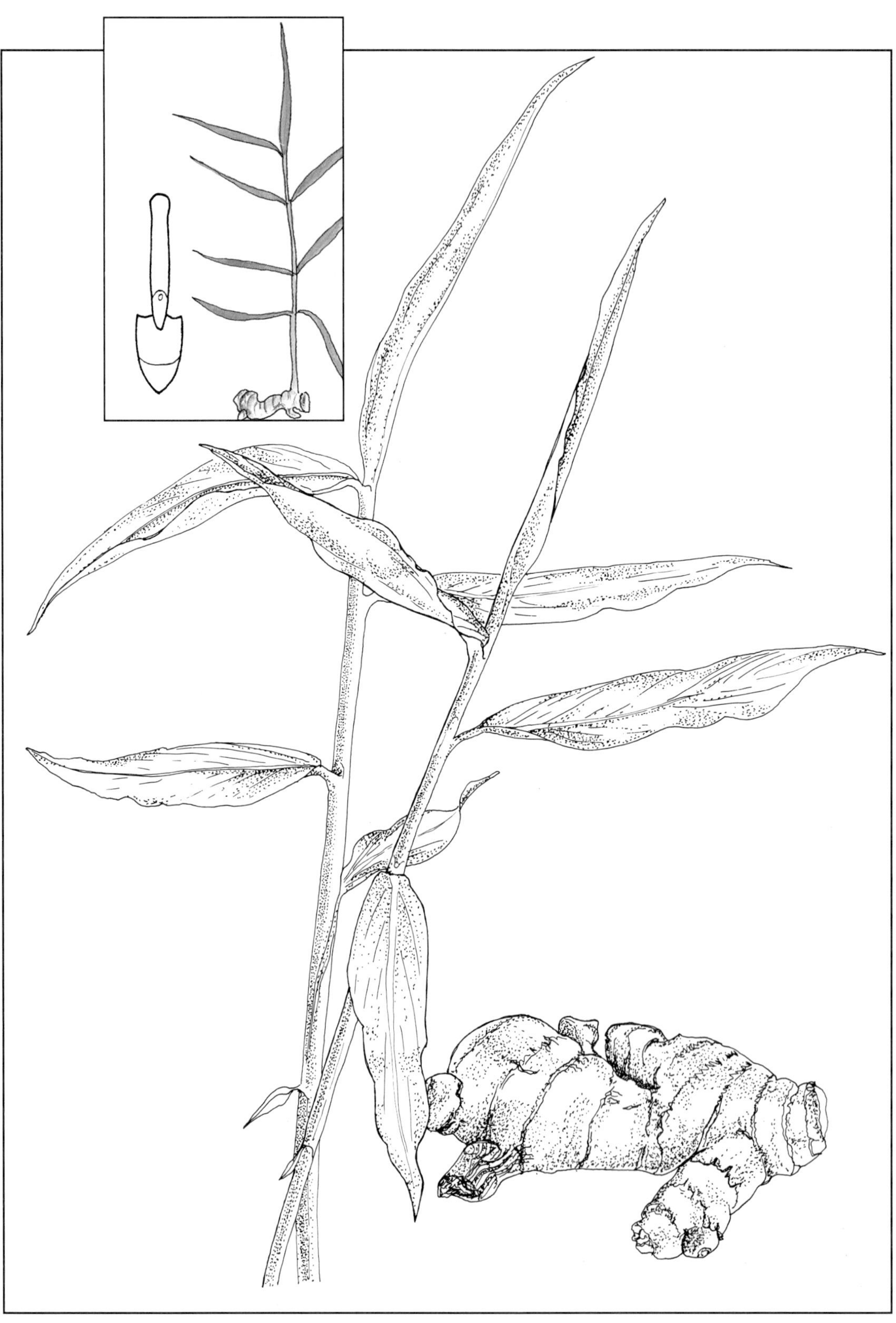

GINGER

HORSERADISH

wavy edges. As the leaves grow up the stem they become much smaller. In its second year a 60-90 cm (2-3 ft) stem grows from the root. On this, the panicles of white, scented flowers are borne. The root is very invasive.

Parts used: Root.

Uses: Charts 1, 2, 3, 5, 6, 12, 15, 16.

Interest: While living on the farm we grew lots of horseradish. One day we lifted a huge amount of the roots and began to process them but the incredibly pungent fumes made our eyes stream so we hit upon the idea of wearing diving masks. Of course, we were caught by visitors, adding further to our reputation for eccentricity. You will find a recipe for horseradish cream on page 239.

Caution: Horseradish can act as an emetic if used in large amounts.

HYSSOP *Hyssopus officinalis* Family: Labiatae

Description: A perennial which can grow to 90 cm (3 ft) under the right conditions. The whole plant is bushy, with square, woody stems and opposite, linear leaves of dark green, which have a sweet scent when bruised. The flowers are pink, blue or white, growing in whorls in the axils.

Parts used: Whole herb.

Uses: Charts 1, 2, 3, 4, 5, 6, 7, 15.

Interest: The name is derived from the Greek *azob* or *ezob,* meaning a holy herb, as it was used as an infusion for cleansing rites in holy places. There seems to be considerable confusion regarding the hyssop mentioned in the Bible — some scholars maintain that the herb was not *Hyssopus* but either caper or oregano.

LANDCRESS See **WATERCRESS.**

LAVENDER *Lavandula officinalis* Family: Labiatae

Description: There are nearly 30 known species of lavender. The one most commonly cultivated for its precious oil is *vera,* now known as *angustifolia.* This is a 60-90 cm (2-3 ft) plant with many straight, four-sided stems. The leaves are greyish-green, opposite, sessile, lanceolate and covered with soft, downy hairs. The lilac flowers borne in clusters or whorls at the top of long spikes are characteristically bilabiate. There are other lavenders which are worth cultivating: *Lavendula spica* or spike lavender, a similar but coarser looking plant, the oil of which is not as powerful as the *vera; Lavendula dentata* which, as the name suggests, has a dentate leaf. This

HYSSOP

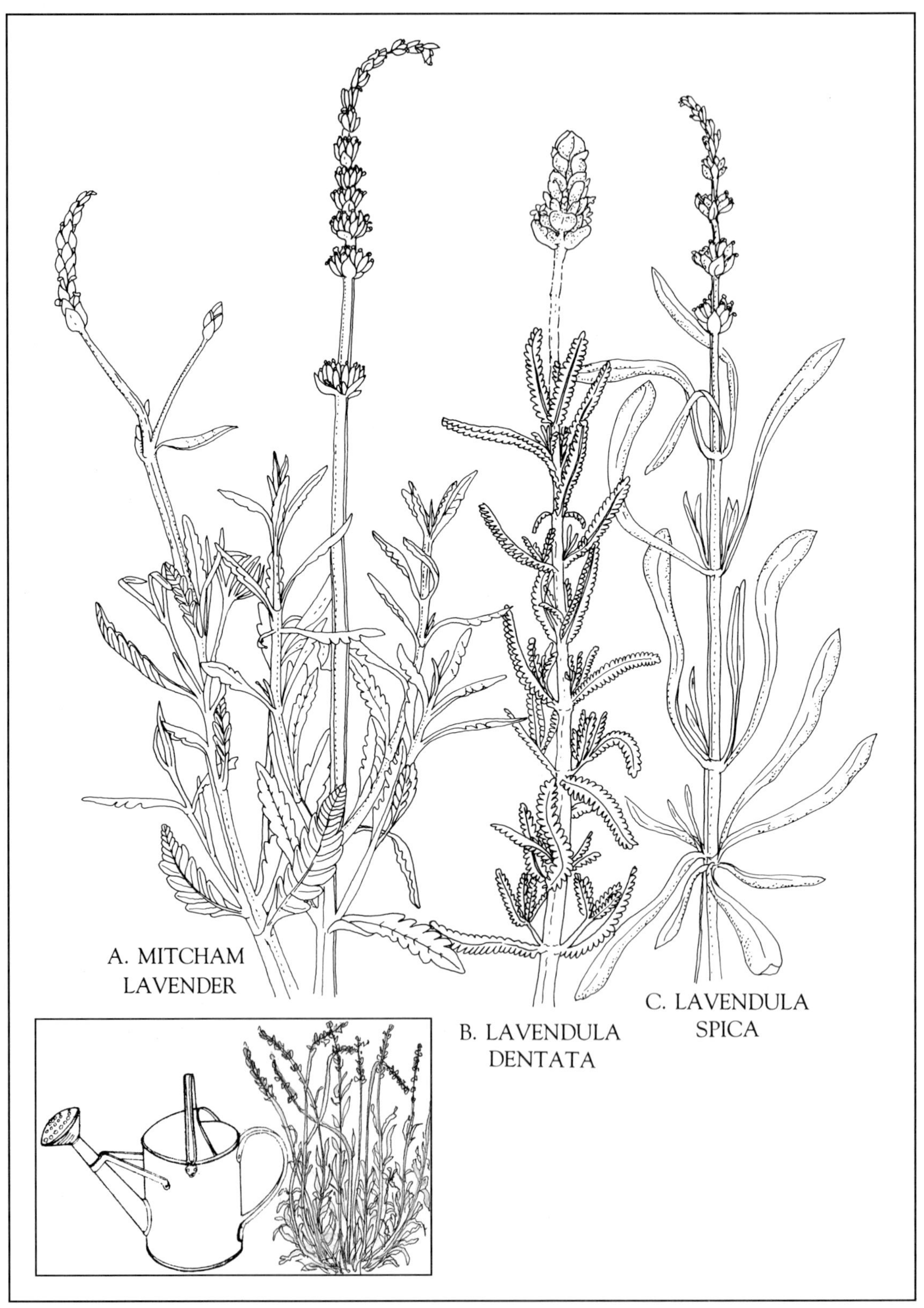
A. MITCHAM
LAVENDER
B. LAVENDULA
DENTATA
C. LAVENDULA
SPICA

grows into quite a large shrub and is useful for hedging, provided it's pruned each year after flowering to prevent it from becoming bare and woody at the base.

My favourite lavender is *Lavendula allardi* or *mitcham*. This is not always an easy lavender to obtain but it's worth persevering as it has the benefits of the other lavenders in one plant. It can grow up to about 150 cm (5 ft). The flower heads are long and borne on tall spikes. The leaves are grey-green, long and dentate, looking like a cross between the French and English lavenders which, in fact, I believe them to be.

Parts used: Flowers, leaves.

Uses: Charts 1, 2, 3, 5, 6, 8, 9, 10, 11, 12.

Interest: There is an old belief that if you want to remain chaste and virginal you must dry lavender flowers and sprinkle them upon your head. I rarely use lavender as an internal remedy but it has many external uses and to me the scent of lavender alone would make it worth growing and using in the home. The following extract from Izaak Walton's book *The Compleat Angler* says it all.

Good master, let us go to that house, for the linen looks white and smells of lavender, and I love to lie in a pair of sheets that smell so.

LEMON BALM *Melissa officinalis* Family: Labiatae

Synonyms: Balm, honeyplant, bee balm.

Description: A medium-sized perennial growing 60-90 cm (2-3 ft) tall. The stem is branched, square and somewhat hairy. The leaves are opposite, light green, ovate and serrated. The small, white, labiate flowers grow from the axils in small bunches. The plant is loved by bees.

Parts used: Whole herb.

Uses: Charts 1, 3, 5, 7, 10, 11, 12, 13, 14, 15, 16.

Interest: The name 'Melissa' is derived from the Greek name for bee. There are many records both ancient and modern which suggest planting lemon balm near to beehives and also rubbing the inside of the hive with leaves to keep the bees happy. To quote Gerard's *Herball* (1597): "It is profitably planted where bees are kept. The hives of bees being rubbed with the leaves of bawme, causeth the bees to keep together, and causeth others to come with them."

This is another herb suitable for children as it is mild, gentle and delicious.

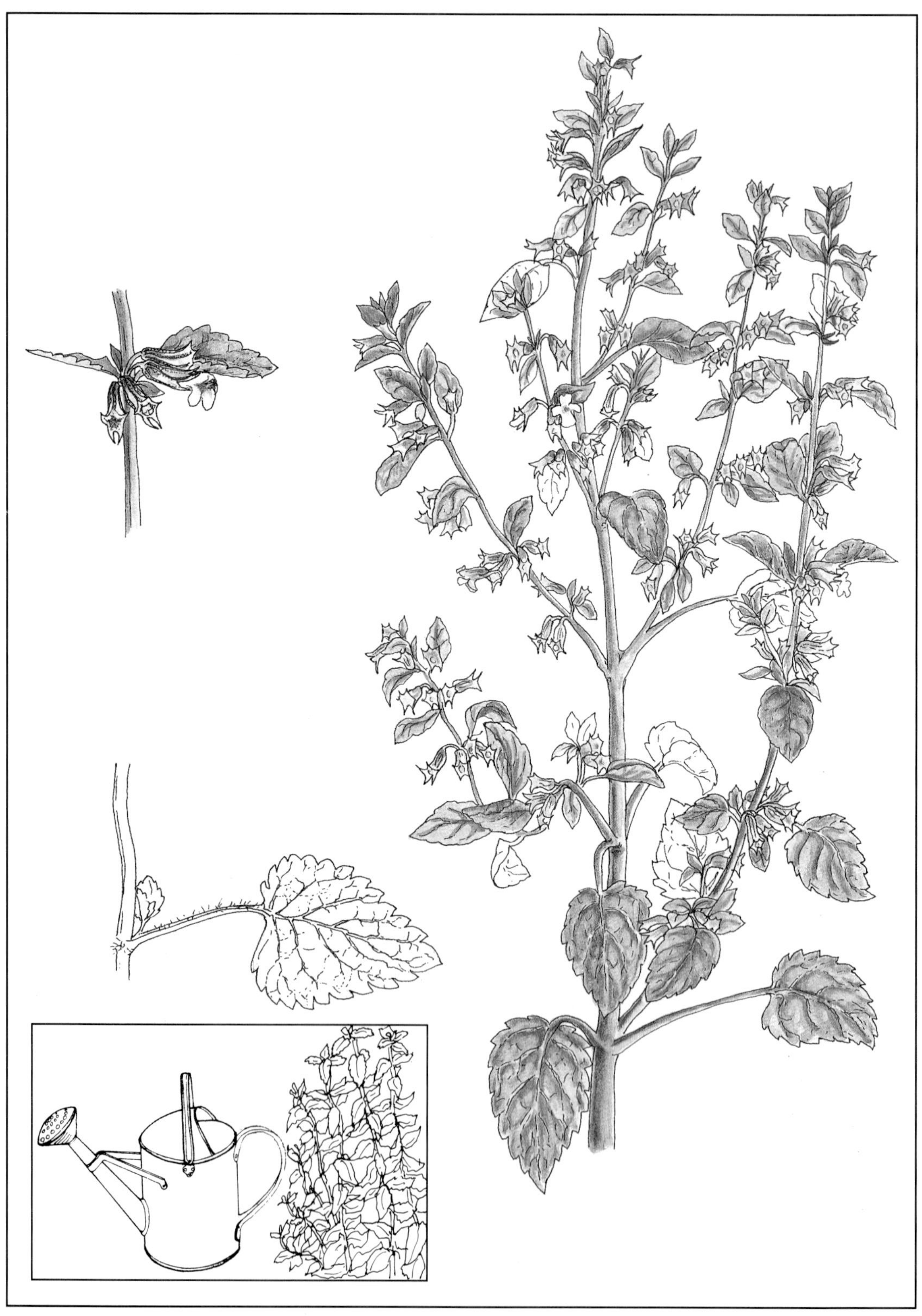

LEMON BALM

LEMON GRASS

LEMON GRASS *Cymbopogon citratus* Family: Graminacae

Description: A semi-hardy perennial which grows in clumps to about 1 m (3 ft) in height. The leaves grow from the base, are pale green and reed-like. This plant doesn't like its feet to be either cold or dry. It dies back in winter, becoming quite straggly and sad looking and is one of the last plants to 'get going' in spring. I believe this plant grows a flowering stem in its native habitat. I've been growing it in South West Australia, which is a sub-tropical area, for 14 years and have never seen it flower so I can't comment on the appearance or seed-setting properties.

Parts used: Leaves.

Uses: Charts 1, 3, 5, 7, 9, 11, 12, 14, 15.

Interest: There are very few records of this plant other than its being Asian in origin. The whole base of leaves is used as seasoning in Thai dishes, especially peanut and saté sauces, and is removed after cooking. I find it a good herb for children, for refreshing drinks and for ornamental value in the garden. I have it growing by my garden pond where it looks very much at home with its tall, reed-like leaves reflected in the water. I am always interested in hearing from people who have experiences to relate with this and other herbs.

LIQUORICE *Glycyrrhiza glabra* Family: Leguminosae

Synonyms: Licorice root, sweet licorice.

Description: A perennial plant, growing very slowly in its first two years, then spreading rapidly. I believe it can reach a height of 2 m (6 ft) tall but have never seen it this height myself. The roots, which are the important part of this plant, are made up of two parts, the first being long, brown, cylindrical and many-branched. The second comprises horizontal rhizomes which run just below the ground and throw up shoots, causing the plant to spread over a large area. Both these types of root are used. From the roots rise many stems which are round at the base, becoming more angular further up. The leaflets are dark green and graceful, borne in 3-7 opposite pairs on a midrib growing from the stem. At night, these leaflets hang down on either side of the midrib. The flowers are borne in racemes growing from the leaf axils and can be mauve, pale blue or yellowish in colour.

Parts used: Root.

Uses: Charts 1, 5, 6, 7.

Interest: I hesitated about including liquorice in this book. I use the root in two forms. One is the extract, which I buy from a pharmacy, as extraction is a complex process that can only be done easily by factories set up for this use. The second form is the root dried and ground into a powder or chopped. This process can be done at home but, as the root is best harvested at the beginning of its fourth year, you would have a long wait; it is much quicker to buy it from your local health food store. It's an

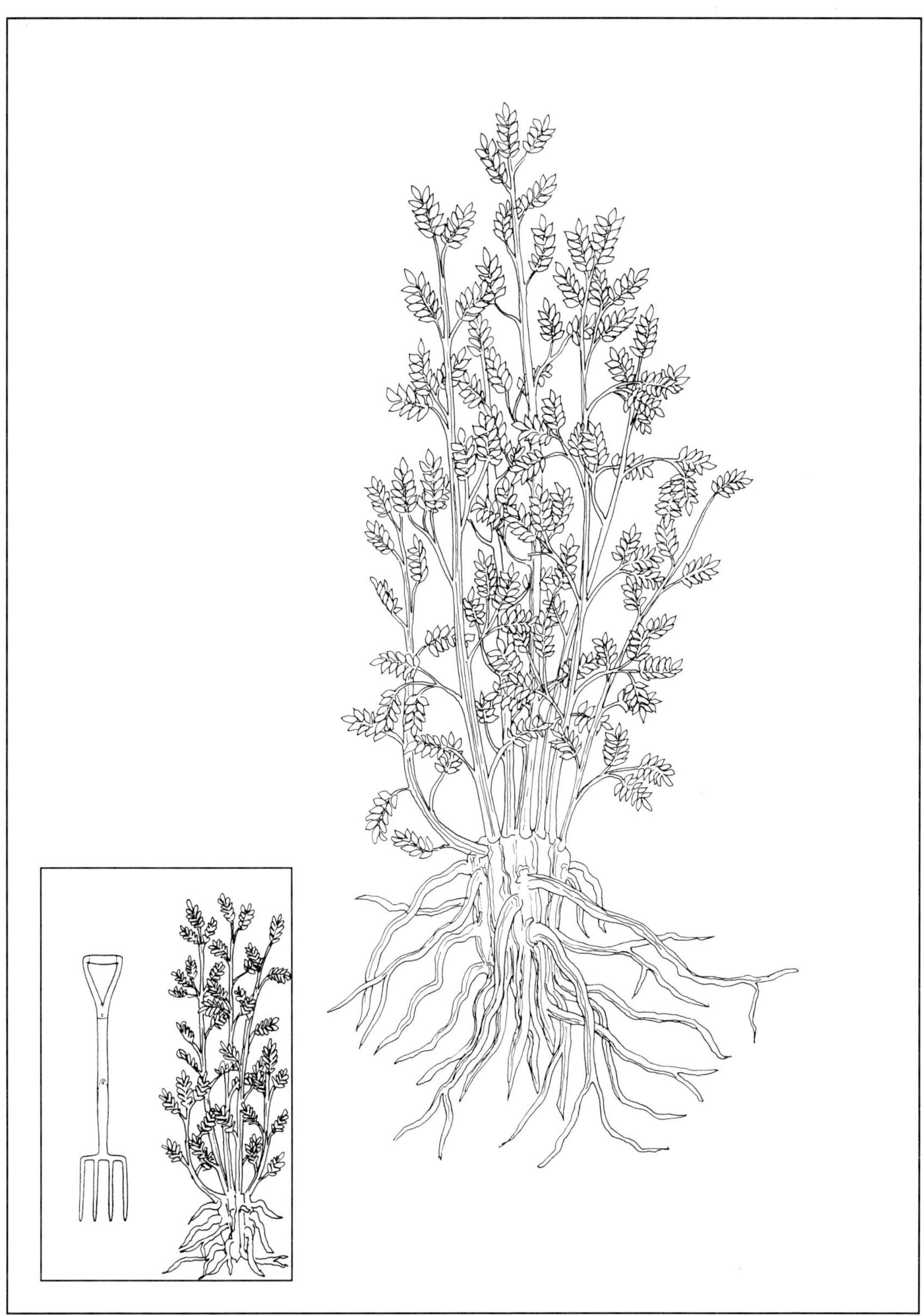

LIQUORICE

invaluable herb and one for which it's not easy to find an alternative. As well as its healing properties, it makes quite putrid-tasting herbs more acceptable to the palate, in tinctures, infusions and decoctions. This is of particular importance when treating children as they are very resistant to unfamiliar tastes but accept liquorice readily.

I would still urge you to find a plant and grow it. After all, if you don't plant it, in four years you won't have a large, handsome plant ready to use.

Caution: There is a possibility that regular or large doses of liquorice could create difficulties for people with cardiovascular problems, diabetes or kidney problems. Certain of its constituents have an aldosteronic effect.

MALLOW *Althaea spp.* Family: Malvaceae

Synonyms: Common mallow, musk mallow, dwarf mallow.

Description: The common mallow is the one used most often because of its availability. It can be seen almost everywhere, including roadsides and rubbish dumps. It is a biennial or perennial of quite straggly habit. It is branching with coarse, rounded, crenate, slightly lobed leaves on long petioles. The flowers grow in the axils and are pink to mauve with dark purple vein markings on each heart-shaped petal. The root is the most important part of the plant, and is thick, fleshy and greyish-white on the outside.

Parts used: Root, leaves, flowers.

Uses: Charts 1, 4, 5, 6, 7, 10, 11, 12, 13, 14.

Interest: Marshmallow sweets were once made from the sticky extract of the mallow root and must have been very beneficial. Now, however, they are far from being healthy as they are composed of sugar, gelatine, artificial colour and flavour. Pliny said: "Whosoever shall take a spoonful of the Mallows shall that day be free from all diseases that may come to him."

MARJORAM *Origanum marjorana* Family: Labiatae

Synonyms: Sweet marjoram, knotted marjoram, joy of the mountains.

Description: A perennial which is best treated as an annual because of a tendency to become straggly in its second year. It grows to about 30 cm (12 in). The stem is many-branched and square, bearing greyish-green, small, almost round, opposite leaves. The flowers look like clusters of little knots, hence the synonym.

Parts used: Whole herb.

Uses: Charts 1, 2, 3, 4, 5, 6, 9, 12, 13, 14, 15.

Interest: The perfume is so intense in this herb that it was a favourite for 'strewing'

MALLOW

MARJORAM

in medieval days. One trembles to think what their houses must have smelt like to need such strong-smelling herbs underfoot. This powerful scent has a modern day application as a 'smelling salt' to restore the faint or dizzy. Just holding a few crushed sprigs under the nose will restore them. Marjoram and oregano have similar properties, the major one for me being their antiseptic power which can act in a prophylactic manner if used frequently in cooking. A good example of preventive medicine.

MINTS Family: Labiatae

A. Spearmint *Mentha viridis*
B. Peppermint *Mentha piperita*

Synonyms: Garden mint, Our Lady's mint, lamb mint, brandy mint.

Description: A. Spearmint is a perennial with a creeping rootstock, growing to about 30 cm (12 in) tall. The stems are square with bright green, short-petioled, ovate-lanceolate leaves with irregularly serrated edges. The pale lilac flowers are borne in several interrupted whorls at the top portion of the stem.

B. Peppermint is in many ways similar to spearmint, but the peppermint leaves are much darker green, the stems have a purple tinge, the flowers are darker and the whole plant has a distinctive menthol odour.

Parts used: Leaves and stems (both varieties).

Uses: Charts 1, 2, 3, 5, 6, 7, 9, 12, 13, 14, 15, 16.

Interest: With all varieties of mint it is essential to pick off all flower heads as they bloom or they will cross-pollinate each other and the plant will become a coarse-leaved and not so useful 'bastard' mint, lacking any distinct flavour or perfume of peppermint or spearmint.

MULLEIN *Verbascum thapsus* Family: Scrophulariaceae

Synonyms: Great mullein, lady's foxglove, blanket herb, flannel plant, and many more.

Description: A tall handsome biennial growing to a height of 2 m (6 ft) in good conditions. The base leaves are huge, grey-green, woolly and ovate or obovate-lanceolate. The tall, straight stem grows in the second year and may be simple or branched. The leaves further up the stem are alternate and smaller. The flowers are bright yellow and heavily clustered on the last 30 cm (12 in) of the stem.

Parts used: Leaves and flowers.

Uses: Charts 1, 4, 5, 6, 7, 13, 14.

Interest: In medieval days, the tall flower stalk of the mullein would be dried, dipped in melted tallow and lit, to carry through the streets as a torch lighting the way for processions.

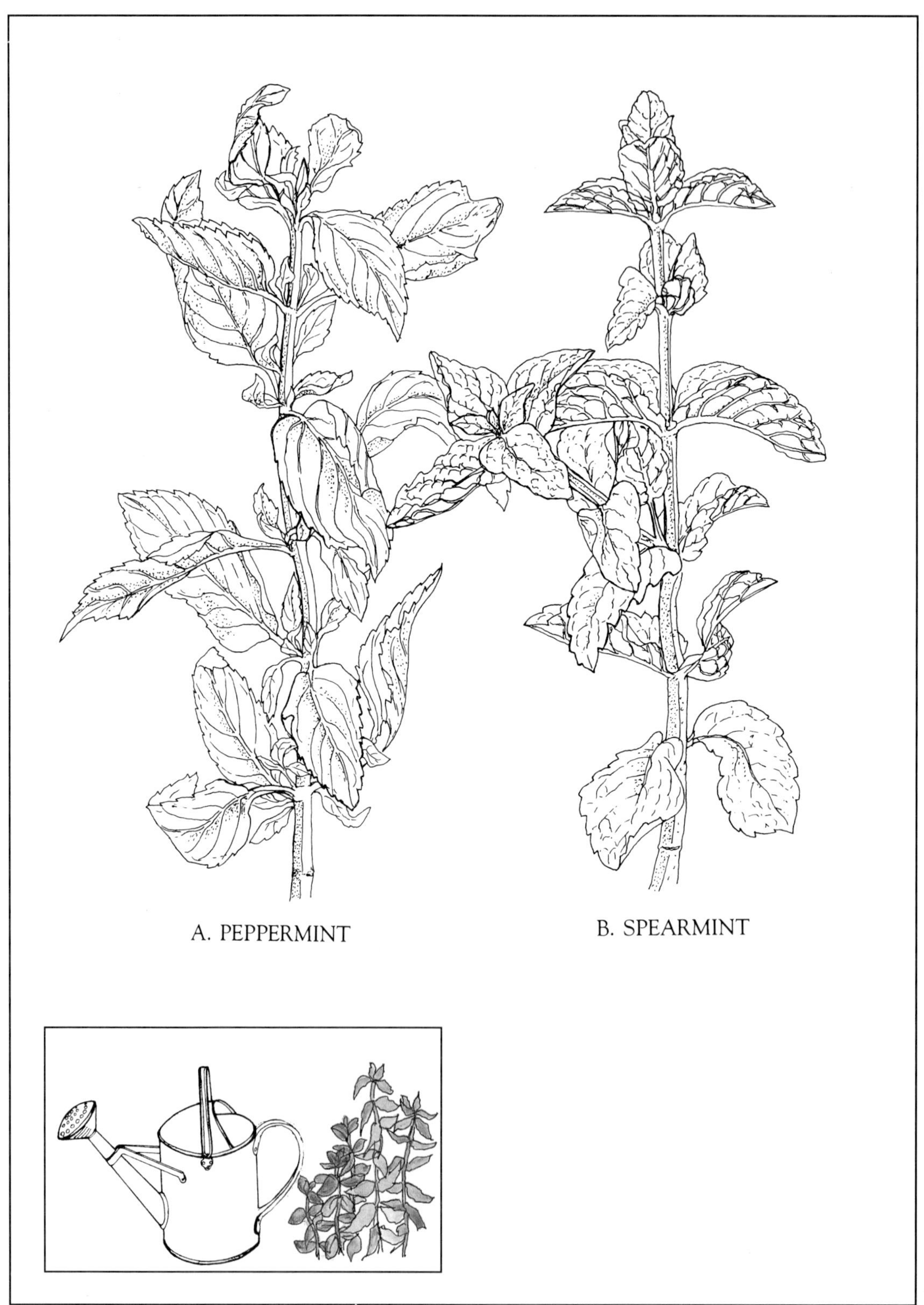

A. PEPPERMINT B. SPEARMINT

MULLEIN

It's worth looking for wild mullein if you can find it in a clean, unpolluted area. The wild variety is shorter with much smaller, dark green leaves. Its medicinal properties are reputed to be more powerful than the cultivated variety. Please make sure you get qualified identification before using this or any wild herb.

Caution: Infusions made from mullein must be carefully strained through muslin to trap the fine hairs. These could cause severe irritation and choking.

NASTURTIUM *Tropaeolum majus* or *minus* Family: Cruciferae

Synonym: Indian cress.

Description: An annual, self-seeding, creeping and climbing plant. The leaves are round, flat, smooth and pale green. The flowers are bright, showy trumpets ranging in colour from pale yellow through to dark red.

Parts used: Leaves, flowers, seeds.

Uses: Charts 1, 2, 3, 5, 12, 13, 15, 16.

Interest: Nasturtium belongs to the same family as watercress and has the same peppery 'bite'. The seeds, after treatment, may be pickled and used instead of capers (see p240). Nasturtium has an antibiotic action and for this reason is included in our food as often as possible. It is a lovely and useful herb to grow in your garden but can become a pest by growing so rampantly that it suffocates and chokes any plants in its path. Overcome this problem by pinching off the tips of all shoots when they are a suitable length for you, or buy seeds of the new 'non-running' varieties.

NETTLE *Urtica dioica* Family: Urticaceae

Synonyms: Stinging nettle, common nettle.

Description: There are two types of nettle. One is an annual with a delicate pale green leaf and shallow root system, rarely growing more than 25-30 cm (10-12 in) tall. The other is a perennial with a much coarser, darker leaf and a creeping rootstock. The leaves of both are opposite, hairy, deeply serrated, and pointed. The whole plant is covered with sharp stinging points which cause intense irritation and local swelling. In Britain (and maybe elsewhere) there is usually a stand of dock growing near nettle patches. A crushed leaf rubbed onto the sting gives instant relief. An old rhyme goes:

Nettle in, dock out.
Dock rub nettle out!

Parts used: Whole herb.

Uses: Charts 1, 3, 5, 6, 10, 11, 13, 14, 15.

Interest: To most people this is a despised weed and yet it deserves a place of honour in your garden, maybe in a corner where it can quietly grow and multiply without stinging anyone. It is a most wonderful herb, full of

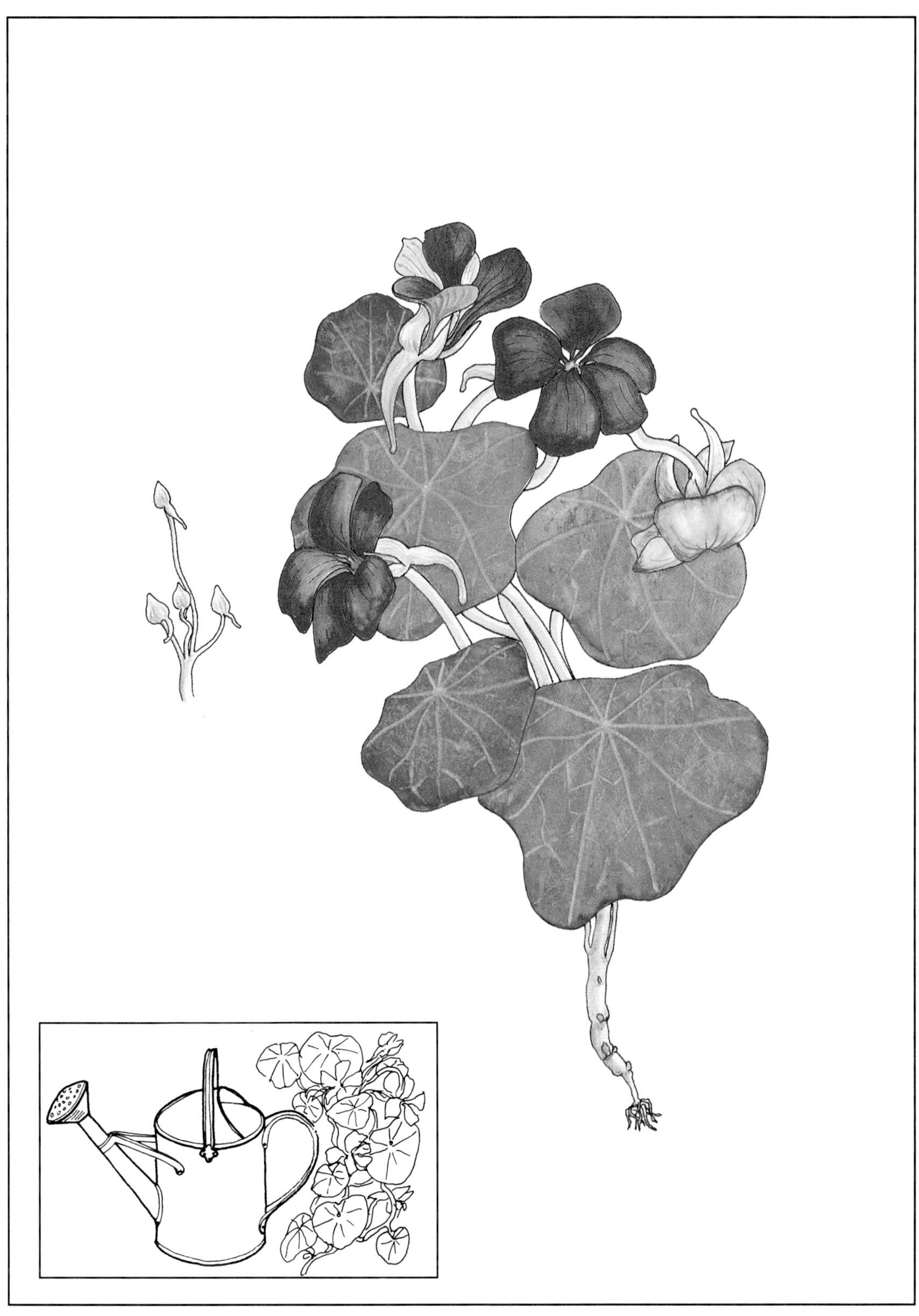

NASTURTIUM

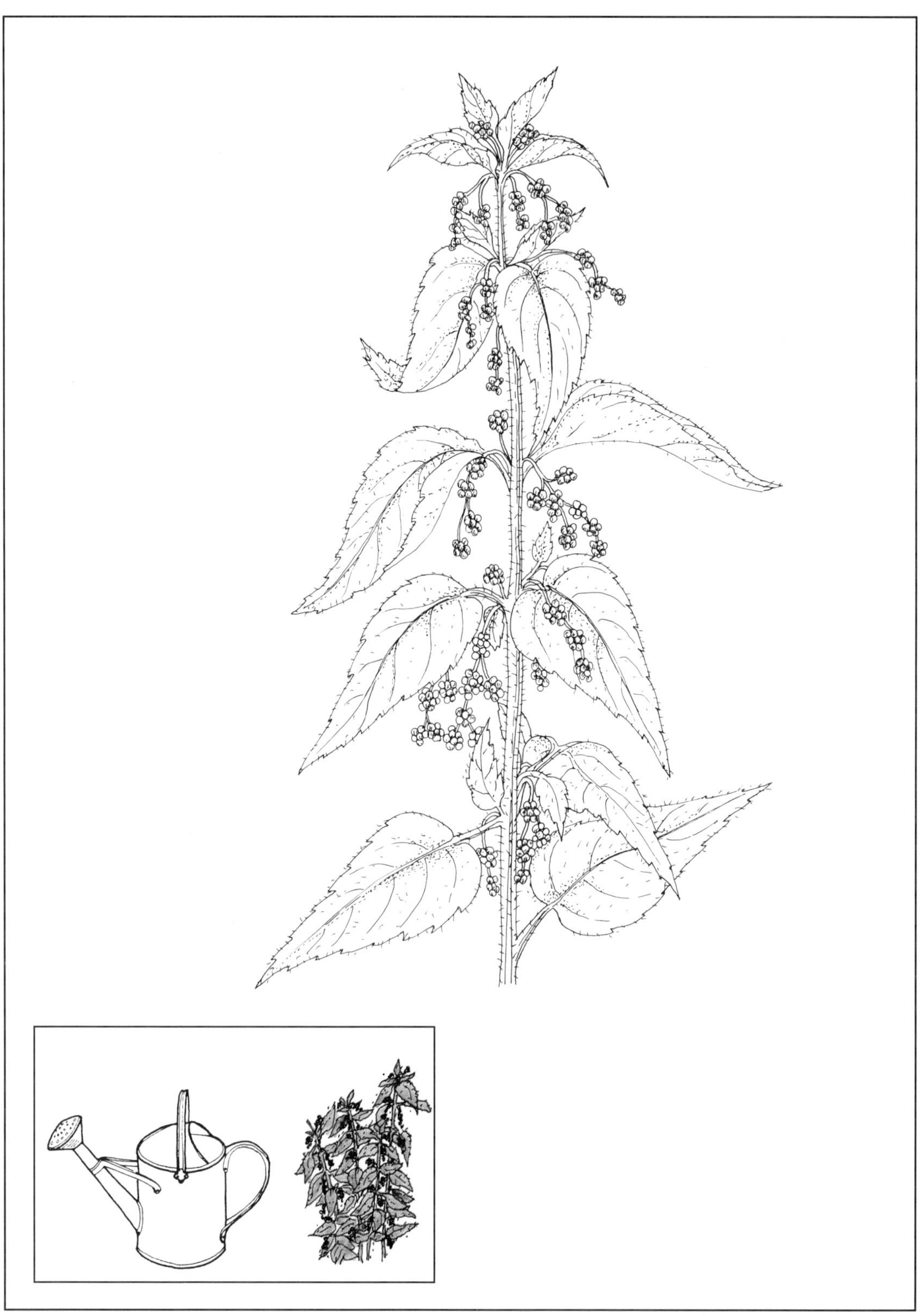

NETTLE

vitamins and minerals. It makes a delicious soup and a first-rate treatment for hair and its uses extend even to the making of a cloth very similar to linen.

In Scotland I have eaten nettles, slept in nettle sheets and dined off a nettle tablecloth. My mother thought nettle cloth more durable than any species of linen.

Cambell

OREGANO *Origanum vulgare* Family: Labiatae

Synonyms: Wild marjoram, mountain mint.

Description: A perennial plant with a creeping rootstock. The purple-tinged woody stems rarely grow taller than 60-70 cm (24-28 in) and bear opposite, ovate, bright to dark green rough-textured leaves. The white or pale purple flowers are bilabiate and grow in terminal clusters. The flowers are as full of flavour as the leaf in this plant.

Parts used: Whole herb.

Uses: Charts 1, 2, 3, 4, 5, 13, 14, 15, 16.

Interest: Argument continues among botanists and herbalists as to the identity of the 'true' oregano. There are so many varieties that my tip would be to find the one with the strongest flavour and perfume and stick to that. Oregano and marjoram are among the few herbs that retain their pungent and distinctive aroma after drying. The flowers also carry the perfume, to an even greater extent than the leaves. This is rare in the herb world and means that the plant can be collected while in full flower and both flowers and leaves dried for use.

PARSLEY *Petroselinum crispum* Family: Umbelliferae

Synonyms: Persely, persele, common parsley.

Description: Of the many types of parsley available, the *crispum* is the most widely used. It is a biennial with bright green foliage. The leaves are deeply divided, curling over at the edges to give a pretty appearance. The flower stem appears in the second year and has compound umbels of white/green flowers. To prolong the life of the plant, cut the stem right back or the plant will go to seed and die.

Parts used: Root, leaves, seeds.

Uses: Charts 1, 2, 5, 6, 11, 12, 13, 14, 15, 16.

Interest: It seems unnecessary to describe parsley, as there can be few people who don't recognise and use this herb. I think, though, there are many who don't recognise its potential. When we owned 'The Prancing Pony' restaurant we used a large variety of herbs in both cooking and garnishing the food. We impressed upon our customers that everything on their

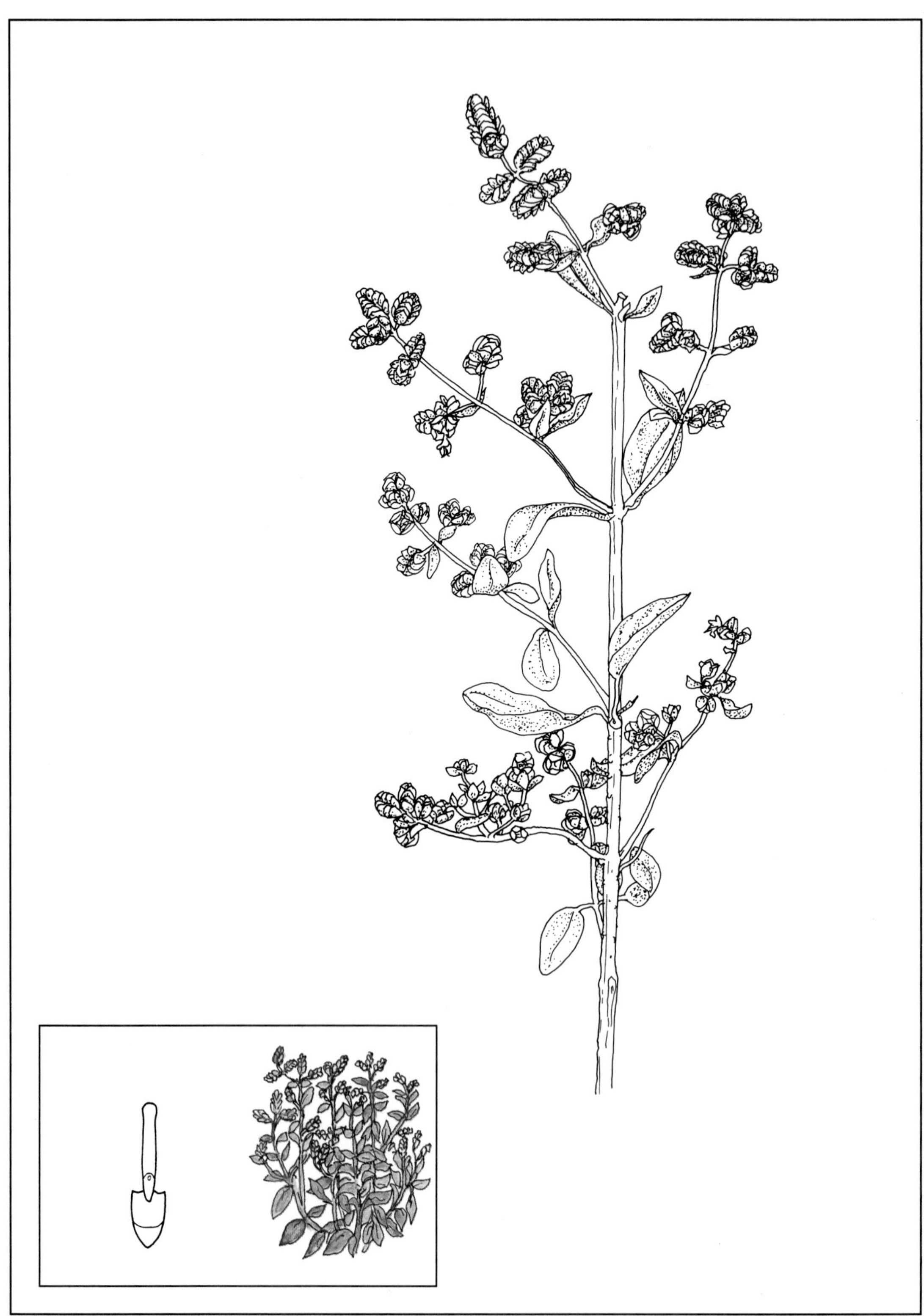

OREGANO

PARSLEY

plate was edible and delicious but it was rare for anyone to eat the garnish. This was a pity, as the parsley sprig would have ensured well digested food, sweet breath and a good supply of minerals and vitamins.

There are many myths surrounding parsley — one is that it will only grow in gardens where the woman is 'master' of the household. Another, that the seed has to go to the devil and back seven times before it will germinate.

Caution: Parsley must never be used where there is inflammation of the kidneys. The correct dosage must always be adhered to as excessive quantities of apiol and myristicin can create severe liver, kidney and other problems.

PENNYROYAL *Mentha pulegium* Family: Labiatae

Synonyms: European pennyroyal, lurk-in-the-ditch.

Description: A perennial herb with a creeping rootstock, growing 20-30 cm (8-12 in) tall. The stems are weak and so tend to be prostrate. They root very readily where nodes touch the ground. The leaves are opposite, small and bright green, bearing no resemblance to others of the mint family. The flowers of pale purple are bilabiate, growing in axillary whorls or clusters.

Parts used: Whole herb.

Uses: Charts 1, 3, 5, 10.

Interest: Pennyroyal has a reputation for driving fleas away. Pliny called this herb *pulegium* as *pulex* is the Latin word for flea. The synonym lurk-in-the-ditch is very apt. I know a watery ditch down a little-used lane which is rampant with pennyroyal in the spring. I collect armfuls and drive home with the car windows open; otherwise the powerful scent gives me a headache.

Caution: **Pennyroyal should not be used during pregnancy.**

PLANTAIN A. *Plantago major* Family: Plantaginaceae
B. *Plantago lanceolata*

Synonyms: Common plantain, broad-leaved plantain, lanceleaf plantain, ribwort, white man's foot.

Description: A. *Plantago major* is a perennial 'weed'. It has a radial rosette of wide, ribbed, greyish-green, hairy leaves which can grow 25-30 cm (10-12 in) long. The flower stalk is erect and 30-40 cm (12-16 in) tall. The flowers grow up the last part of the stalk; they are greyish-green but inconspicuous because of the light brown sepals and bracts which almost cover them.

B. *Plantago lanceolata* is the more common plant in Australia. The leaves grow from a radial rosette, are bright green, lanceolate and ribbed. The grooved flower stalks rise up in various heights from 20-60 cm (8-24 in) and are topped with a flower head 1-2 cm (½ in) long. The corolla can scarcely be seen; the most prominent aspects are the pale brown, dried looking sepals

PENNYROYAL

B. LANCELEAF PLANTAIN
A. BROADLEAF PLANTAIN

and the slim white filaments tipped with greenish-yellow anthers forming a halo round the base of the head.

Parts used: Leaves, seeds.

Uses: Charts 1, 4, 5, 6, 7, 8, 12, 13.

Interest: One of the 'nine sacred herbs' (see chamomile), plantain grows everywhere in the world where the white man has been and this has led to the synonym, white man's foot. This plant, like the nettle, is treated as a pest by those who don't know its worth. Make a place for it in your garden and learn to appreciate its many virtues. It is one of my favourites.

RASPBERRY *Rubus idaeus* Family: Rosaceae

Synonyms: Red raspberry, hindberry, wild raspberry.

Description: A well known plant with perennial roots and prickly biennial stems growing to a height of 1-2 m (3-6 ft). The leaves are opposite, pinnate, with 3-7 dentate lobes, green above, whitish-green and hairy beneath. The flowers are loose, small, greenish-white corymbs. Red compound fruits ripen during the summer, strongly scented and delicious.

Parts used: Leaves and fruit.

Uses: Charts 1, 5, 6, 7, 12, 13, 14.

Interest: I often took my dachshunds walking in the woods in Dorset. The dogs would race ahead chasing real or imagined rabbits, but in late summer and early autumn the hunt became serious. I would hear high-pitched barking and know they had found raspberry bushes. They were far too shrewd (and also too short) to pick the berries — this chore was left to me — but they would eat the berries for as long as I was prepared to pick them. This led me to the discovery that dogs love fruit if it's offered to them from an early age.

RED CLOVER *Trifolium pratense* Family: Leguminosae

Synonyms: Purple clover, trefoil.

Description: A perennial with 30-60 cm (1-2 ft) stalks rising from the short rootstock. The leaves, whose stalks grow from stipules, are bright green, trifoliate and sometimes minutely toothed on the leaflets. The flowers grow in dense globular heads and vary considerably in colour from deep red to white.

Parts used: Flowers or sprouted whole herb.

Uses: Charts 1, 5, 6, 7, 11, 12, 13, 14, 15, 16.

Interest: This is one of the well known fodder and soil improvement plants. It is a nitrogen fixer and is used by farmers in many countries. It is also a very valuable plant to the herbalist, having wide application. Because of the amount of space needed to grow any reasonable quantity, I suggest you buy seeds and sprout them in the same way as alfalfa (see p217).

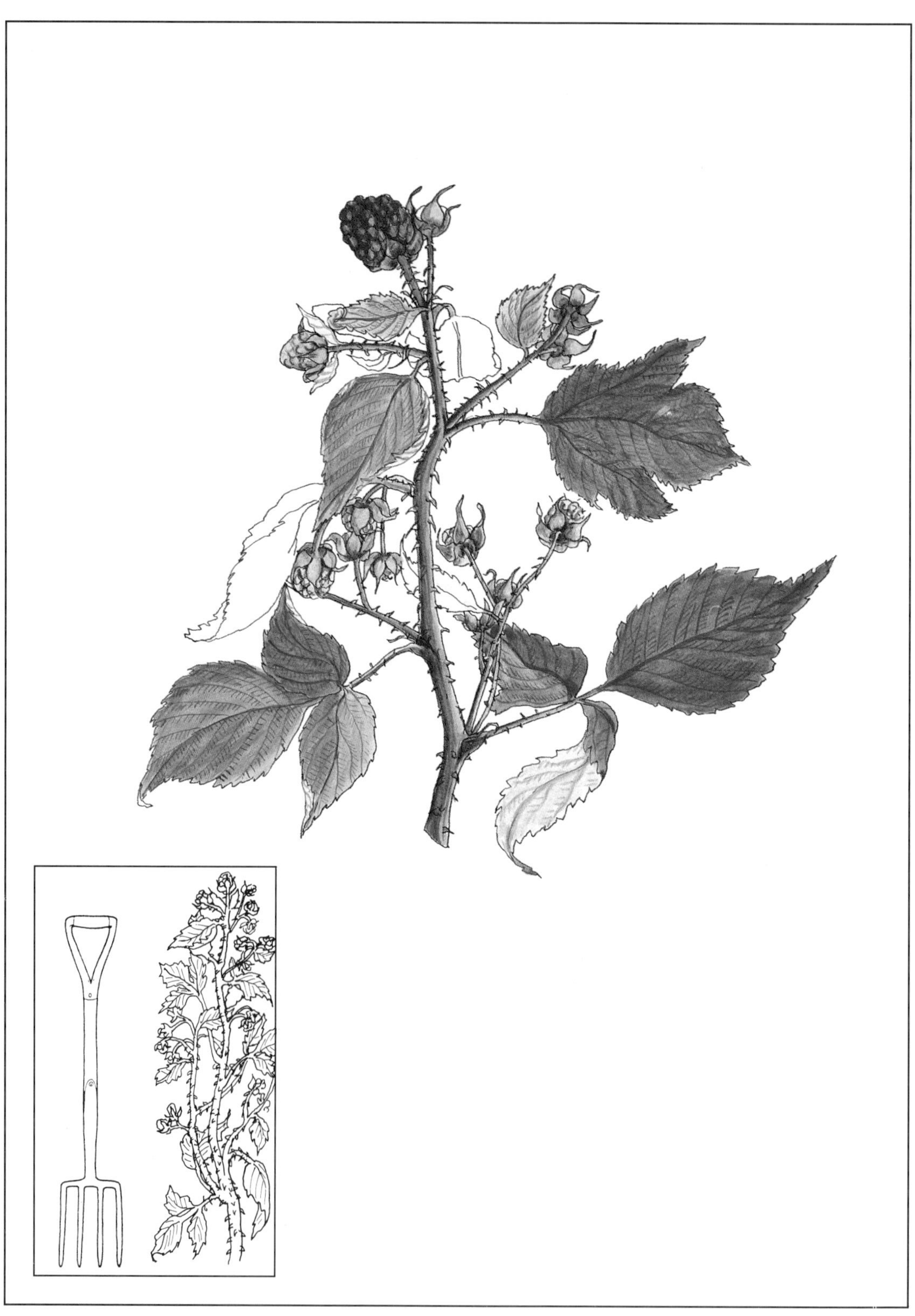

RASPBERRY

RED CLOVER

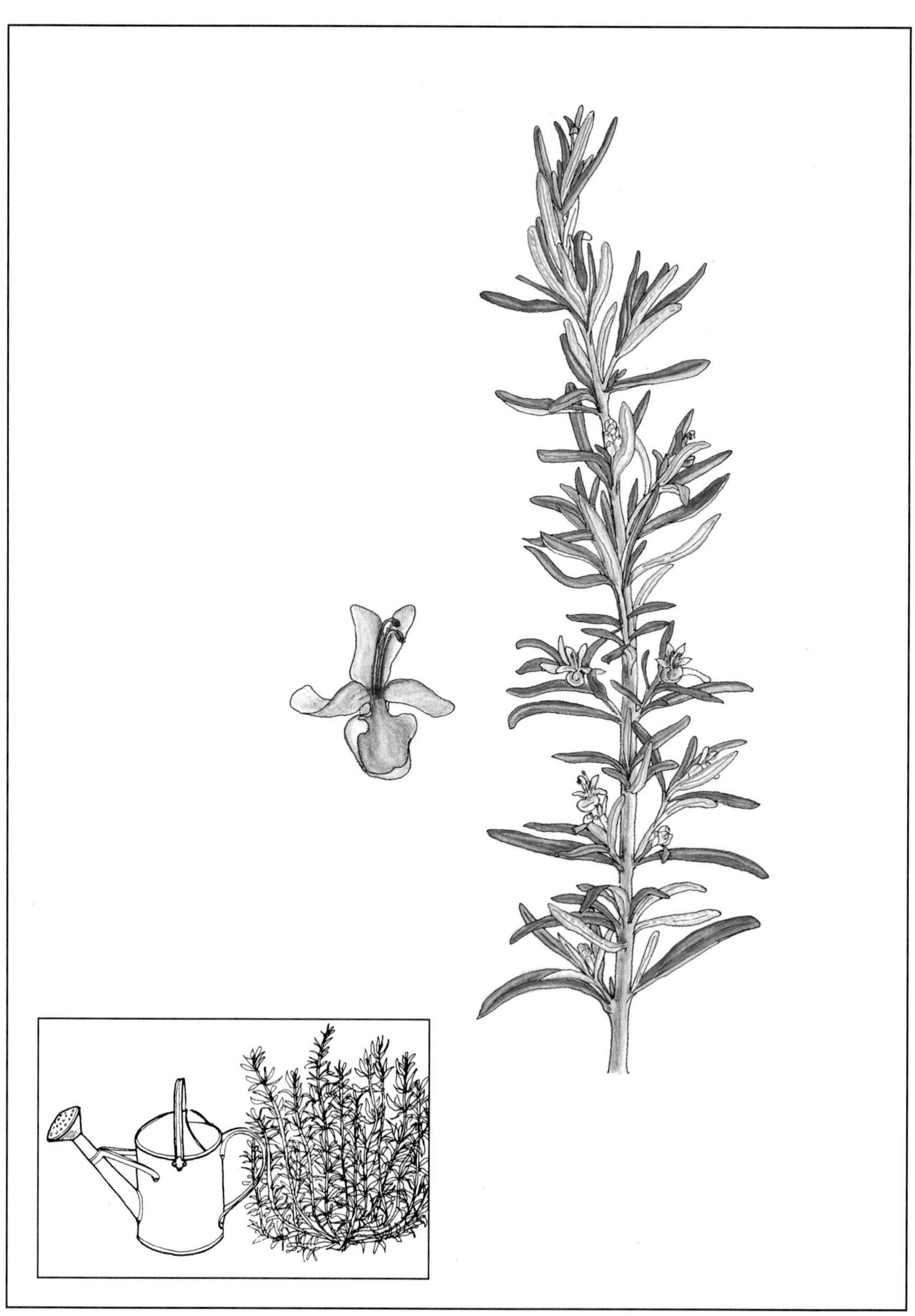

ROSEMARY

ROSEMARY *Rosmarinus officinalis* Family: Labiatae

Synonyms: Compass plant, romero, polar plant, herb of remembrance.

Description: One of the best known and loved herbs, rosemary is a perennial shrub growing up to 2 m (6 ft) under good conditions. It is many-branched with opposite, narrow, shiny, leathery leaves which are a rich dark green on top and pale underneath. The flowers are small, pale blue and grow in axillary racemes. The whole plant is very aromatic if bruised and the leaves exude a sticky resin when stripped from the branches.

Parts used: Leaves, flowers.

Uses: Charts 1, 2, 3, 4, 5, 6, 8, 9, 10, 11, 12, 13, 14, 15, 16.

Interest: Rosemary is known as the 'herb of remembrance' and is dedicated to lovers. However, this herb is used medicinally to improve brainpower and failing memory so perhaps this is the origin of the name — not so romantic but maybe more accurate. It was always included in bridal bouquets as the herb of love and loyalty and used on many occasions when solemn vows of honour and fidelity were being sworn. In Wales, where I was born, it was the custom to carry a sprig of rosemary to a funeral and throw it on the coffin as it was being lowered into the grave.

Caution: Rosemary should not be taken in large doses or over extended periods of time. The oil must never be taken internally.

RUE *Ruta graveolens* Family: Rutaceae

Synonyms: Herb of grace, herby grass, herb of repentance.

Description: A shrubby little perennial with a smooth, pale green, branched stem bearing alternate bi- or tri-pinnate leaves of an unusual metallic blue-green. Panicles of yellow flowers grow terminally. The plant rarely grows more than 60-80 cm (24-32 in) high. Almost every book I have read complains about the smell of rue — it is certainly pungent — but I really enjoy the scent.

Parts used: Leaves.

Uses: Charts 1, 2, 3, 5, 6.

Interest: Rue has been in use for more than 2000 years. It seems to have been the main herb used against plague and witchcraft. Judges in court were, until quite recently, given 'tussie mussies' (small bouquets) or sprigs of rue. It was believed that the perfume would protect them from the jail fever being carried by the prisoners. Rue was one of the ingredients in the 'vinegar of the four thieves'. The four thieves were a band of robbers employed by a pharmacist in France to rob the bodies and homes of the dead during the plague. He devised the vinegar as a wash to prevent the thieves catching the disease. We never learn how effective it was but I use herbal vinegar (see p190) a great deal as an air spray, wound wash and bath additive and find it excellent.

Caution: Rue should not be used in large quantities or over an extended period of time. **Not to be used during pregnancy.**

RUE

SAGE

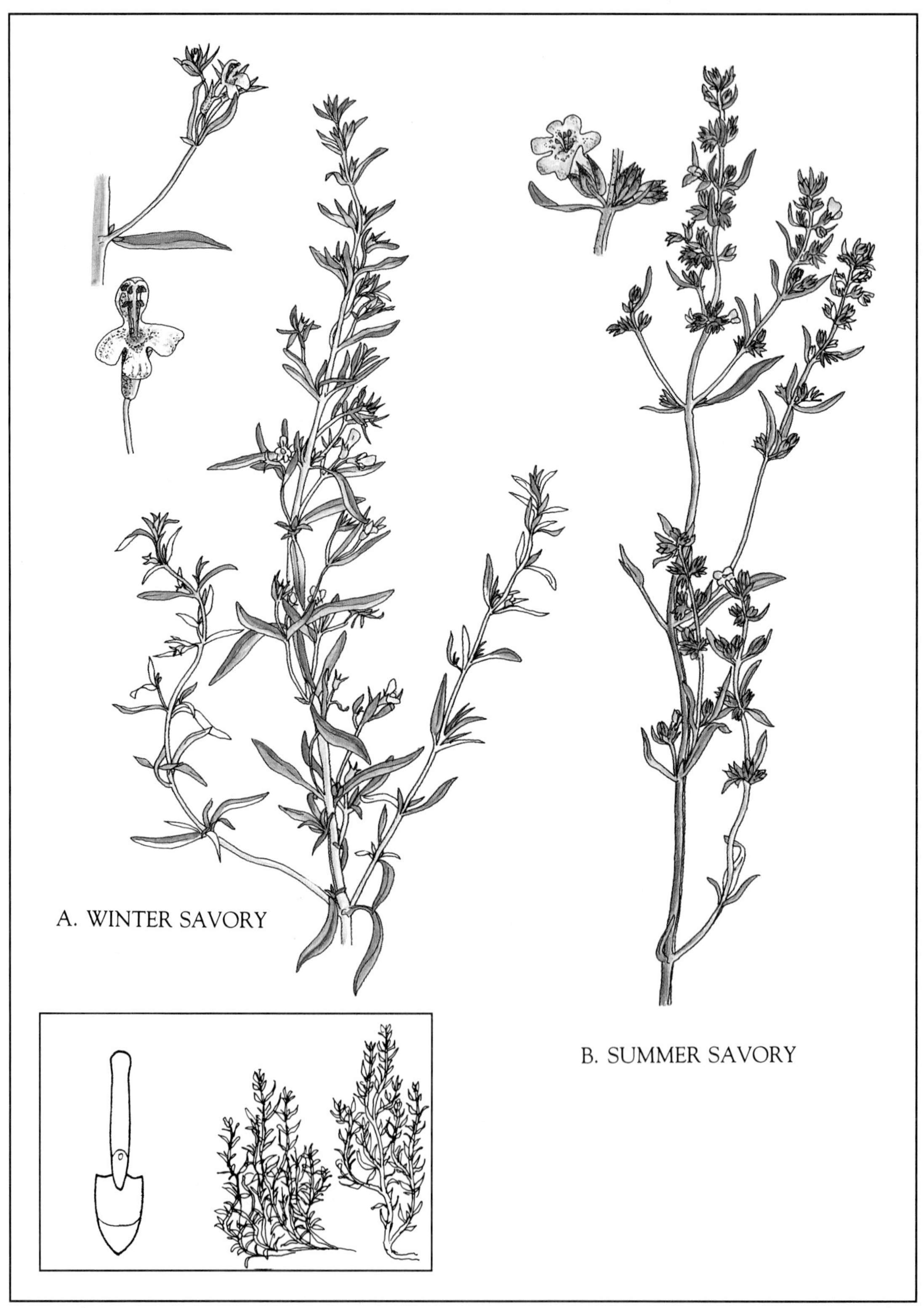
A. WINTER SAVORY
B. SUMMER SAVORY

SAGE — *Salvia officinalis* — Family: Labiatae

Synonyms: Garden sage, sawge.

Description: A hardy perennial of shrubby habit growing to about 30 cm (12 in) in height. The leaves are opposite, slightly hairy, greyish-green and oblong. The flowers are bilabiate and purple, and grow in terminal whorls.

Parts used: Leaves.

Uses: Charts 1, 2, 3, 4, 5, 6, 7, 9, 10, 11, 12, 13, 14, 15, 16.

Interest:

He who would live for aye,
must eat sage in May.

Old English proverb

Tis a plant indeed with so many and wonderful
properties as that the assiduous use of it is said
to render men immortal.

John Evelyn

I don't know about the above statements, they seem a bit extravagant, but I keep a very strong sage infusion in my freezer for rapid relief from any mouth or throat problems. One of my grand-daughters was plagued with mouth ulcers. After a few treatments with sage ice cubes they became progressively less and now she has no problem with her mouth at all.

SAVORY, SUMMER — *Satureia hortensis* — Family: Labiatae

Synonym: Bean herb.

Description: An annual plant of bushy growth, about 60 cm (2 ft) high. The leaves are opposite, about 1 cm (½ in) long, oblong and linear. The flowers are pinkish-mauve and labiate, growing in clusters in the axils.

Parts used: Leaves.

Uses: Charts 1, 2, 3, 5, 10, 14, 15, 16.

SAVORY, WINTER — *Satureia montana* — Family: Labiatae

Description: A small shrubby perennial, much smaller than the summer variety. It is branched and woody with oblong, linear, dark green glossy leaves. Racemes of creamy white, labiate flowers are borne in profusion from midsummer until end of autumn.

Parts used: Leaves.

Uses: Charts 1, 2, 3, 5, 10, 14, 15, 16.

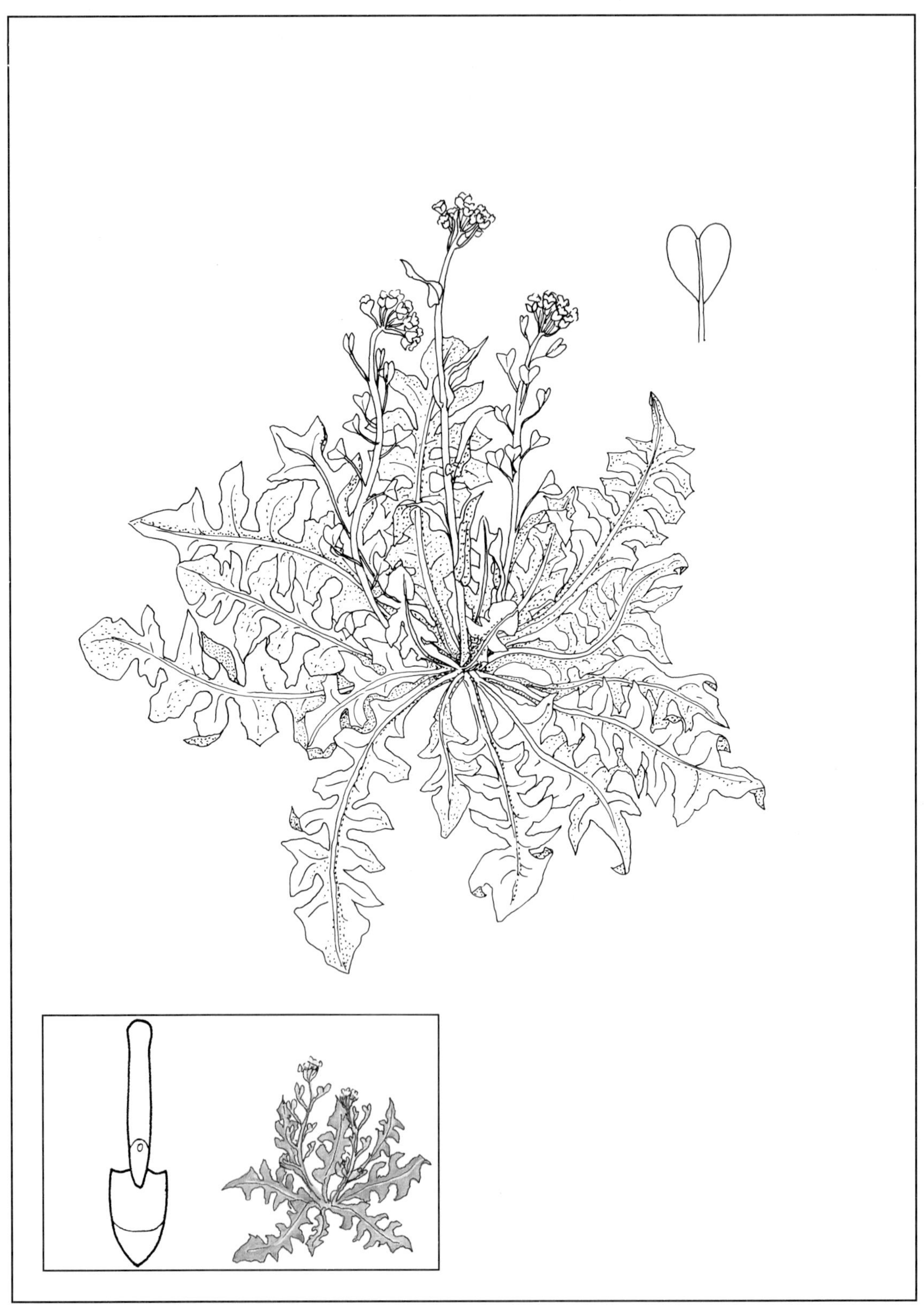

SHEPHERD'S PURSE

Interest: *Keep it dry, make conserves and syrups of it for your use; for which purpose the summer kind is best. This kind is both hotter and drier than the winter kind. It expels tough phlegm from the chest and lungs, and quickens the dull spirits in lethargy.*

Source unknown

SHEPHERD'S PURSE *Capsella bursa-pastoris* Family: Cruciferae

Synonyms: Shepherd's bag, lady's purse, pickpocket, toywort.

Description: An annual which can vary 15-30 cm (6-12 in) in height depending on the growing conditions. The main leaves form a basal rosette and are green, rough, and pinnatifid, entire or toothed. The stem is erect and can be either simple or branched with a few small leaves. The tiny flowers are borne in terminal inflorescences and are inconspicuous and white. The fruits are the best way to identify this plant — they are small, flat, heart-shaped pods looking like old-fashioned purses.

Parts used: Whole plant.

Uses: Charts 1, 5, 6, 8.

Interest: Another invaluable herb which is described as a weed. I looked in several dictionaries for definitions of the word 'weed' and found the following: 'a small useless plant'; 'anything useless or obnoxious'; 'any wild herb'. I would only be able to agree with the last statement as most of my favourite herbs have been described as pests or weeds by the uninformed. Give shepherd's purse a special place in the 'wild' area of your garden. It can be used to prevent haemorrhage and could save your life in an emergency.

SOUTHERN-WOOD *Artemisia abrotanum* Family: Compositae

Synonyms: Old man, lad's love, garderobe.

Description: A small perennial shrub rarely exceeding 90 cm (3 ft) in height. It has grey/green finely divided leaves and a very strong, aromatic, lemony smell which makes it a fine insect repellant. The pale yellow flowers bloom in summer in small, loose, inconspicuous bunches.

Parts used: Leaves.

Uses: Charts 1, 2, 3, 8.

Interest: The main stories about this plant seem to concentrate on its reputed hair-growing properties. Used as an ointment and rubbed on the chin, it was said to grow beards on young men, making them more attractive to the girls. Small bouquets would be taken to church and sniffed to ward off sleepiness during lengthy sermons. The sharp scent would certainly achieve this.

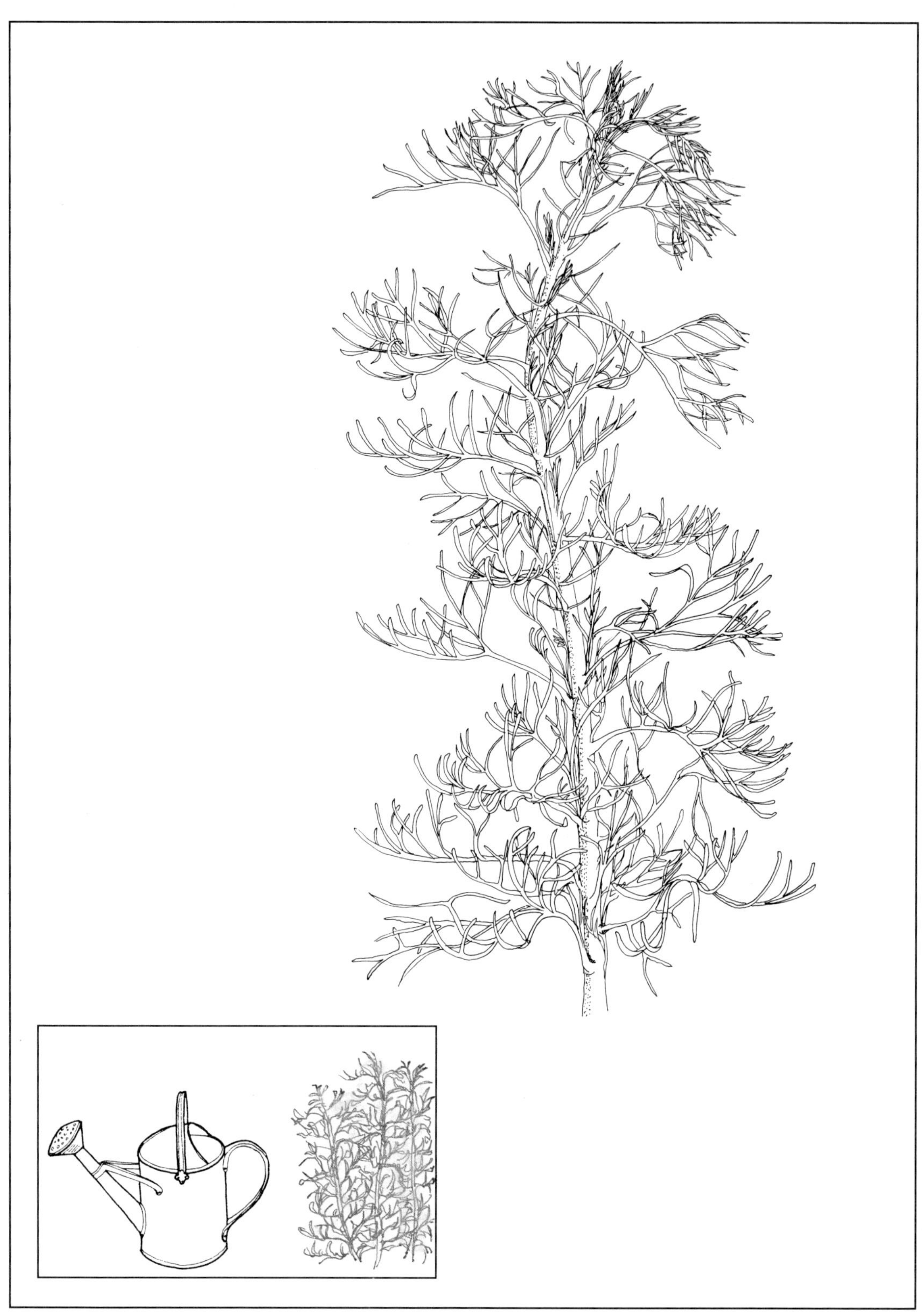

SOUTHERNWOOD

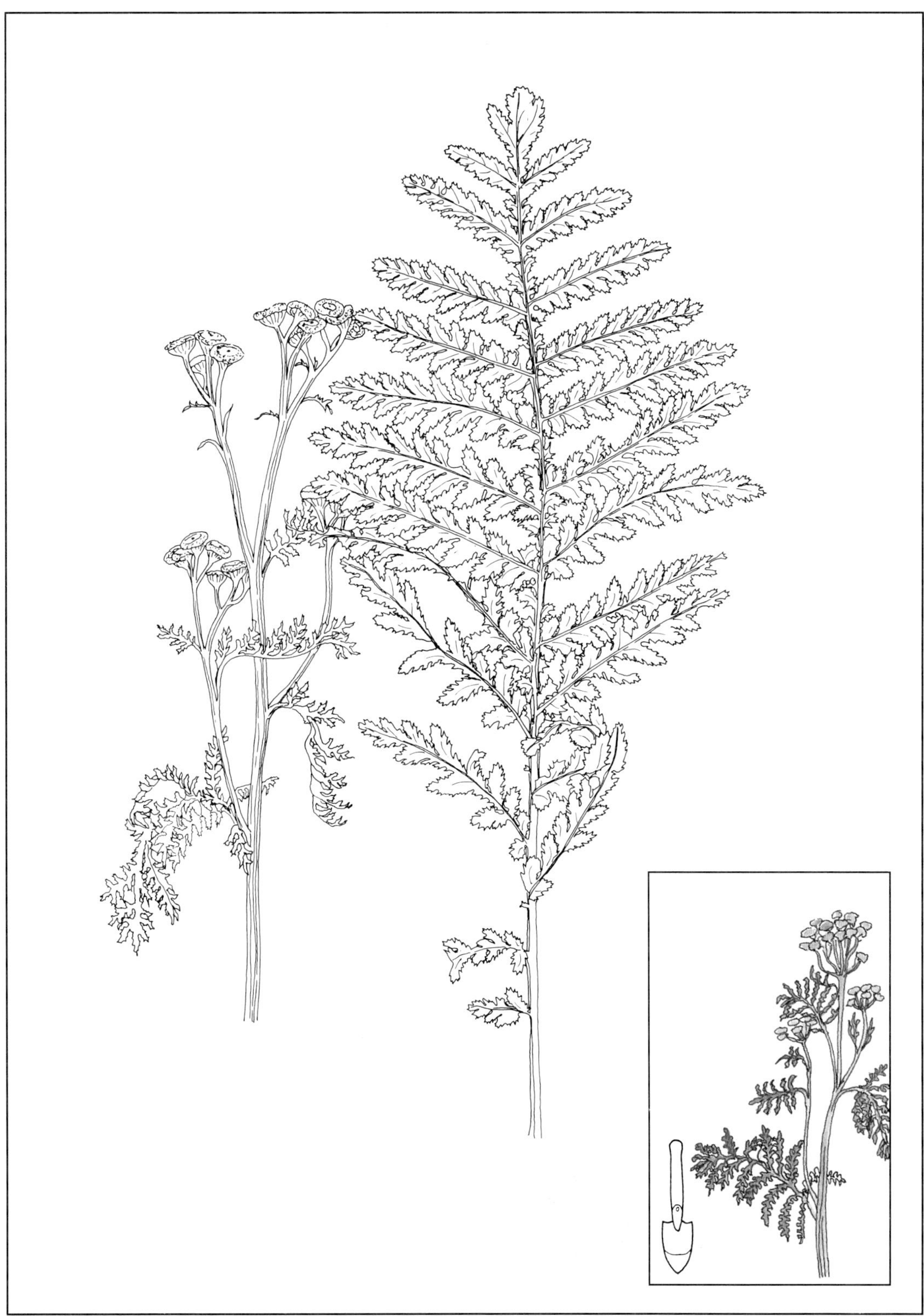

TANSY

TARRAGON

TANSY *Tanecetum vulgare* Family: Compositae

Synonyms: Buttons, bachelor's buttons, stinking willie.

Description: Tansy is a hardy perennial which spreads from runners. It is almost as invasive as the mint family. The rootstock sends up an erect, grooved, leafy stem which grows to a height of about 90 cm (3 ft). The leaves are alternate, dark green, pinnately divided with dentate segments. They have a fern-like appearance. The attractive flat, yellow clusters of button-like flowers develop in early autumn.

Parts used: Whole herb.

Uses: Charts 1, 2, 3, 4, 5, 6.

Interest: One of the most interesting uses of tansy in the past was as an embalming agent and a meat preservative. It is a useful herb for those with pets. In South West Australia there is a constant battle with fleas. They breed in the sand and jump onto the dogs who carry them into the house to breed in the carpets. I use a spray containing tansy for my carpets and dogs which, if used *frequently*, keeps the flea population under control.

Caution: Over-large doses of tansy can be fatal. **Do not use internally except with professional advice and under supervision.**

TARRAGON *Artemisia dranunculus* Family: Compositae

Synonyms: Little dragon, estragon, French tarragon.

Description: A semi-hardy perennial, tarragon grows to about 70 cm (28 in) in height. It is bushy but has a rather sprawly habit. The leaves are dark green, lanceolate to linear, and can be either toothed or entire. The flowers, growing in terminal panicles, are small and quite insignificant. Don't let yourself be fobbed off with Russian tarragon — it is very inferior in flavour.

Parts used: Leaves.

Uses: Charts 5, 14, 15, 16.

Interest: True French tarragon will rarely grow from seed. The inferior Russian tarragon grows readily from seed but, when I have seen packets of seeds, there is never a mention of variety. So beware — much better to beg or buy a piece of root from an established plant.

THYME *Thymus vulgaris* Family: Labiatae

Synonyms: Garden thyme, common thyme.

Description: A small, bushy perennial with hard, branching stems growing about 25 cm (10 in) high. The leaves are very small, opposite, ovate to lanceolate and greyish-green in colour. The light purple, bilabiate flowers are borne in terminal whorls from late spring onwards.

Parts used: Leaves.

Uses: Charts 1, 2, 3, 4, 5, 6, 7, 8, 9, 10, 11, 12, 13, 14, 15, 16.

Caution: Take no more than 15 g (½ oz) daily of the dried leaf. Not to be taken for longer than three weeks at a time.

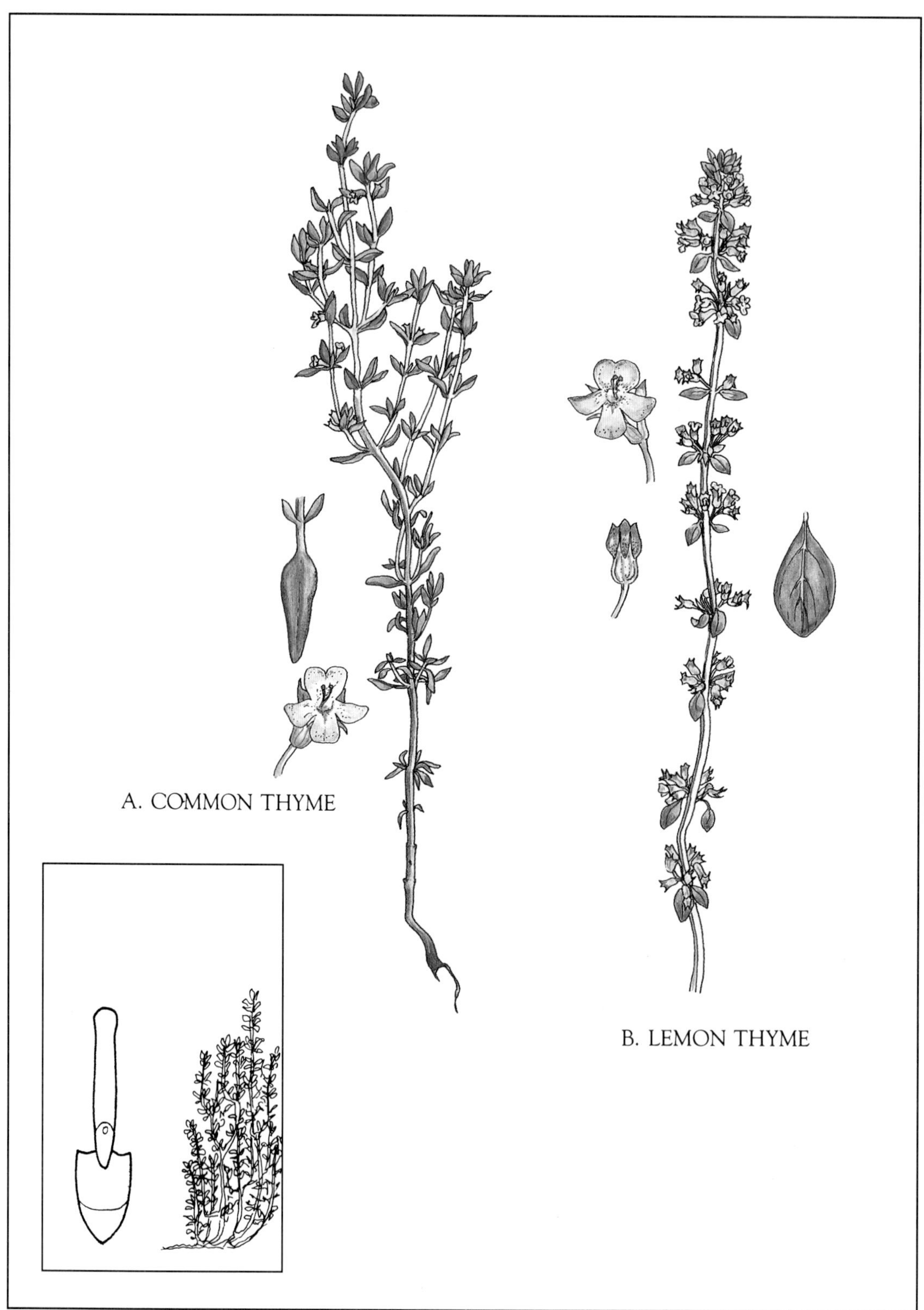
A. COMMON THYME
B. LEMON THYME

THYME, LEMON — *T. citriodorus* — Family: Labiatae

Description: Very similar to garden thyme, but slightly lower in height, brighter green foliage and a slightly darker mauve flower. It's not as strong medicinally but is such a wonderful culinary herb that I urge you to grow it.

Parts used: Leaves.

Uses: Charts 1, 2, 3, 10, 14, 15, 16.

Interest:

I know a bank whereon the wild thyme flows,
Where oxlips and the nodding violet grows;
Quite over canopied with lush woodbine,
With sweet musk roses and with Eglantine.

Shakespeare: *Midsummer Night's Dream*

VALERIAN — *Valeriana officinalis* — Family: Valerianaceae

Synonyms: Setwall, all-heal, amantilla, fragrant valerian.

Description: A hardy perennial with one hollow, furrowed stem rising to a height of about 100 cm (40 in), usually in the second year of growth. The leaves are pale green, opposite and pinnate with lanceolate, serrated leaflets. These vary in number from 6-12 pairs. The stem divides to form flower stems with clusters of small pink flowers at the top.

Parts used: Root (end of second year of growth).

Uses: Charts 1, 5, 6, 10, 14.

Interest: The flowers of this plant smell bad and the root even worse. It is this evil-smelling root, containing valerianic, formic and acetic acids, pinene and borneol plus isovalerianic acid (this gives the evil smell), that provides us with one of nature's finest nervine and antispasmodics. I have included it in the 'Teas' chart but I use it almost exclusively in compounds as it is easier to disguise the taste in this way. The story about valerian that I like best is that it was used by the Pied Piper of Hamelin to lure rats out of the city. The scent of the bruised root does seem to attract them.

VIOLET — *Viola odorata* — Family: Violaceae

Synonyms: Sweet violet, garden violet.

Description: This little perennial plant must surely be known by everyone. It has heart-shaped leaves and sweet-scented flowers in colours ranging from pink through to royal purple. Propagation is by runners and unless the plant is regularly divided it will produce very few flowers.

Parts used: The whole plant.

Uses: Charts 1, 4, 5, 6, 7, 16.

Interest: In both ancient and modern days, in the East and the West, the violet has always been a favourite flower. In France, during the days of troubadours, the prize awarded to the best poet was a golden violet.

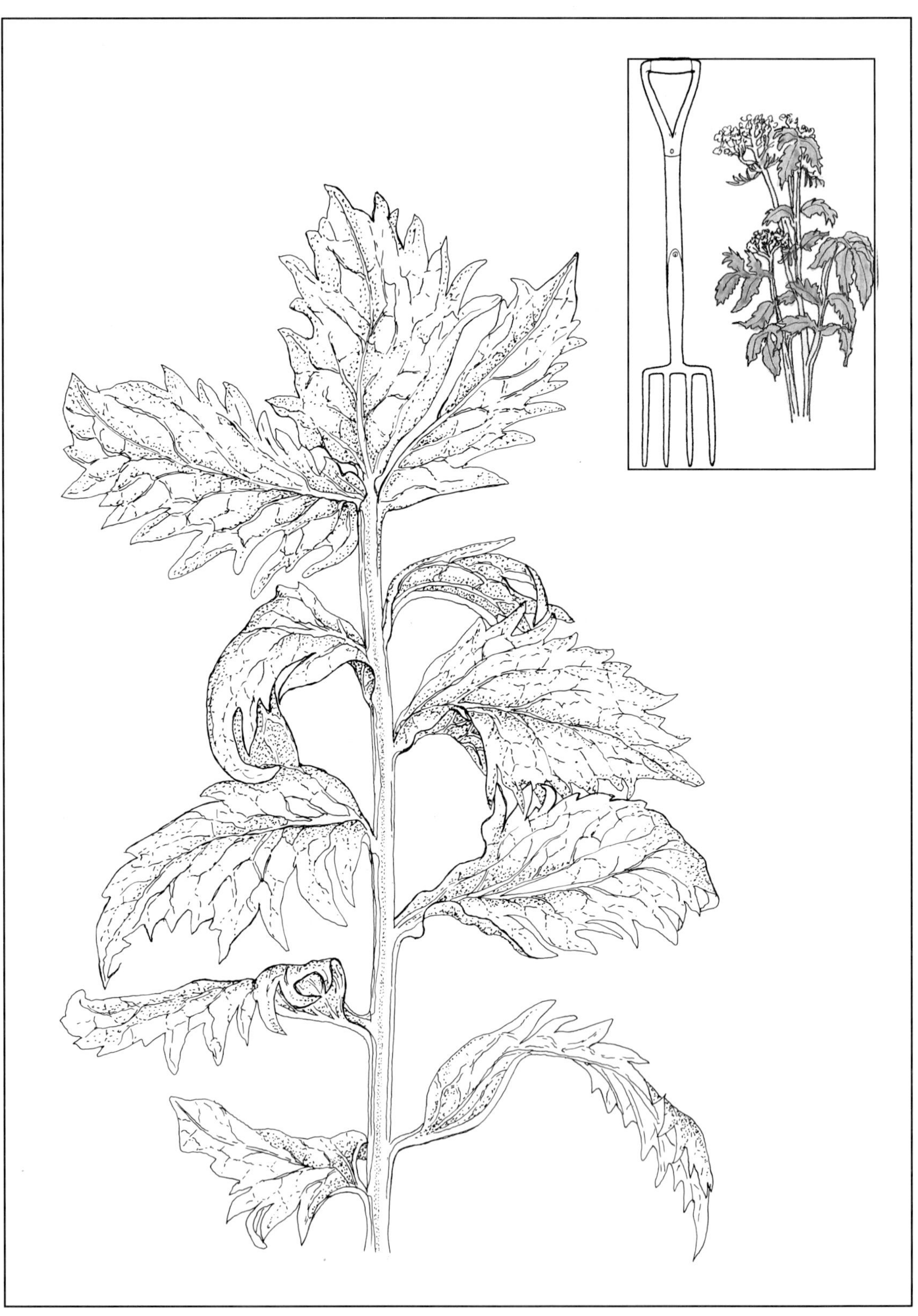

VALERIAN

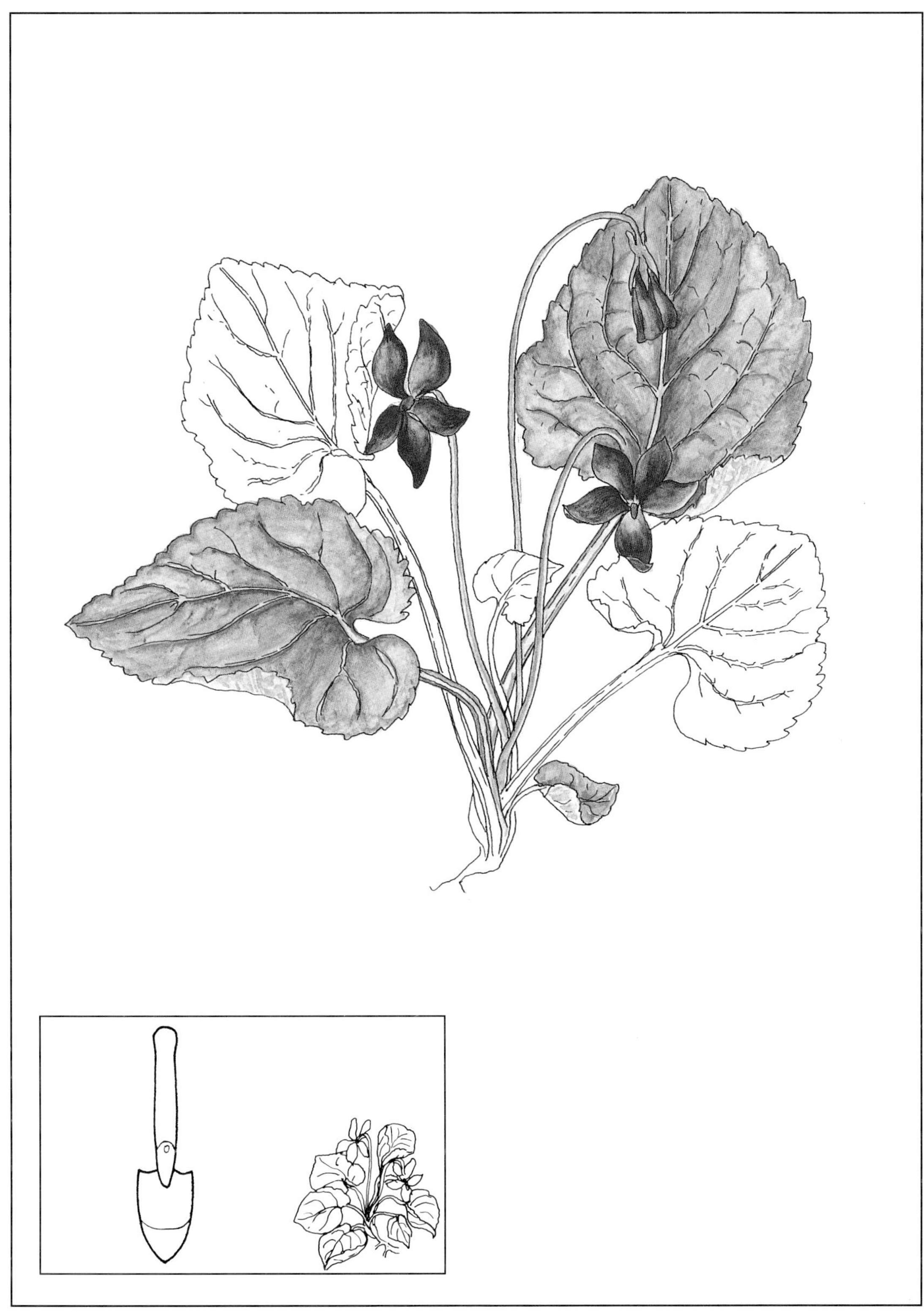

VIOLET

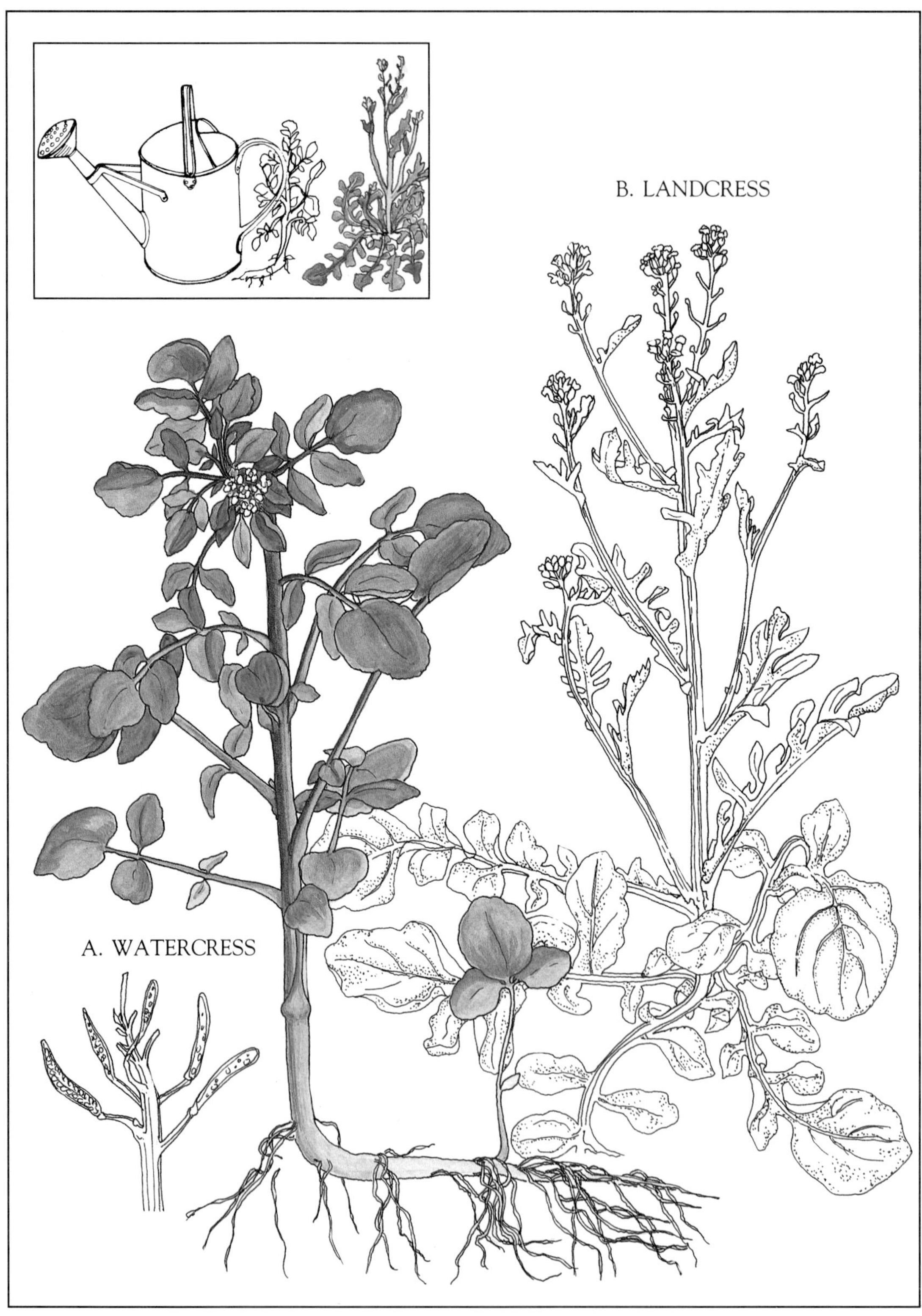
B. LANDCRESS
A. WATERCRESS

WATERCRESS *Nasturtium officinalis* Family: Cruciferae
LANDCRESS *Lapidium sativum*

Description: Watercress is a perennial plant of creeping habit, which needs running water to grow. The leaves are glossy, brownish-green, pinnatifid, with ovate, cordate leaflets. The flowers are small and white, blooming in terminal racemes.

Landcress, also known as American upland cress, is much easier to grow than watercress. It is an annual with dark green, shiny leaflets growing up a pale green, sappy, grooved stem. The flower stalk rises above the leaves and has small yellow blooms. The flavour is more pungent than that of watercress. This herb should not be eaten while flowering. If you don't want to save the seeds you can cut the flower stalks off to ensure a continuing supply of leaves for the table.

Parts used: Whole herb.

Uses: Charts 1, 5, 6, 13, 15, 16.

Interest: Be very careful if you are collecting watercress in the wild as it can harbour liver fluke. Check with your local Agriculture Department to find out if this pest is in your neighbourhood.

WORMWOOD *Artemisia absinthium* Family: Compositae

Synonyms: Old woman, green ginger, absinthe.

Description: A bushy perennial growing about 1 m (3 ft) high. The stems and leaves are covered with fine whitish hairs, giving the plant a silvery appearance. The leaves are alternate, bi- and tri-pinnatifid. The numerous, small, yellow, round flower heads are borne on erect leafy panicles.

Parts used: Leaves, flowering tops.

Uses: Charts 1, 3, 4, 5, 6, 11.

Interest:

For the lips of a loose woman drip honey,
and her speech is smoother than oil:
but in the end she is bitter as wormwood,
sharp as a two edged sword.

Proverbs, 5.3-4

While Wormwood hath seed, get a handful of twaine,
To save against March, to make flea to refrain:
When chamber is sweep'd, and wormwood is strowne,
No flea, for his life, dare abide to be known.
What savour is better, if Physic be true,
For places infected than wormwood or Rue?
It is a comfort for heart and the brain,
And therefore to have it is not in vain.

Thomas Tusser: *Five Hundred Point of Good Husbandry,* 1573

Caution: Excessive or prolonged use of this plant can cause poisoning.

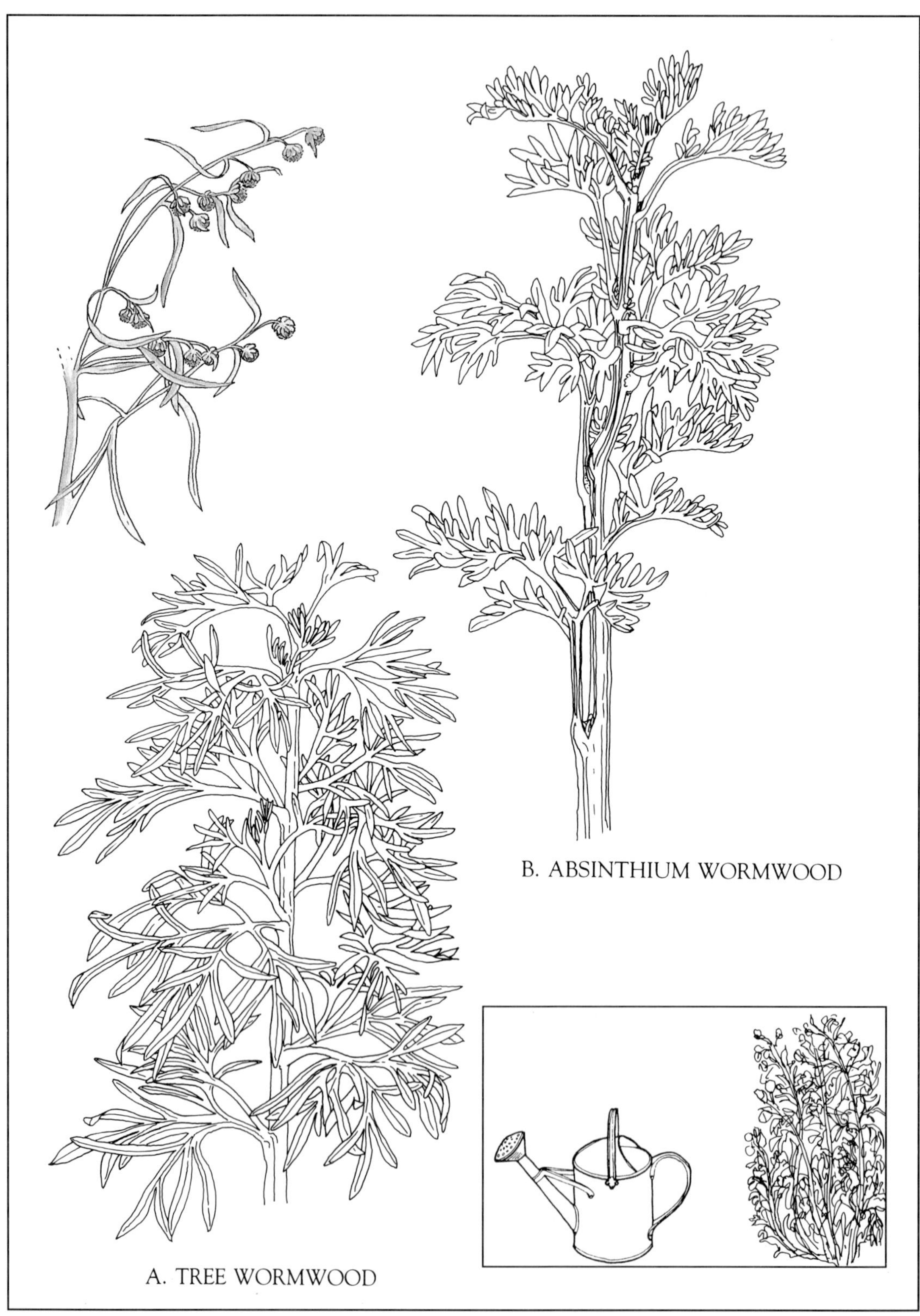
B. ABSINTHIUM WORMWOOD
A. TREE WORMWOOD

YARROW — *Achillea millefolium* — Family: Compositae

Synonyms: Milfoil, thousand leaf, nosebleed.

Description: A perennial plant growing 30-40 cm (12-16 in) in height. The leaves are alternate, bipinnatifid and so finely cut that they are like feathers. The flowers are white, small and daisy-like in flattened terminal heads. There is a variety of yarrow with much coarser, larger leaves and scarlet heads — I grow and use this in the same way as milfoil.

Parts used: Leaves and flowers.

Uses: Charts 1, 3, 4, 5, 6, 7, 10, 12, 13, 14.

Interest: In *The Herball* (1597), Gerard writes that Achilles used this plant to stem the bleeding wounds of his soldiers, hence the name *Achillea*. Bancke's Herbal (1525) also had the following to say:

> *Kynge Achyllis found this herbe, and with it he heled his men that were wounded with yron. For woundes stampe this herbe with Swynes grece, and playster it to the wounde and it shall hele it. And the same it is for ache in the back or in the side.*

To this day the stiff, straight flower stalks are dried and used in the casting of the *I Ching*, an ancient Chinese oracular tradition.

The classic colds, flu and fever remedy among herbalists is an infusion made of yarrow, peppermint and elderflower.

Caution: Extended use of this herb may make skin 'light-sensitive'. This means an intolerance to sunlight is created, causing pigmentation of the skin.

YELLOW DOCK — *Rumex crispus* — Family: Polygonacae

Synonyms: Curled dock, narrow dock, garden patience.

Description: A perennial plant whose stem grows 30-90 cm (1-3 ft) in height. The root (which is the important part of the herb) grows very deep, 23-30 cm (9-12 in) long, and about 1 cm (½ in) thick. It has a rusty brown, quite thick bark with whitish flesh. It is very difficult to eradicate, hence its unpopularity with gardeners. The light green leaves have crisped or wavy edges, are lanceolate to oblong-lanceolate and become progressively smaller up the stem. The flowers are pale green, loosely whorled and are borne in axillary spikes. The seeds are brown with three angles.

Parts used: Root.

Uses: Charts 1, 5, 6.

Interest: If you want to prevent this plant from spreading right through your garden it's best to cut the flower heads off as they develop. If you can find plants growing away from roads or other sources of contamination, then you are fortunate, as you won't have to risk this most important herb becoming a 'nuisance' in your garden.

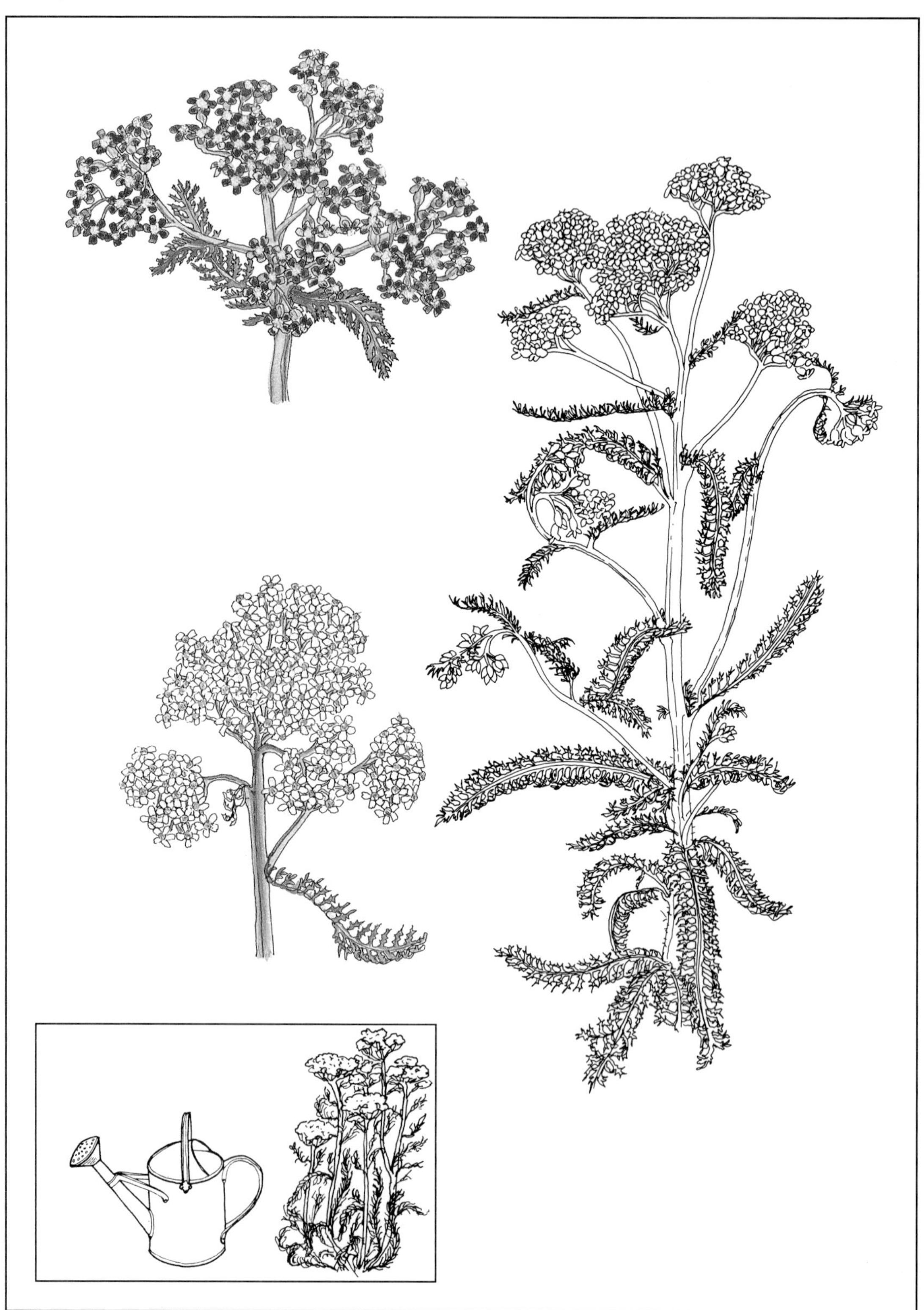

YARROW

YELLOW DOCK

CHAPTER TWO

GROWING, HARVESTING AND STORING HERBS

I have a garden plot,
Wherein there wants nor hearbs, nor roots, nor flowers:
Flowers to smell, roots to eate, hearbs for the pot,
And dainty shelters when the welkin lowers:
Sweet smelling beds of lillies, and of roses,
Which rosemary banks and lavender encloses.

There growes the gilliefloure, the mynt, the dayzie
Both red and white, the blue-veyned violet;
The purple hyacinth, the spike to please thee,
The scarlet dyde carnation bleeding yet:
The sage, the savery, and sweet margerum,
Isop, tyme and eye-bright, good for the blinde and dumbe.

The pinke, the primrose, cowslip and daffadilly,
The hare-bell blue, the crimson cullumbine,
Sage, lettis, parsley, and the milke-whyte lilly,
The rose and speckled flowre cald sops-in-wine,
Fine pretty king-cups, and the yellow bootes,
That growes by rivers and by shallow brookes.

Richard Barnfield, *The Affectionate Shepherd,* 1594

As I write these words I remember my home in North Wales when I was a teenager. Grey stone walls with windows overlooking heather-purple mountains, valleys and caves where foxes raised their cubs, and the north window framing the turbulent, exciting ocean between us and Ireland. In the kitchen there was a dark oak Welsh dresser, beeswaxed until it reflected the blue and white pots standing on it, and a floor of red quarry tiles washed with buttermilk which gave it a rich warm glow in the firelight. Hanging from the black oak beams were home-smoked hams, strings of black puddings and bunches of herbs gathered from the meadows, river edge and hillsides.

The larder off the kitchen was built into the hill, making it as cold as any refrigerator. It had a huge marble bench on which red salmon (caught in the river by my father), fresh milk and buttermilk stayed cold and delicious. It also housed home-churned butter wrapped in sorrel leaves, a bowl of fresh eggs and, if we were lucky, a clove and apple pie with a fragrance to make your mouth water. Hanging from the ceiling was a pheasant and a rabbit or two, tribute to my father's prowess with the gun and also to his delicacy — he never took from the sky, river or fields more than his family could eat or trade with friends. On the floor stood stone bottles of dandelion and burdock wine which I was allowed only in medicinal doses. How I longed for more.

I look back with nostalgia on these days of my youth which I took so much for granted — I remember complaining at the dinner table, "Not pheasant *again!*" We can't return to our childhood, but we can do as much as we are able to create a safe, wholesome and happy environment for our families.

It has been said that wild herbs are more potent than herbs grown in a garden and this may well be true, but these days they are also more contaminated. In the following pages you will find many ways to ensure that your plants are full of vigour and goodness. You will discover how to grow your herbs, how to harvest, dry and store them, and how to use them as companion plants and insect repellants.

If you wish to begin with only a few plants you can work your way through the charts, pinpointing the herbs that are repeated most often. In this way, you will begin with a selection that has wide application. If you have very little space you can use the charts to find a selection of small herbs that will suit you. For instance, if you have a pocket-sized garden you are not going to find it possible to grow angelica, bay or elder. My family has found an answer to this problem: we have a communal vegetable garden and share the cost, work, picking and eating. It might be possible for you to find friends who also want to grow herbs and to divide the cost and growing between you. You will benefit in lots of ways — shared interest, expense and space.

If you have never grown herbs before, you are about to experience a very joyful time as you watch the plants grow, gather them and turn them into all the exciting things in this book. You will also see the benefits to your garden as the herbs give their minerals to the soil and their essential oils to the air.

Many people think that a garden is made up of a herb patch, some flower beds and the vegetable plot. I have a garden where a border may be woolly yarrow, parsley or some other low-growing herb, and silver beet grows cheek by jowl with roses and borage — a great colour combination. Tomatoes, capsicums and other vegetables share very happily with the herbs and flowers. The only precaution you need to take is to make sure the vegetables get the extra space and food that they need.

From now on, be very careful of well-wishers who offer to do some weeding for you. It's more than likely you will find your precious dandelions, shepherd's purse and plantain in a dying pile and your friend very happy at having done such a good job. You will develop a whole new attitude towards 'weeds' when you realise they are all valuable, though not necessarily in the position they have chosen to grow. Give them their own place and watch them flourish.

Glossary of gardening terms

This is a very short list of terms, sufficient for the scope of this book. If you want to know more, consult one of the many good books on organic gardening which are now available. I mention a few I like in the booklist on p250.

Acid Soil, water etc, with a pH level below 7.0, indicating the absence of lime. A simple soil test can be done at home using litmus paper. Put a tablespoon of soil in a dish, cover with water, and when it has settled dip the paper into the water. If the paper is red then the soil is acid, if blue it is alkaline. If you'd like a more accurate test you can buy a testing kit. The application of good compost balances most soils. However, if you have azaleas or other acid-loving plants in your garden, you must remember to mulch them with pine needles, sawdust or other acidic materials.

Alkaline Soil, water etc, with a pH above 7.0. See **Acid.**

Annual Completing a whole life cycle in one year.

Biennial A plant which fruits in its second year and then dies.

Damping off A condition in which a seedling rots at the base where it touches the soil. 'Damping off' is usually a fungal problem.

Deciduous Plants which lose their leaves during the winter season.

Drill A channel made in soil to sow seed, usually twice as deep as the circumference of the seed.

Humus Decomposed organic matter.

Litmus paper See **Acid.**

Mulch Material laid around plants to protect the roots, conserve moisture, or deter the growth of unwanted plants, e.g. straw, grass clippings, newspaper, rocks.

Node A sometimes swollen joint where a leaf joins a stem.

Perennial A plant which lives for more than two years.

Slaked lime Otherwise known as hydrate of lime. This is quicklime which has been treated with water, making it less caustic and more readily available to the soil.

Vermiculite A water-absorbing substance made from mica. It is very useful for mixing with soil in pots and as a medium for growing seeds and cuttings, as it helps to hold water and air in the soil.

Measurements in the garden

We once had a very knowledgeable horticulture graduate working with us at the farm. She planned some very beautiful vegetable gardens which were weeded, dug over, composted and made ready for the big day of first planting. When I went into the garden to help I found her planting beans with the aid of a tape measure. Well... to each his own, but I'm sure tape measures weren't invented when Adam was a boy so here is the easy way to measure, taught me by my father who was a wonderful gardener. The measurements below are of my body; I am quite tall and have long fingers so your 'body ruler' might be different. It really doesn't matter as plants can't read rulers.

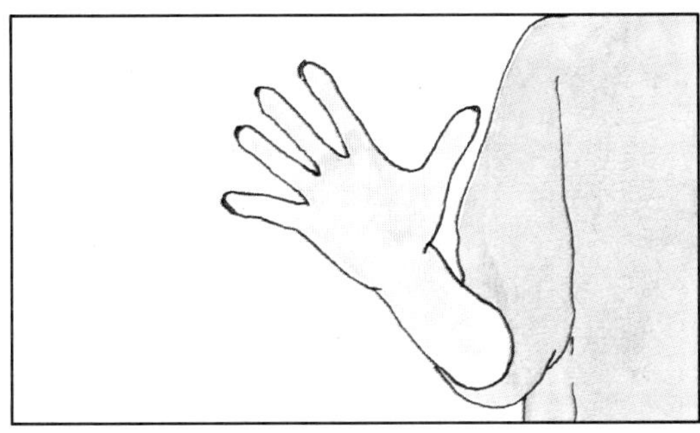

Handspan = 20 cm (8 in)

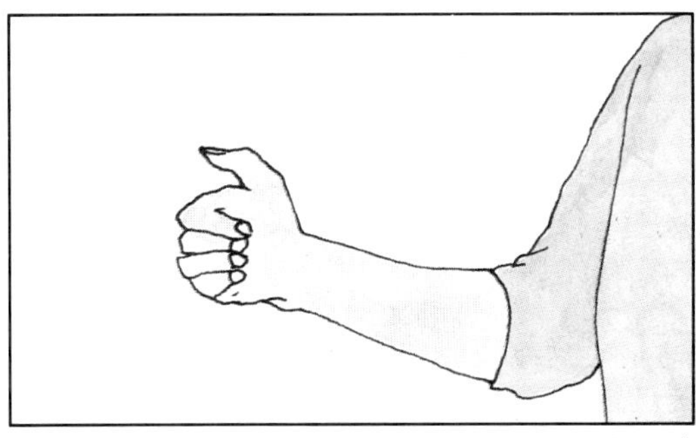

End of thumb to first joint = 2½ cm (1 in)

End of fingers to elbow = 43 cm (17 in)

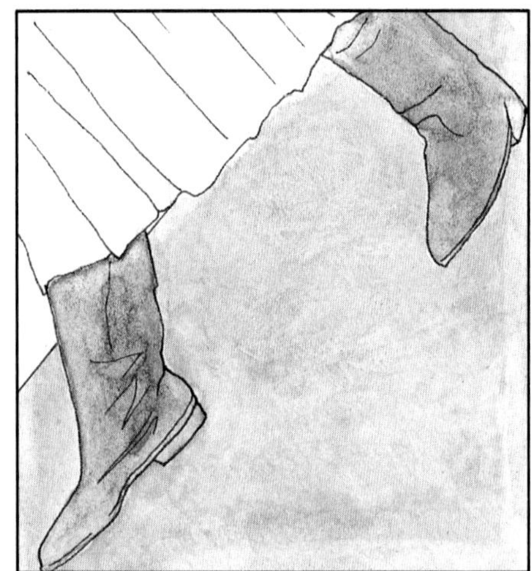

Big stride (heel to heel) = 90 cm (36 in)

Suggestions for garden equipment

Buy the best you can afford.
Fork
Spade
Shovel
Plastic grass rake

Metal rake
Secateurs
Trowel
Hand fork
Wheelbarrow
Plastic buckets
Selection of stakes
Watering can
Plastic garbage bins (for compost, liquid sprays and fertilisers)
Craft/pop sticks for marking rows of seeds, etc.
Spray bottles
Soft twine for tying up plants
Garden sieve
Garden hoses
Gardening gloves
Plastic pots
Small jars for storing seeds
Large jars for storing dried herbs
Cheesecloth bags
Old flyscreen windows for drying herbs
Sharp garden knife and scissors
Black plastic
Fine-tip waterproof marker
Selection of trays etc, for seed sowing

Growing from seed

Seeds can be planted in containers and then transplanted, or sown directly in the garden where you want them to grow. The decision depends on several factors such as size of seed, difficulty of transplanting, and weather conditions. These factors have been taken into consideration in the planting charts.

Make drills and sow seeds

Cover the seeds with finely sieved soil

You will need a bag of good quality potting mix or some sieved compost, and some seed trays. The trays need to be at least 3 cm (1¼ in) high and have good drainage. I find that egg cartons make good seed trays as you can cut up the carton when the plant is 1-2 cm (½ in) tall and plant each portion with its little seedling without disturbing the roots. The carton will rot, adding humus to the soil. I also use the little trays in which seedlings are sold, and other favourites of mine are square 2 litre (3½

Firm down gently with the back of your hand

pint) ice cream containers. I cut these down to a suitable height and punch lots of holes in the bottom with a skewer. Things you would throw out as rubbish are often useful as seed trays.

Fill the container to within 1 cm (½ in) of the top after firming; water it down with chamomile spray (see p122) and make drills (channels) in which to sow the

Label immediately using a waterproof pen

seed. (If you are using egg cartons the drills aren't necessary.) Sprinkle the seed as thinly as possible and cover with very finely sieved soil to about twice the thickness of the seed. If possible, place the tray in water when needed rather than watering from above, as there is less chance of disturbing the seed. Occasionally, give a spray of chamomile to prevent 'damping off'.

The seeds will need good light to germinate, but mustn't be left in full sun. A shadehouse or similar is ideal. The surface of the soil should never be allowed to dry out completely. Nor should it be sodden, or the seeds and/or seedlings will rot. I cover the seed tray with a sheet of plastic or glass which I remove for an hour early morning and evening. This helps to prevent drying out and keeps the seeds warmer. The plastic

Thinning the seedlings

or glass should be removed as soon as the plants show through.

The seedlings should be thinned out as soon as possible. Do this by nipping off surplus plants at surface level until there are no plants touching each other. Transplant when they are about 2-3 cm (¾-1¼ in) high, being very careful not to damage the delicate roots as you take them from the soil. I use a wooden tool shaped like a delicate two-pronged fork, but a wooden craft or 'pop' stick is fine. Water the hole before planting the seedling, and water again after planting. Firm the soil round the plant and finish with a dose of one of the sprays on page 122 to ensure a good start.

Transplanting

Cuttings

The advantage of growing a plant from a cutting is that you will get an exact replica of the parent, i.e. a 'clone'. The best time of day to take cuttings is the early morning before the sun has made the plant soft and limp. Late spring is the best time of year to start cuttings of non-deciduous plants and winter for plants which lose their leaves during this season. Some plants are so obliging that any time seems all right. Sandy soil, river sand or vermiculite may be used to strike the cuttings. There is a hormone powder available which is called 'rooting powder'. It's supposed to assist and hasten the growth of roots. I can't comment on the efficiency of this powder as I've never used it but if you have problems with cuttings you might like to try it.

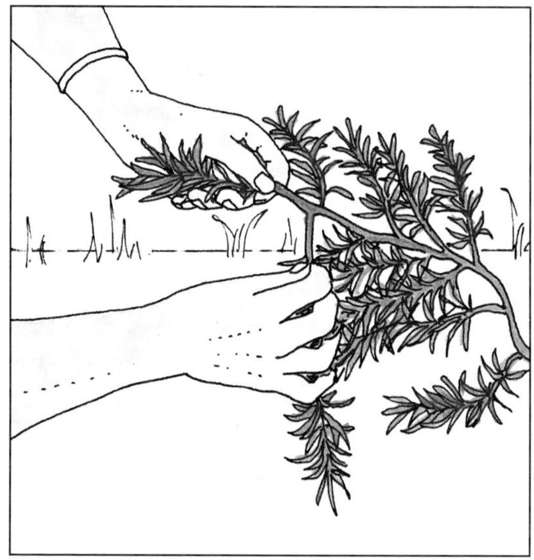

Taking a 'heel' cutting

Taking a 'tip' cutting

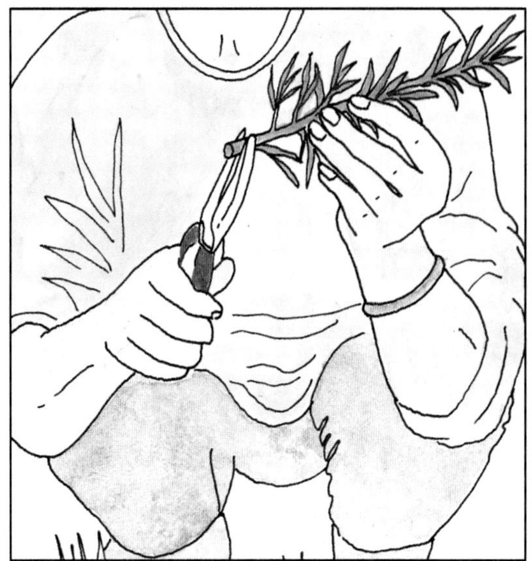

Trimming at an angle, just below a node

Cut the top leaves back to half their length

Strip off the remaining leaves

Cuttings enclosed in a plastic bag 'greenhouse'

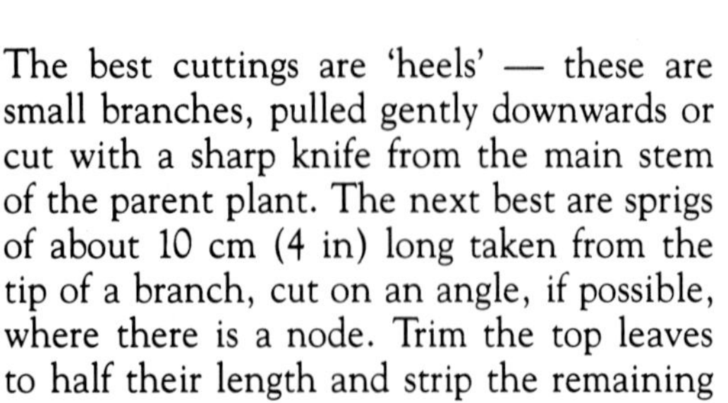

The best cuttings are 'heels' — these are small branches, pulled gently downwards or cut with a sharp knife from the main stem of the parent plant. The next best are sprigs of about 10 cm (4 in) long taken from the tip of a branch, cut on an angle, if possible, where there is a node. Trim the top leaves to half their length and strip the remaining leaves off the stem. Using a stick, make holes in the potting mixture, put the cuttings in the holes and firm in well, leaving about 5 cm (2 in) showing.

You can put a lot of cuttings in each pot — in fact, they seem to prefer this to being alone. When the pot is full, water it, put in a plastic bag and seal the top of the bag.

This stops the cuttings from drying out. Leave the pot in a semi-shaded position for 3-4 weeks, when the new plants should be ready to plant out. Open the plastic bag every 3-4 days to give the plants some fresh air and prevent moulds from developing. Plant in the same way as seedlings. Keep the roots cool and moist while they are waiting their turn.

I live on sandy soil and often put cuttings straight in the ground where they are to grow. I cover them with a plastic bag with some holes punched in it, weigh the edges down with stones or rocks and leave it on until I see some new top growth. Take the bag off for about an hour, three times a week, to give a good airing to the plant. This works very well and saves time for me and trauma for the plants as their new roots are very delicate and can be easily broken when you take them out of the pot.

Root division

The best time for this method of propagation is early spring when the new growth is just beginning to appear. It is not only desirable but necessary to divide perennials, as it gives them a new lease of life and prevents clumps from becoming too big and straggly.

Using a spade to divide a tough clump of roots

Pulling a clump of roots apart

Here is a really easy way to grow new plants — simply lift the whole clump and pull or cut it into new plants, each one having its own piece of root. Trim the tops and roots back equally to avoid stress to the new plant. Replant as quickly as possible and water in very well. If for some reason you can't plant immediately, be sure to cover the roots with a wet sack or similar to prevent drying out.

There are some plants, particularly comfrey and horseradish, which can be propagated by chopping their roots into several parts (each part must have an 'eye'). These separate pieces of root will each grow into a plant.

Mounding

Some plants (see planting chart) may be very easily propagated by mounding. The best time to do this is in the autumn. The plant is mounded over with soil and then shaken lightly to enable the soil to get right down among the branches. About 12-15 cm (5-6 in) of the top of the plant must be left exposed. Leave the plant over the winter, topping up with soil if needed. In the spring, lift the whole plant and with secateurs cut away all the new rooted cuttings.

Mounding is a good system to use with plants which have become leggy and bare at the base — thyme, lavender, small rosemaries and winter savory are some of the plants which benefit from being treated in this way.

Mounding a plant with soil

Freeing the tips of a mounded plant

Using a peg to layer a branch

Covering the pegged area with soil

Herbs growing indoors

Layering

This is similar to mounding, but only single stems are treated.

Pegs are needed to hold the stem or branch on the ground and all but the tips are covered with soil. After a few weeks the soil may be removed and the rooted stem cut away from the main plant. The pegs may be pieces of wire about 10 cm (4 in) long bent into a 'peg' shape.

Indoor growing

It's possible to grow some herbs in pots, either indoors or out: the charts will tell you which are the most suitable. The soil is a most important factor as it needs to retain plenty of moisture but also to drain well. I use half-and-half compost and sandy loam. The sandy loam could be replaced by a bought potting mix. Just a word on proprietary potting mixes — most of the ones I have tried are very poor; they seem to be mainly immature sawdust with a bit of peat moss thrown in. If you have a good nursery nearby, take the advice of the owner or gardener and then buy only a small bag to start with.

Herbs grown indoors never seem to get as big or strong as those grown in the garden. Let's face it, there is no such thing as an indoor plant. There are only plants which will tolerate being indoors or which need to be wintered indoors because they are not in their native habitat. With all this in mind you can still 'have a go'; some people have more success than others.

The prime requirements are good light (but not burning heat through glass), fresh air without a draught, and not much artificial heat. Try to give them a day every now and again in a shadehouse or other sheltered place out of doors.

Herb planting

The planting chart will give you some idea of the conditions under which your herbs will flourish. Please don't imagine that you have to avoid growing the plant if your soil doesn't conform to the suggestion on the chart. These headings are guides only to the best liked conditions. The soil at 'Rivendell Farm' was rich, quite heavy, chocolate loam. My present garden at 'Amberwood' is very light and sandy. The herbs I have growing now are the same ones that I transplanted from the farm and are just as happy here as they were before. Plants will, as a general rule, adapt to different soils and different amounts of sunlight; they will often tolerate some shade, even if they are specified as 'full sun' plants on the chart.

The area in which herbs seem very unwilling to change their habits is the amount of water they need. Too much water on a sage or lavender will cause them to die very quickly as they, and several other herbs, hate having wet feet. If you deprive angelica or the mints of water their growth will be very stunted or they will die. Try to arrange your garden so that plants which like plenty of water live together and the ones which enjoy drier conditions are in their own area.

KEY to Chart 1

I Invasive because they seed so readily. Create a corner to restrain or plant in large, deep containers. Easy to control by giving surplus plants away!

W Collect from the wild if possible. Make sure the source is uncontaminated by traffic or chemical sprays.

O Seed viable for a short time only.

B Bottom heat needed to strike cuttings.

Chart 1 Planting

	Annual	Biennial	Perennial	Compact growth	Spreading habit	Frost tender	Frost resistant	Height, short - 30 cm	Height, medium - 90 cm	Height, tall - over 90 cm	Invasive - see note	Lots of water	Medium water	Little water	Grow from seed	Grow from cuttings	Grow from root division	Grow from mounding/layering	Grow from runners	Grow from suckers	Seeds may be sprouted	Soil, acid-loving	Semi-shade	Shade	Sun	Suitable for indoors	Winter dormant
Alfalfa			X	X			X		X				X		X						X						
Aloe			X	X		X			X					X						X					X	X	
Angelica		X		X			X			X		X			O								X				
Anise	X			X		X			X				X		X										X		
Basil	X			X		X		X					X		X										X	X	
Bay			X	X			X			X			X			B									X		
Bergamot			X		X		X		X				X				X		X				X				
Borage	X			X			X		X		I		X		X										X		
Calendula	X			X		X		X			I		X		X										X		
Caraway	X	X		X			X		X				X		X										X		
Catnep			X	X			X		X				X		X	X	X	X							X		
Cayenne		X		X		X			X				X		X										X		
Chamomile, Roman			X		X		X	X					X		X		X		X			X	X				
Chamomile, German	X			X		X			X				X		X										X		
Chives			X	X			X	X					X		X		X								X	X	
Comfrey			X		X		X		X		X		X				X								X		X
Coriander	X			X		X			X				X		X										X		
Dandelion			X	X			X	X			I			X	X										X		
Dill	X			X		X			X				X		X										X		
Elder			X	X			X			X			X			X									X		
Fennel		X	X		X		X		X	X				X	X										X		
Feverfew			X	X			X		X		I		X		X										X		
Garlic			X	X			X	X					X				X								X		
Ginger			X		X	X			X				X				X								X		
Horseradish			X		X		X		X		X		X				X								X		X
Hyssop			X	X			X		X					X	X	X	X	X							X		
Landcress		X		X			X	X			I	X			X						X				X		
Lavender			X	X			X		X					X		X		X							X		
Lemon, Balm			X	X			X		X				X		X	X	X	X					X			X	
Lemon, Grass			X	X		X			X			X					X								X		

Chart 1 (cont) Planting

	Annual	Biennial	Perennial	Compact growth	Spreading habit	Frost tender	Frost resistant	Height, short - 30 cm	Height, medium - 90 cm	Height, tall - over 90 cm	Invasive - see note	Lots of water	Medium water	Little water	Grow from seed	Grow from cuttings	Grow from root division	Grow from mounding/layering	Grow from runners	Grow from suckers	Seeds may be sprouted	Soil, acid-loving	Semi-shade	Shade	Sun	Suitable for indoors	Winter dormant
Liquorice			X		X		X			X	X		X		X		X			X					X		
Mallow	X		X	X			X		X					X	X										X		
Marjoram			X	X		X		X					X		X	X		X							X	X	
Mints			X		X		X	X			X	X			X				X				X			X	
Mullein		X		X			X			X			X		X										X		
Nasturtium	X				X	X		X					X		X										X		
Nettle	X		X		X		X	X			W		X	X	X										X		
Oregano			X	X			X		X				X		X		X								X	X	
Parsley		X	X	X		X		X					X		X										X	X	
Pennyroyal			X		X		X	X				X			X		X							X		X	
Plantain			X	X			X		X		W		X	X	X										X		
Raspberry			X		X		X			X	X		X			X									X		
Red Clover			X	X			X		X				X		X						X				X		
Rosemary			X	X			X			X				X		X		X							X	X	
Rue			X	X			X		X					X	X	X									X		
Sage			X	X			X	X						X	X	X									X		
Savory, Summer	X			X		X			X				X		X										X	X	
Savory, Winter			X	X			X	X					X		X	X		X							X		
Shepherd's Purse	X			X		X	X	X			W		X	X	X										X		
Southernwood			X	X			X		X					X		X									X		
Tansy			X		X		X		X				X				X								X		
Tarragon			X		X		X		X				X				X								X		X
Thyme, Garden			X		X		X	X					X		X		X	X							X	X	
Thyme, Lemon			X		X		X	X					X				X	X							X	X	
Valerian			X		X		X		X				X				X								X		X
Violet			X		X		X	X					X						X					X			
Watercress			X		X		X	X			W	X							X		X	X	X				
Wormwoods			X	X			X			X			X			X									X		
Yarrows			X		X		X		X		X		X	X			X								X		
Yellow Dock			X		X		X		X		W		X	X	X										X		

Compost

Now that you are growing your herbs you will be wondering how to fertilise them. Compost and herbal sprays, if well made, are the only nutrition they will ever need. Compost is a home-made fertiliser made from rotted organic ingredients. It is cheap, natural and adds humus to the soil. It improves drainage in a heavy soil and holds moisture in a sandy or light soil. None of these advantages is to be gained by using artificial fertilisers.

If you are trying to avoid the use of chemicals or other pollutants in your garden you should be very careful about the raw materials you use in the compost heap. The fragrant grass clippings from your local lawn-mowing man could well be from lawns which have been sprayed with weed killers or other poisons. The rich, wholesome looking animal manure may be from animals which have been treated with antibiotics or chemical drenches. Seaweed washed up after a storm may contain heavy metals or other undesirable elements introduced into the ocean from factory effluent or ships. There is no need to become paranoid about this problem but you should maintain an awareness and ask potential suppliers what, if anything, has been used. It has been my experience that no offence is caused if the questions are asked diplomatically. In fact, the people concerned show a great deal of interest as it frequently hasn't occurred to them that the recycling of these chemicals could cause a problem.

If you become a 'compost addict' (a very easy addiction to form) you should visit your local library and browse among the many books on compost making. I have included a few in the booklist on page 250. I am a rather lazy gardener and an impatient one as well so I look for both the quickest and the easiest way. The methods which follow have been working well for me for years.

These methods are known as 'aerobic' composting, as the introduction of oxygen by regular turning speeds up the decomposition of the pile and keeps the compost smelling sweet. If an aerobic pile smells nasty or isn't heating up then it's not working properly and you need to consider what you may be doing wrong. It could be too much or too little water or sun, not enough nitrogenous matter (i.e. manure, grass clippings), or you may not be turning it enough. The most common error is overwatering. This is easily rectified by adding more dry material such as sawdust or straw.

Collect the materials in separate piles or bins: use grass clippings, manure (dog and cat manure is okay if left to mature for a long time), weeds, leaves (not from non-deciduous trees such as eucalypts), food scraps, vacuum cleaner contents, hair, hay, straw, sawdust etc. Avoid the addition of fat as it takes a long time to decompose. The finer all the materials are, the quicker the pile will be complete.

When you have enough, choose an area near to a tap, which gets some sun daily but not too much (filtered light under a tree is ideal) and which is not too close to the house. I arrange for lawn clippings and horse manure to be delivered on the same day if possible. All household scraps and green waste from my garden have been accumulating in bins with some soil sprinkled over to deter marauding possums, rats and cats. When everything is ready, plus a bag of garden lime to sweeten the pile, I can begin.

This method has the advantage of not using bins as the basis of its construction but could make a neat, small garden look a bit messy. This may not bother you if, like me, you are so proud of your compost that guests in their 'glad rags' are led down the garden path to admire the compost pile before they get to eat!

Building a compost heap

1. Dig over the soil, insert a central pole for aeration and watering.
2. Put a layer of loose material (e.g. leaves) to assist aeration.
3. Spread a 5 cm (2 in) thick layer of manure.
4. Add a small handful of lime.
5. Put on 30 cm (12 in) grass clippings, vegetable scraps etc, plus finely chopped herbs (see page 116).
6. Cover with 2-3 cm (¾-1¼ in) of soil.

Repeat these layers until the pile is 1-2 m (3-6 ft) high, finishing with a thicker layer of soil. The minimum size for a heap is 1 x 1 m (3 x 3 ft). If it's any smaller it won't heat up. Try to have the base of the pile the same size as the height for optimum efficiency. Remove the stake and water the pile. It is impossible to tell you how much water to add. The pile needs to be as moist as a squeezed-out sponge.

Cover with a sheet of black plastic with a few holes punched in and weigh this down with rocks or bricks. During the next week turn the pile twice. Have an identical patch dug next to it ready for turning the pile onto, and then watch it go. It will

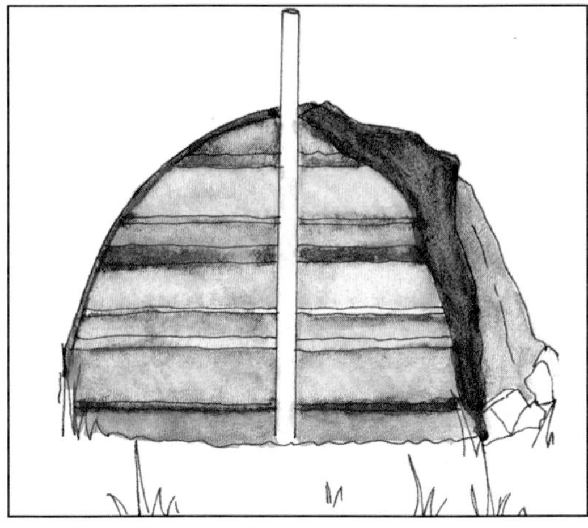

A section through the compost heap; notice the layers and the pole

begin to heat up very quickly and it is possible for a heap to reach a temperature of 75°C (165°F) which will kill diseased organisms and seeds. Don't forget to keep it moist. After the first two weeks, turn only about once weekly.

After about two weeks the pile will have cooled and it is at this stage that you add the final refinement to give you a perfect compost heap. Poke holes in the

Turning the pile

pile and introduce as many worms as you can beg, borrow or buy. They will do miraculous things in a very short time. They chew up the raw materials and pass them out the other end as fine castings full of nitrogen, phosphorus, potassium, magnesium and calcium. Look in your local telephone directory for 'Worm Farms' and the owners will be able to advise you how many you will need. If the materials were finely cut and the weather is warm, you should have compost in about 6 weeks. The pile will end up about a quarter of its original size.

The second method involves the building of bins. If you want aesthetically pleasing bins you can make wooden ones. If, however, the bin area is out of sight and you are looking, like me, at 'recycled, quick and cheap', the following idea might be what you need.

It is good to have two or even three bins side by side, so that the mix can be turned from one into the other with the minimum of labour. As you can see from the diagram, a visit to the local rubbish dump or demolition firm can furnish the raw materials.

The diagram shows two bins side by side, made of corrugated iron and metal fence posts (star pickets). If these are not available, any 150 cm (5 ft) hard wood stakes will do. The corrugated iron sheets are about 100 cm (3½ ft) wide and 200 cm (7 ft) long. The stakes are hammered into the ground and the tin slotted down between them. If three bins are wanted, an extra sheet of iron or a longer sheet is used across the back and front. If the back of the bins are situated against a fence or a wall, the iron backing may not be needed. The front sheet needs to be removable (this is not shown in the diagram); it is held in place in the same manner as the side sheets, allowing for easier access to turn and collect the compost.

The bins may be covered by a further sheet/s of iron or black plastic. The building and treatment of the compost in the bins is exactly the same as that described above for a compost heap.

I tend to have both a compost heap and compost bins. The heap seems to be a little quicker, but the bins are useful for storing while you are waiting to accumulate sufficient materials and they keep your

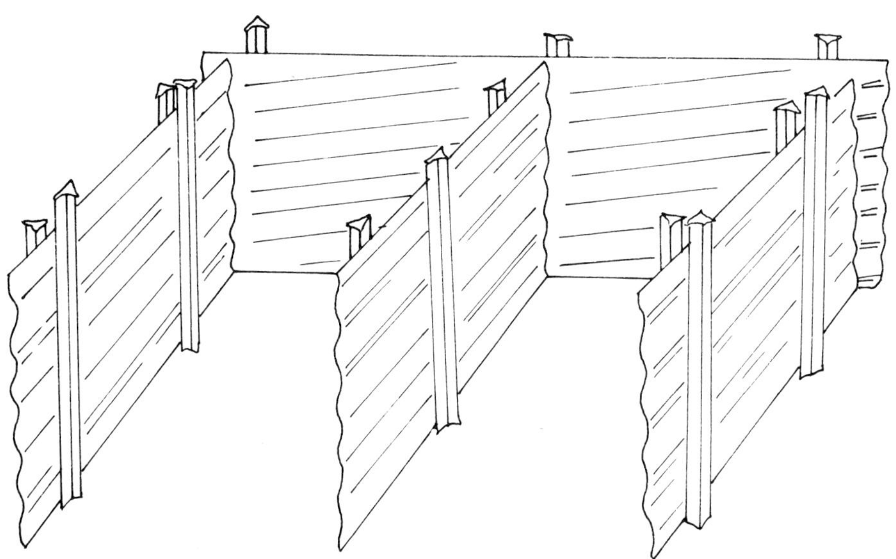

Compost bins

compost in one place if you aren't going to use it all at once.

This compost is what you are going to use for potting and to pile on your garden, adding humus and nutrients to the soil and plants. It is the only fertiliser, humus and mulch you will need apart from herbal sprays. I think we need to be thankful that composting methods have changed over the years. The recipe which follows doesn't appeal to me at all!

Compost

2 Barrowsful of goose dung,
steeped in bullocks blood,
2 Barrowsful of sugar-bakers scum
2 Barrowsful of night soil,
2 Barrowsful of fine yellow loam.

Isaac Emmerton, *Culture and Management of the Auricula,* 1815

Herbs to use in the Compost Heap and their main Nutrients

Comfrey	Adds calcium, nitrogen, potassium.
Yarrow	One chopped leaf in each layer will accelerate the pile. Yarrow contains copper, nitrates and phosphates.
Nettle	Adds iron, copper and calcium.
Dandelion	Adds iron, copper, potassium, sulphur and manganese.
Chamomile	'Sweetens' the pile, rich in calcium.

I am not suggesting that you should use only the above herbs in the compost heap but mention these particularly as they are very rich in the minerals needed. All herbs will add vital nutrients. I often trim the herbs and scatter the clippings directly onto the garden to rot and act as mulch, humus and fertiliser.

Biodynamic herbal fertiliser

This fertiliser is an adaptation of one being used extensively in New Zealand and other places with very successful results. It is best to use dried herbs, but if you don't have dried herbs in stock you can use double the quantity of fresh. Spray or water this solution on to your garden every two weeks during spring and autumn.

Cow/horse manure, dried **Rain water**	*1 teaspoon* *5 litres (1 gallon)*	Mix well, leave in the sun for 2 days
Chamomile, dandelion leaves, nettle, plantain, sage, yarrow	*1 cup of each*	Take 1 cup liquid from above, add to herbs plus 22 litres (5 gallons) water (rain if possible). Leave in the sun for a further 2 days. Strain before using.

Some suggestions for garden planning

Herbs loved by bees and butterflies

Plant these throughout your vegetable garden, under fruit trees or anywhere that you want good pollination to take place.

Anise	Basil	Mallow	Marjoram
Bergamot	Borage	Mints	Rosemary
Catnep	Dandelion	Sage	Thyme
Lavender	Lemon Balm	Valerian	Yarrow

Colour in the garden

Grey or silver herbs

Catnep	Lavenders	Rue
Sage	Southernwood	Wormwoods

Blue, mauve or purple flowers

Borage	Catnep	Chives
Hyssop	Lavender	Pennyroyal
Rosemary	Thymes	Violet

Red/pink flowers

Bergamot	Clover	Comfrey
Coriander	Mallow	Savory, Summer
Valerian	Yarrow	

Yellow/orange flowers

Aloe	Calendula	Dandelion
Dill	Nasturtium	Rue
	Tansy	

White flowers

Anise	Basil	Caraway
Catnep	Chamomile	Elder
Feverfew	Lemon Balm	Marjoram
Savory, Winter		Yarrow

Aromatic herbs

Angelica	Basil	Bergamot
Catnep	Chamomile	Coriander
Lavender	Lemon Balm	Marjoram
Mints	Rosemary	Southernwood
Tansy	Thymes	Wormwood

Flowers for salads

Bergamot	Borage	Calendula
Dandelion	Elder	Fennel
Nasturtium	Rosemary	Violet

Chart 2 Companion Planting

	Apple trees	Apricot trees	Asparagus	Beans	Broccoli	Brussels sprouts	Cabbage	Cauliflower	Carrots	Celery	Cucumber	Grapes	Kohlrabi	Lettuce	Parsnips	Peach trees	Potatoes	Radishes	Raspberries	Roses	Silverbeet	Strawberries	Tomatoes	Zucchini
Anise			O	O	O	O	O	O	O	O	O			O	O			O			O	O	O	O
Basil		O	O									O											O	
Borage																						O		
Calendula				O										O			O			O			O	
Chamomiles							O																	
Chives	O								O		O												O	
Coriander							O		O															
Dill							O			O													O	
Fennel				X									X										X	
Horseradish	O	O															O							
Hyssop							O					O						X						
Garlic	O			X			X								O	O				O		X		
Lavender																					O			
Marjoram											O													
Mints							O																	
Nasturtium	O				O	O	O	O			O	O	O					O						O
Oregano							O				O													
Parsley			O																	O			O	
Rosemary							O		O								X						X	
Rue							X																	
Sage							O		O													O		
Savories				O																				
Southernwood		O																						
Tansy	O	O					O	O				O				O			O	O				
Thyme					O	O	O	O																

KEY to Chart 2

O Plants which are good companions.

X Plants which are bad companions.

Companion planting

Chart 2 gives you a general idea which plants like or dislike each other. The reasons for these preferences are many and sometimes it's impossible to know why they exist. Some plants exude such strong essential oil perfumes that they disguise the smell of other neighbouring plants, thus protecting the plants from predators. Other herbs give off secretions from their roots which are of benefit to nearby plants, or their roots penetrate the soil to such a depth that nutrients are brought up into the upper soil. These deep-rooted plants have the additional benefit of helping to break up heavy soil. Tall plants protect smaller plants from wind and sun. Some plants are visited by bees and other insects, thus helping to attract pollinating insects to the vicinity.

A lot of companion planting is plain common sense and learning to know your herbs and what conditions they like. You will make mistakes initially. We have all done so in the past, and will do so in the future, but these mistakes are sometimes the best way of learning. I make every effort not to move self-sown plants which often appear, seemingly from nowhere, in my garden. These plants are almost always stronger and bigger than the plants which I put into the ground with such care! When I go for walks, I find it of great interest to see where plants choose to grow in the wild. I learn a lot from these observations.

The average garden is a far cry from the forests of Europe, the dry, hot cliffs of Greece or the lush meadows and hedgerows of Britain. The best we can do is to be as sensitive as possible to these plants and their needs. They will repay us many times over for our efforts.

Insect repellant herbs

The term 'insect repellant' is rather misleading as it suggests the aim of the gardener is to rid the garden of insects. What a disaster that would be! Pollination would slow down dramatically if there was just the wind to rely on. I suppose, if we are truthful about what we really want, we are asking for a pest-free garden, undamaged fruit and vegetables, aphis-free roses and baby plants growing free from the threat of slugs and snails; all this without resorting to the use of poisonous sprays.

What we need to aim for is not to kill insects but to discourage them from destroying the plants. This can be achieved with time, effort, a few 'tricks', and a lot of herbs.

Snails and slugs are a real threat only to young seedlings and these are fairly easy to protect. I cut the bottoms out of a number of plant pots, push these into the soil around each young plant and remove them only when the plant is well established. They get plenty of light and seem to appreciate the protection, not only from snails but from wind. Fresh grass clippings around young plants also deters snails as well as providing mulch to keep their tender roots cool.

Chart 3 shows you which herbs are good for repelling certain insects. These are not going to work if you plant one solitary basil near a rose bush and trust that every aphid in the vicinity is going to leave. You need to plant enough of the herb you have chosen to form a reasonable barrier near the plant you want to protect. For instance, if a border of feverfew is planted around a bed of carrots, the strong scent will mask the smell of the carrots; the carrot fly will then fly over your garden to your next door neighbour's.

I have noticed that self-sown plants are rarely bothered by insects or disease. There is a valuable lesson to be learnt here. A strong, healthy plant, growing in the right position, in good soil, can put up its own resistance. If you want a good vegetable garden you need to

Chart 3 Insect Repellant Herbs

	Ants	Aphis	Apple scab	Bacteria	Beetles	Black fly	Cabbage moth	Cabbage worm	Carrot fly	Caterpillars	Cucumber beetle	Cutworm	Eelworm	Fleas	Flies	Fruit moth	Fungus	Insecticide	Indoors	Mice	Mildew	Mosquitoes	Moths	Potato bug	Rose beetle	Spiders	Snails & slugs	Silverfish	Woolly aphis
Anise	General benefit to most plants																												
Basil		/													/	/			/			/							
Bay																			/				/					/	
Borage	Increases resistance to disease																												
Calendula													/																
Caraway		/													/	/			/			/							
Catnep					/															/									
Chamomile				/				/															/						
Chives		/	/														/												
Coriander		/					/	/	/																				
Dill							/																						
Elder		/								/																			
Fennel														/															
Feverfew	General protection																												
Garlic	General protection																												
Horseradish			/														/							/			/		
Hyssop	General protection. Good in sprays																												
Lavender					/										/				/										
Lemon balm	Use in general sprays																												
Marjoram	/			/																									
Mints							/			/										/									
Nasturtium		/			/																								
Nettle	Use in general sprays																												
Oregano	/			/																									
Pennyroyal	Use on pets. Rub dried powdered herb in coats																												
Rosemary					/		/		/					/															
Rue	/													/	/												/		
Sage							/		/																		/		
Savories					/																								
Southernwood	General protection																												
Tansy	/	/			/		/					/						/	/										
Thyme				/		/	/																						
Wormwood					/		/		/									/	/								/		
Yarrow	General protection																												

avoid growing crops in the same position more than once every four years. This is known as crop rotation. It has the double benefit of not encouraging insect pests to reach plague proportions by constantly encouraging them to breed in the same patch. It also prevents the ground from being depleted of the particular nutrients taken from it by that crop.

You will see that some of the herbs are of general benefit and protection to plants. It's good to plant these among your vegetables and flowers and also to use them in sprays. We have a very good garden spray: it has a long hose leading from the spray barrel and the end of the hose rests in a bucket, so it's possible to make and use a large quantity of spray if needed. Such a large unit was needed when we first went to the farm as every insect in the district seemed to live there. As time went on, we had less and less use for it and now I use a small spray bottle if I don't have more than one plant to take care of. This can be a recycled, well washed kitchen or bathroom cleanser bottle, with a spray nozzle on it.

If you use compost to keep your soil in top condition, plan to include herbs which will attract birds and bees, and import a lizard or two. You will be doing your part to create the balance that nature intended.

I'm afraid, however, that there will always be an ongoing battle with the snails. My father used the 'torch and gumboot' deterrent for snails. You wait till evening (moist if possible), put on gumboots, grab a torch, go into the garden and stamp on snails!

Type of spray bottle suitable for use in the garden

KEY to Chart 3

/ Interplant or surround the garden bed with herb to mask the odour of the plants you wish to protect.

Garden sprays

Chamomile

Make a 3x infusion (see p129). Stand for 24 hours. Strain, dilute to a weak tea. Use to give a lift to sick plants or water onto young seedlings to prevent 'damping off'.

Elder

Make as for chamomile (above). Spray on young plants to protect from insects and caterpillars.

Garlic

Garlic cloves **Onions** **Chilli peppers**	*100 g (3 oz)* 6 6	Blend all well.
Paraffin oil	*to cover*	Add, stand for 2 days.
Water **Skim dried milk powder**	*4 cups* *1 cup*	Add, mix well, strain through a fine cloth.

Dilute 1 part spray to 50 parts water (stronger if needed) and use to spray against aphis, ants, spiders, caterpillars.

Nettle

Cover nettles with water, put lid on container and leave until rotted and fermenting. Strain before use. Nettles add valuable vitamins and minerals to the soil.

General spray

Southernwood, mint, tansy, feverfew, chamomile, nettle, parsley, sage, borage	Mix the herbs together. Make as nettle spray. Will repel insects and give general health to plants.

Gathering herbs

The exciting thing about your herb garden is that you are going to be able to use it almost immediately. Herbs love being picked and will grow much better if 'pruned' regularly. The difference to the taste buds between shop-bought dried herbs and your own carefully dried or freshly picked herbs is very pronounced. You also have the satisfaction of knowing that they are as uncontaminated as you could manage to make them.

To ensure a regular supply of herbs you will need to harvest and preserve your own as they reach their peak. This is usually just as they come into flower.

Choose a warm, sunny morning to harvest, before the sun is too strong, but after every trace of moisture has dried from the plant. The picking time is critical as the sun causes the plant to 'expire' its precious essential oils. These oils are what gives the plant most of its perfume and flavour and must be protected at every stage from picking to using. I talk more of this in other chapters.

LEAVES

Cut a whole branch or stem just as the plant is coming into flower, cutting the stem just on or above a leaf node. Take only as much as you can process quickly as the plant can deteriorate very soon after picking. Pick over the material, discarding all dead or discoloured parts. It's pointless storing anything but the best.

FLOWERS

Cut just before they are at their most fully open.

SEEDS

Cut whole heads as they turn beige to brown. If there is a danger of the seed falling before you gather it, the head may be enclosed in a paper or muslin bag until the seeds are ripe (see 'Drying' below).

ROOTS

These are usually collected in the plant's most dormant season when there is not much leaf growth.

Drying the herbs

The quicker you dry your herbs, the better the colour and flavour will be. However, they must never be dried in direct sunlight or at high temperatures as this destroys the properties of the plant.

Choose an airy, dust-free area or an oven set at its lowest temperature and with the door open. Keep the herbs low down in the oven and turn them regularly. If you have a wood stove in your kitchen you can create a wonderful drying area by making screen racks to fit above the stove. This is the method we used most at the farm as it could be utilised all year round.

Manufacturers maintain that herbs can be dried using microwave ovens. I feel that while the plants may dry satisfactorily, the essential oils would be lost. These oils are very sensitive to heat and need to be treated with the utmost respect. I would therefore hesitate to recommend this form of drying.

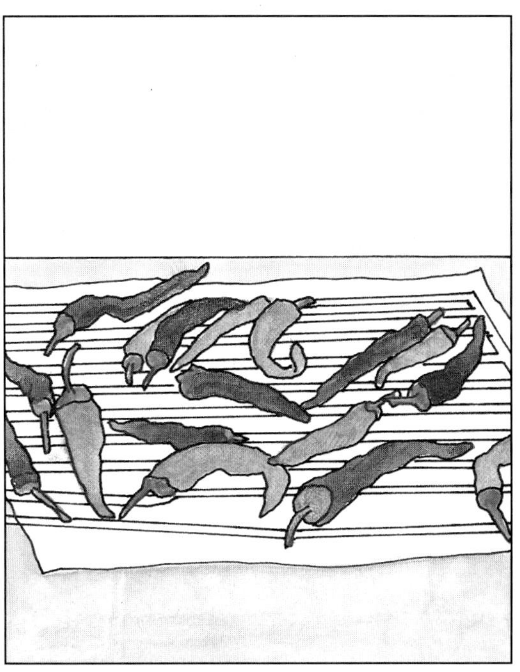

Racks for drying

Leaves and flowers

These can be tied in small bunches and hung in a suitable area. If dust or flies are a problem, enclose the bunches in muslin bags. They can be spread on flywire screens or dried in the oven as described above. If liked, the leaves may be stripped from the stems. The material is dry when it is just becoming crisp. If you are using an oven, watch the herbs carefully to prevent overdrying.

Roots, bark and stems

These parts of the plant usually need to be washed and thoroughly dried, then chopped as finely as possible to speed up the drying process. I find the oven method best for roots but, unlike leaves and flowers, roots may be dried in the sun. If you are doing them in summer, spread on old flyscreens, cover with cheesecloth and put on top of a water tank, shadehouse or similar, where they will be out of the dust. Roots, bark and stems are dry when they snap easily.

Herbs hanging up to dry

Placing seed heads in a cheesecloth bag

Seed heads enclosed in a cheesecloth bag

Seeds

The best way that I have found to dry seeds is to cut the whole heads off, enclose them in a muslin or cheesecloth bag, hang in an airy place and forget about them for about two months. The seeds may be stripped off the heads if preferred, before putting in the bag. Do search the seed heads for insects before putting them in the bag or you may be very disappointed when you open up and find that you have provided a larder for creepies and no seeds are left!

Large leaves and pods

The way to deal easily with large leaves such as borage, comfrey and mullein, and with pods such as chillies, is to thread a large needle with tough linen thread or dental floss and push the needle through the stem of the leaf or pod. Keep them separate so that they don't touch each other and hang the string from each end as shown in the drawing.

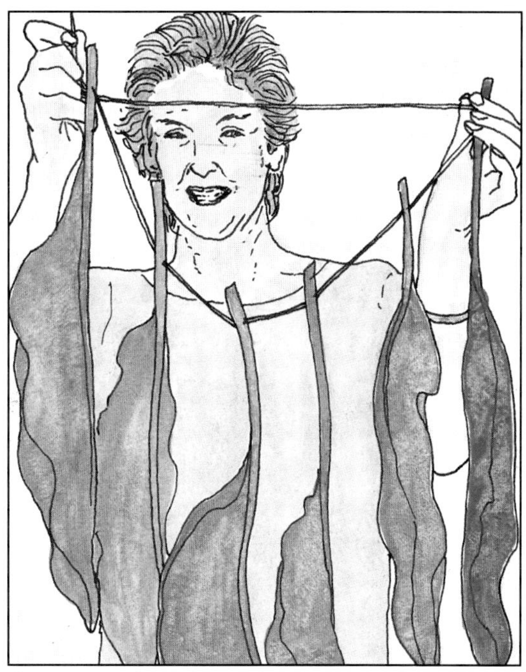

Getting ready to hang the string of leaves

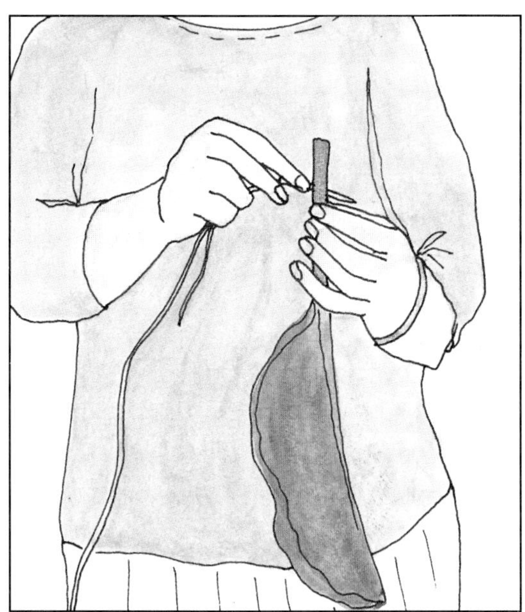

Threading a large leaf onto string for drying

Storage

Over the years I have experimented with several methods of storage and finally settled on glass jars. These give protection from damp, insects and dust and have the advantage of allowing you to keep a close eye on the contents. It's very important to check the jars regularly, particularly in the first few weeks, as any moisture left in the herbs could cause mould to develop.

Try to use appropriate-sized jars. A lot of air in the jar will detract from the keeping qualities of the herbs being stored. Collect sizes from very large to very small. Label your jars very carefully with the common name, Latin name and the date of storage. Don't trust your memory as many herbs smell and look very similar after drying.

For further storage hints see page 220.

COFE
TEA
SUGA

CHAPTER THREE

HERBS THAT HEAL

The great spirit is our father, but the earth is our mother.
She nourishes us; that which we put into the ground she returns to us,
and healing plants she gives us likewise.

Big Thunder, *North American Indian,* 1900

This chapter concerns illness or disease and the part which herbs play in restoring health to the body and mind. Unlike many modern drugs which aim a 'bullet' at a symptom, herbs work in quite a different way by helping the body to rally its defences and regain its balance. The written records of the use of herbs for healing go back about 2000 years. Who knows how far back in time the unrecorded use stretches? Many of the remedies are the same now as then, and I find it awe-inspiring that they should have survived such a test of time. People who deny the value of herbs are those who have either never tried them, or who drank one cup of herb tea and complained that their problem was still with them.

Humans have been slowly evolving over millions of years. For most of this time it has been a natural, unforced, unhurried process, allowing plenty of time for the planet and its inhabitants to adapt to changing conditions. Nature uses floods, famine, plague and predators as natural selectors to ensure the survival of the fittest.

In the last 45 years this situation has changed radically. I was a nurse in the mid-forties when penicillin was introduced. Tuberculosis, pneumonia and many other diseases which had been difficult to cure ceased to be a threat. The sulpha drugs appeared in the early fifties and brought more diseases under control. What has happened? We live longer and many life-threatening diseases can be overcome but we are no healthier — in fact, we appear to have exchanged one set of problems for new and possibly more dangerous ones, such as AIDS.

Along with the discovery of the 'wonder drugs' came the pesticides, herbicides, hormone treatments for animals, artificial fibres, aerosol cans full of insecticides and oven cleaners, air pollution from an increasing number of factories and vehicles ... the list grows alarmingly. Add to this the increasing migration of humans from town to town and country to country and you have a situation where we are unable to adapt sufficiently quickly. Had these changes happened over thousands of years we might have changed with them but our abused auto-immune systems, subjected to chemicals, the overuse of antibiotics, and new climates and pollens, have become confused and given up the unequal battle. AIDS, allergies and candida albicans are some of the illnesses resulting from this breakdown.

What can we do about this situation? We can take preventive measures by making our homes and gardens 'toxic-free zones' and take as much responsibility as possible for our health. We need to learn to be confident in our own capabilities and intelligence. I must say at this point that I am not in any way condemning the medical profession or drugs. I know many dedicated, open-minded doctors who are beginning to look at alternative methods with great interest and who try to restrict the use of drugs (it's the *overuse* of drugs that creates the problem). I have also had experience of charlatans in the alternative fields of healing, who seem to be in the profession merely to make money. The blame can be laid squarely at our own doorstep. Every time we place the responsibility for our well-being on someone else, we are weakening ourselves.

The role of health professionals, as I see it, is to use their diagnostic skills to determine the nature of the problem, attempt to find the underlying cause, and then suggest a course of treatment. The role of the patient is to ask questions and to be prepared to change a lifestyle if necessary, rather than hold out a hand for a bottle of pills. It's not easy to change the living patterns of a lifetime but this is frequently the only way to get the body into a state of 'ease' rather than 'dis-ease'.

It's to be hoped that the next few years will see more of a 'marriage' between allopathic and alternative styles of medicine, each giving of its best to create truly wholistic methods of healing.

This chapter is not intended to be an instant medical 'self-help guide'. The correct use of herbs can be complex and you need guidance from as many reliable sources as you can find. Establish a firm relationship with a reputable herbalist, naturopath, homeopath, doctor or other health professional who will respect your views and, until you have had a great deal of experience with herbs, rely on the experience of your chosen therapist to guide you. The best way to learn about herbs is first to grow them, learning all you can about each one and the way they react with each other. Become accustomed to sharing your life with herbs, using them in as many ways as possible — the chances are you will be so healthy you might never need this chapter!

Note: See page 10 for suggestions on record keeping.

Equipment needed for the recipes in this chapter

Keep separate equipment for making all your recipes. Some things become discoloured or impregnated with the perfume of herb oils, tinctures and teas and would be unsuitable to use for cooking food. Most of these items are not expensive and can usually be picked up for cents at second-hand shops or sales.

2 teaspoons
2 tablespoons
wooden spoons
1 or 2 funnels
coffee filter papers
scales
droppers
sharp knife
scissors
2 sieves, different sizes
2 or 3 measuring jugs
2 or 3 bowls, different sizes
25 ml plastic measure
mortar and pestle or coffee grinder
2 or 3 saucepans, different sizes. Made of glass, steel or unchipped enamel, *not* aluminium. One pan or bowl should fit neatly into another pan to create a double boiler.
cheesecloth (fine, unbleached) for making bags and for fine straining. It's a good idea to make several different-sized bags, varying in size from 8 x 12 cm (3 x 5 in)

up to 18 x 25 cm (7 x 10 in). I use double thickness cheesecloth and make the bags with French seams for strength.
screw-top jars, different sizes and very clean.
labels
waterproof marking pen, fine tip
clean, old tea towels

If you get really involved in making a lot of the recipes you will need Pyrex measuring flasks. These are expensive and can be added one at a time as the need arises.

Methods of herbal preparation

To avoid the problems of varying systems of measurement I have used the teaspoon as a measure where possible. Many books say that 60 drops = 1 teaspoonful = 5 millilitres. We have found that this is not the case. After measuring various sizes of spoons and droppers, the liquid measurement we came up with was:

18-20 drops = 1 ml;
90-100 drops = 5 ml = 1 teaspoonful

INFUSION OR TEA

This is the simplest and most widely used preparation, particularly for the 'beginner herbalist'. This method is used for ground roots and bark, crushed seeds and finely chopped flowers and leaves. Infusions and decoctions are the most suitable preparations to give to children. Your herbal preparations deserve their own special, scrupulously clean, non-metal pot or teapot (aluminium or ordinary tea can taint the delicate taste of infusions).

Infusions can be used in several ways. The most obvious is for drinking, but by increasing the herb by a factor of three or four (shown in future as 3x or 4x), the infusion can be strengthened and used in baths, fomentations, compresses, poultices and ointments.

Making a herbal infusion

To make an infusion (or tea)
Pour 250 ml (1 cup) boiling water over 2 heaped teaspoons fresh, finely chopped herbs, or 1 heaped teaspoon crumbled dried herb. *Cover* and stand for 5-10 minutes; strain and sweeten with honey if liked. Increase or decrease this recipe as required.

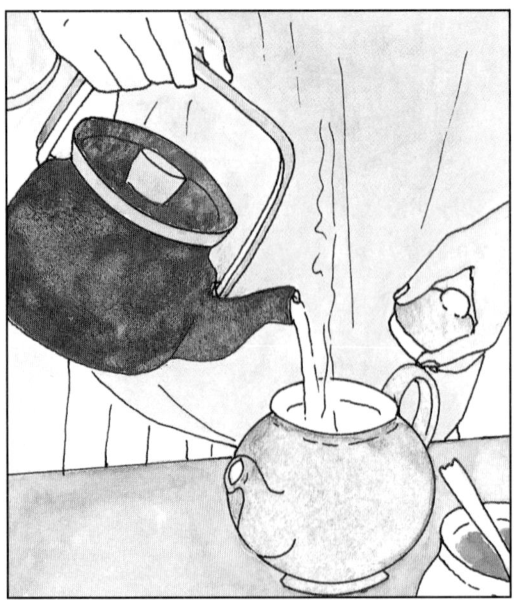
Making and covering a herbal infusion

The covering of any hot herbal preparation is vital. Otherwise, the precious essential oils will escape and the preparation will lose a lot of its healing potential.

Dose

Adults: 125 ml (½ cup) 3 times daily, ½ hour before food.

Children:

30 kg (66 lb) and over	½ adult dose
15-29 kg (33-64 lb)	¼ adult dose
7-14 kg (15-31 lb)	⅛ adult dose

Decoctions

Some plants need to be simmered to extract their properties. Roots and barks are the parts usually treated in this way. Before beginning the decoction, chop the material as finely as possible. This is difficult with some dried roots and barks, but you can resort to a cleaver if necessary.

To make the decoction
To each 250 ml (1 cup) cold water add 2 teaspoons fresh or 1 teaspoon dried herbs. Bring to the boil, cover and simmer for 10-30 minutes, depending on the fineness of the material. Strain and make up to the original 250 ml (1 cup) with fresh boiling water. The best way to make a decoction is to invest in a crock pot or similar very slow stewing pot. The decoction can be left covered for several hours, gradually releasing the herbal properties and retaining the maximum amount of its potency. Sufficient quantity for several days can be made at once by this method. It should be kept in a covered container in a refrigerator and used within 4-5 days.

Dose: see Infusions above.

Tinctures

A tincture is an alcoholic extract of herbs. Tinctures are stronger and more concentrated than infusions or decoctions. There is also the benefit of being able to make them in advance and, if well made and stored, they will keep for years.

Alcohol The keeping qualities of the tincture are largely determined by the strength of the alcohol you use. Pure alcohol is usually only available to professional users but occasionally you will find a pharmacist who will sell you 95% alcohol. If you manage to get this alcohol you will need to dilute it with purified water until it is 70%. Otherwise, you will need to rely on your wine and spirit merchant to advise you on the highest proof vodka, gin or brandy he has in stock. You will need alcohol as near to 70% proof as possible.

Making a tincture

To make the tincture

The tincture methods I have read suggest that it's best to determine the amount of herb used by its weight, but over the years I have found that density is a much more reliable way. For example, 120 g of comfrey root is quite a small amount in volume while 120 g of calendula petals is a large amount and can't be covered by the amount of alcohol specified. So the following is the method I have chosen to use and it makes a very fine tincture.

Leaves and flowers, fresh or dried
Loosely fill a jar with the finely chopped herb, half fill if the material is dried. Cover with alcohol and close the jar with a well-fitting lid.

Roots, bark and seeds
Cover 15-30 g (½-1 oz) herb, depending on density, with 250 ml (1 cup) alcohol.

Mark the jar (not the lid) with the common and Latin name of the plant and a date two weeks hence when the tincture will be ready. Keep the tinctures where you can see them, because they need to be successed twice a day. Succussion means tapping the jar base gently but firmly on a folded cloth for not less than one minute. This releases the properties from the herb into the alcohol.

After two weeks the tincture is ready to be strained through a coffee filter into a dark-coloured glass bottle, labelled with the name, Latin name, date and the symbol ∅, which denotes that it is a Mother Tincture. Store the bottle in a cool dark place and it should last for years. If liked, you can add 1 teaspoon of glycerine to each 250 ml (1 cup) tincture to give additional keeping qualities.

Uses and doses of tinctures

Internal: 5-15 drops taken in 2 tablespoons milk or water three times a day before meals, or added, 5 drops at a time, to infusions and decoctions to strengthen their action. 1 teaspoon of tincture is equivalent in action and strength to 1 cup of infusion or decoction. For further information on internal use refer to Chart 6.

Caution Tinctures are not suitable for children under 7 years of age unless prescribed by a practitioner.

External: Tinctures may be added to poultices, fomentations, compresses, ointments, wound washes and anywhere you may want to increase the strength of the remedy. They may be used undiluted where needed in order to stop infection or bleeding quickly.

Syrups

These are used to disguise unpleasant tasting herbs, or when a cough or sore throat syrup is needed.

To make a syrup
In a non-aluminium pan put 500 g (1 lb) of sugar and 250 ml (1 cup) of water. Heat, stirring, until sugar is dissolved and the liquid is boiling. Remove from the heat, cool, bottle and store in the refrigerator.

To use syrup To each 3 parts syrup, add 1 part tincture; *or* to each 3 parts syrup add 1 part 3x infusion or decoction.

Dose: 20-60 drops as needed, according to age.

Making a syrup

Oxymel

The use of oxymel is the same as syrup but some people, myself included, prefer the honey mixture in oxymel. Honey rots teeth the same as sugar but, unlike sugar, has medicinal properties of its own. It's wise to clean your teeth after taking any of these honey/sugar preparations.

To make oxymel
Boil 5 parts honey and 1 part cider vinegar to a thick syrup, taking care not to burn. Cool. Usage and dose as for syrup.

Ear treatments

Ear pain must always be treated very seriously, especially in a child. It can be a symptom of middle ear infection, mastoiditis or other complaints which need treatment from a professional. Untreated ear problems can lead to partial or complete hearing loss.

During consultation with a professional you could mention the garlic oil treatment recommended in Charts 6 and 7. Dry eczema, excess wax and outer ear infections are some of the problems which are dealt with very effectively by the use of garlic oil. It's an easy process to make your own garlic oil (see p141). The resulting oil won't be as strong as that in capsule form but this can be an advantage when using the oil for children as they cannot tolerate full-strength garlic oil.

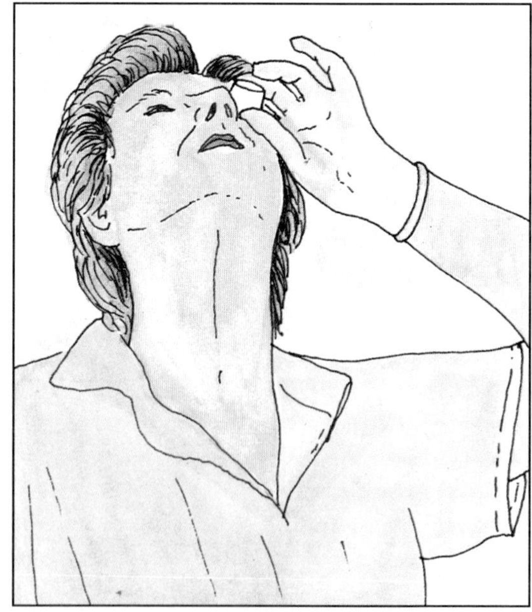

Using an eye bath

Eye baths

There are a few very important things to know about eye baths:

- Everything you use when dealing with eyes must be scrupulously clean and dust-free.

- Made-up eyewash must be kept for only 2 days and must be stored in the refrigerator in a sterilised, well-covered jar.
- If both eyes are infected you should use separate baths or sterilise the bath before treating the second eye.

You can buy special eye cups or eye baths from a pharmacy. Buy more than one. Immerse them in boiling water before and after use. To use the eye bath, fill it three-quarters full of warm infusion or decoction which has been filtered through coffee filters. (If there is a lot of inflammation or swelling the liquid may be used cold.) Hold the bath firmly over the eye, tilt the head back and blink rapidly several times. Use the treatment 2-6 times a day depending on the severity of the problem.

Foot Baths

As the name suggests, this is a bath for the feet but an ideal vessel would be deep enough to cover the calves of the legs as well. The most well known foot bath is the mustard bath but other herbs may be used. Cold foot baths will soothe tired feet and help to stop nosebleeds. See Charts 6 and 10 for more information.

To make herb liquid to add to bath

Boiling water	*2 cups*	Pour over herbs, cover.
Fresh herbs	*12 teaspoons*	Stand 15 minutes.
or		
Dried herbs	*6 teaspoons*	

To use, strain the herbal liquid into the foot bath. Add water which is comfortable heat. A foot bath should last 10-15 minutes.

Gargles

Gargles are preparations for healing and soothing infected or sore throats. They can be made either from tinctures added to boiled water or a strong infusion or decoction. It's a good idea to have suitable dried herbs or tinctures mixed, labelled and stored in your medicine box.

Inhalations

To make an inhalation you need finely chopped herbs, essential oils or menthol crystals (see Chart 8), a heat-proof bowl, boiling water and 2 large towels.

Method Put the bowl on a folded towel. on a table; make sure it is very stable and won't slip. Half-fill the bowl with boiling water, sit in a chair, close to the table and bowl, with the towel draped over your

Putting the towel over before an inhalation

shoulders. Put a handful of finely chopped herbs on the surface of the water or sprinkle with a few menthol crystals or about ten drops of oil. (It's fine to use a mixture of herbs and oils if you like.) Immediately cover your head, shoulders and the bowl and breathe in the medicated steam for 10 minutes. If the mixture seems to be getting weak you can add more herbs or oil.

Don't go out of doors for some time after having an inhalation as your mucous membranes will be sensitive and cold air could have an adverse effect.

Caution If you are giving an inhalation to a very young or very old person you must be very careful to avoid accidents with the boiling water. Stay with the patient the whole time and hold the bowl firmly. If the patient is a baby it's better to fill the hand basin in the bathroom with boiling water, shut the door and let the baby inhale the steam coming from the basin. This is also a good system to use for a frail, very sick or aged person.

Ointments

Making ointments is one of my greatest pleasures. Collecting the herbs from an early morning garden and transforming them into a wonderful healing cream always feels like magic and, indeed, these homemade salves do seem to work in a special way. Friends have taken my healing

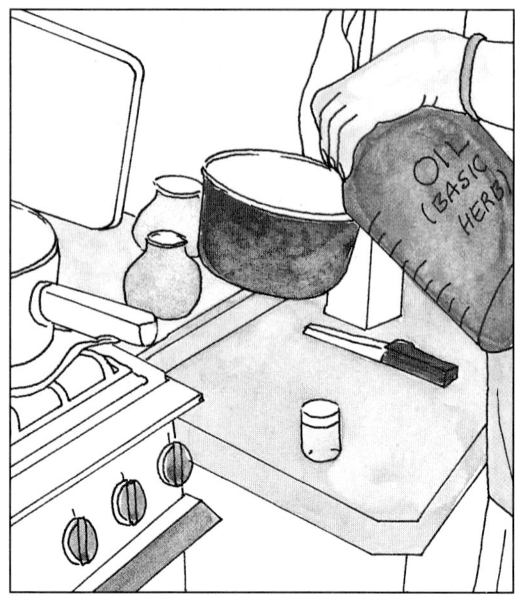

Adding herb oil off the heat

cream all over the world as their panacea for all things external and I hear wonderful stories about cures to dogs, cats and even chickens. Very satisfying, even if a little unexpected.

The ointment recipe given here will make a 100 g (3 oz) jar. However, it's much easier to make larger quantities which may be given as gifts. The tincture of benzoin is used for its healing and preservative properties and the other tincture can be chosen by looking in Chart 5 under 'Vulnerary'. The herbs in the oil can be

To make the ointment

Beeswax	*6 g (½ cube)*	Melt *gently* in a small pan.
Vaseline or lanolin	*40 g (1½ oz)*	Add and melt.
Herb oil	*40 ml (2 tablespoons)*	Add *slowly*, don't re-harden the wax. Take the pan off the heat, cool slightly.
Herb tincture **Tinc. benzoin**	*10 ml (2 teaspoons)* *2 ml (½ teaspoon)*	Add both tinctures, stir until the mixture thickens slightly. Pot at once.

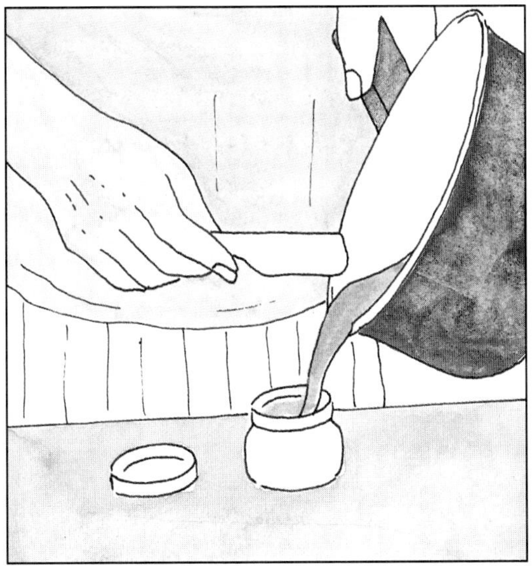

Pouring the ointment

chosen in the same way.

The first step is to make a quantity of base herb oil which can be used in massage oils, facial preparations, baths and ointments (see p170 for recipe).

I have always used lanolin in my preparations but have recently decided to change to petroleum jelly. Lanolin is now polluted due to the use of chemicals on the coats of the sheep. Only a proportion of these chemicals is removed during the cleansing of the wool fat. The Nursing Mothers Association has recently issued a warning against using lanolin on nipples because of the chemical content. A pharmacist assures me that the amount of contamination is minimal but I prefer not to take the risk.

Poultices, fomentations and compresses

These are ways of applying heat, cold, stimulation, moisture or the healing properties of various agents to areas of the body. They can be used to draw pus or foreign bodies from flesh and are a fine treatment for relieving congestion. As a general rule a cold compress is used for withdrawing heat from an area, soothing abrasions, etc. Hot fomentations and poultices ease pain, relax spasms, draw pus and relieve congestion. They are very simple to use.

The methods of preparation will be found following Chart 4. The number one rule when using a hot fomentation or poultice is **Don't burn your patient.** Test the temperature on the inside of your wrist before putting it on the person you are treating. Remember also that a sore, bruised or abraded area will be able to tolerate less heat than undamaged flesh and skin.

Poultices

A poultice is made with mashed or blended herbs, hot fluid, and tinctures (if liked). It is applied as a pack to the skin and used to draw pus or foreign bodies from a wound. It also relieves congestion.

To make a poultice

Mash or blend fresh or dried herbs. Make into a paste by adding boiling water,

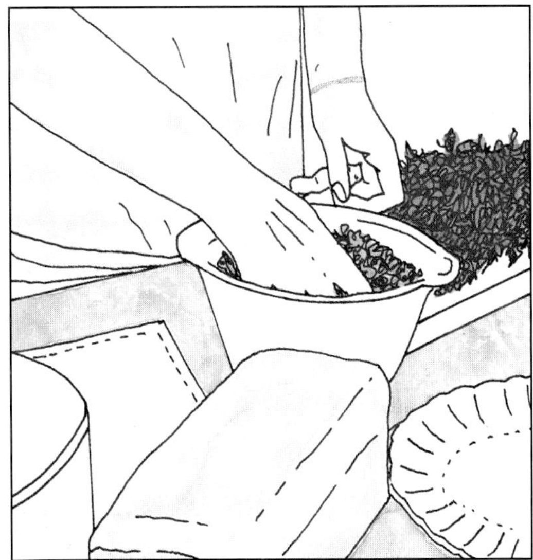

Beginning to make a herb poultice: mixing bread and herbs in a bowl

Chart 4 Poultices, Fomentations, Compresses

	Calendula	Cayenne	Chamomiles	Cider vinegar	Comfrey	Garlic	Ginger	Hyssop	Mallow	Marjoram & Oregano	Mullein	Plantain	Rosemary	Sage	Tansy	Thyme	Violet	Witch hazel	Wormwood	Yarrow	Yellow dock
Abscesses						W		W		W				W						W	
Arthritis				F	W						F					F					
Boils					M		M					M									
Bruises			C		W			B	W	B								C		C	
Bronchitis											F					F					
Bursitis				F							F										
Black Eye								W				C						C			
Cysts		W		A							W	W									
Cystitis		F	F									F							F		F
Earache			W			W				W											
Glands, swollen											F	F								F	F
Inflammation	C							C	C	C	C				C			C			
Neuralgia		F	F								F								F		
Nipples, sore	C				W															C	
Pain	H		H				H		F	C	H										
Rheumatism				W				W			W					W			W		
Ringworm						M						M									
Skin, cuts & tears	C				C					C			C		C	C				C	
Sores, running	M				M							M	M	M		M	M			M	M
Sore throats		F		F				F			F									F	F
Sprains	C		C	C	C		C		C	W					C				C		W
Stings & bites					W				C			C	C								
Swellings			C	C	C				C	W		C						C			C
Ulcers	W				W				W					W		W	W				
Varicose Veins	C											C		F	F			C			
Whitlow							M														
Wounds	H				H				H	H		H	H	H						H	

KEY to Chart 4

M Mash chopped or powdered herbs with oats, bran or bread and hot water to form a paste.

W Poultice or fomentation.

F Fomentation.

C Compress.

B Blend or mash to form a cold paste.

A Add to other herbs.

H Use as liked, e.g. poultice, compress or fomentation.

Cayenne Use only ⅛ the amount of other herbs (1 teaspoon of cayenne = 8 teaspoons of other herbs). A valuable but very potent herb. Too much can cause blistering.

Note: Use Chart 4 to select herbs for use in poultices, fomentations and compresses.

Mixing the bread and herbs with boiling water

Putting the mixture on a folded cheesecloth bag or folded cloth

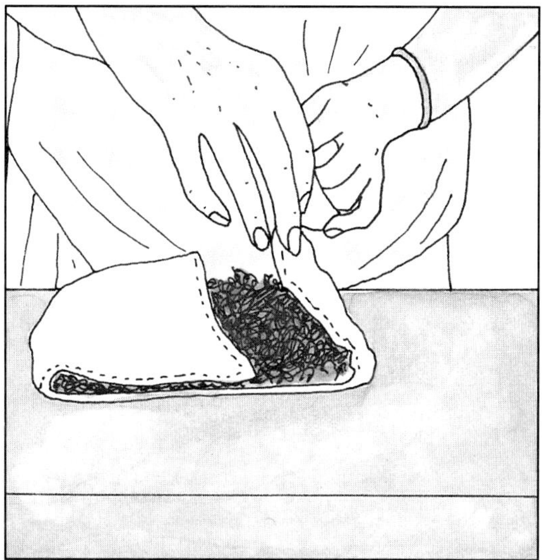

Folding in the ends

infusion or decoction. A few drops of tincture may be added for extra strength. If liked, you can add bread to this mixture as it enables it to stay hot longer and gives it a good consistency.

Put the mixture into a cheesecloth or

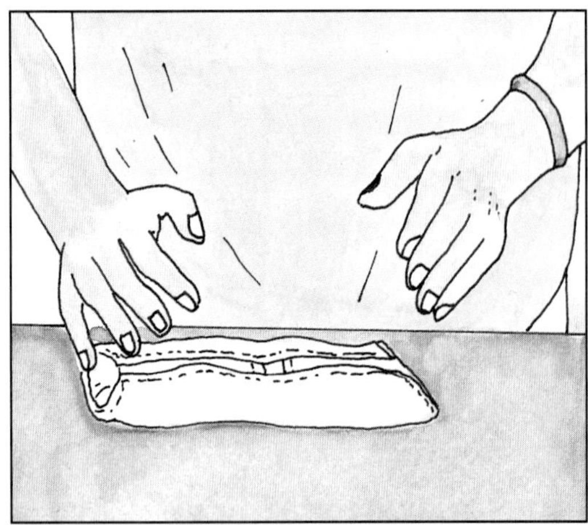

Folding the sides to the middle to enclose the contents

muslin bag, flatten it out and test it for heat on the inside of your wrist. Place on affected part. *Be very careful not to burn your patient.* Cover with plastic wrap and a towel or similar to keep in the heat.

The poultice may be reheated between two plates over a pan of boiling water. It's not necessary to make it afresh each time unless it's contaminated with pus or blood. The poultice will need to be changed often for the first two hours or until some improvement is seen.

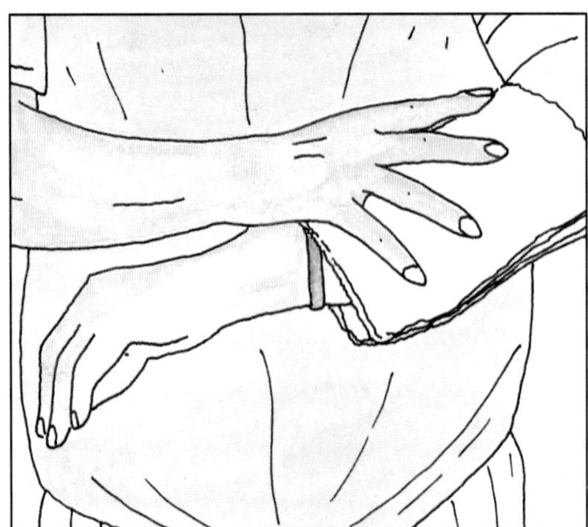

Testing the heat on your own inner wrist

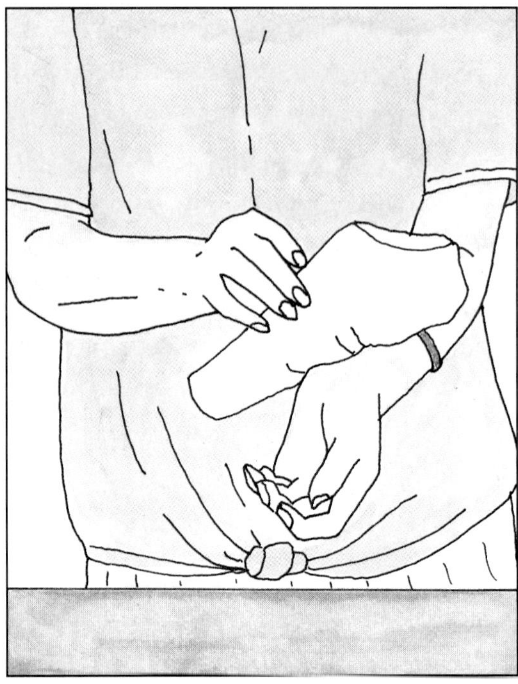

Placing the poultice on the affected part

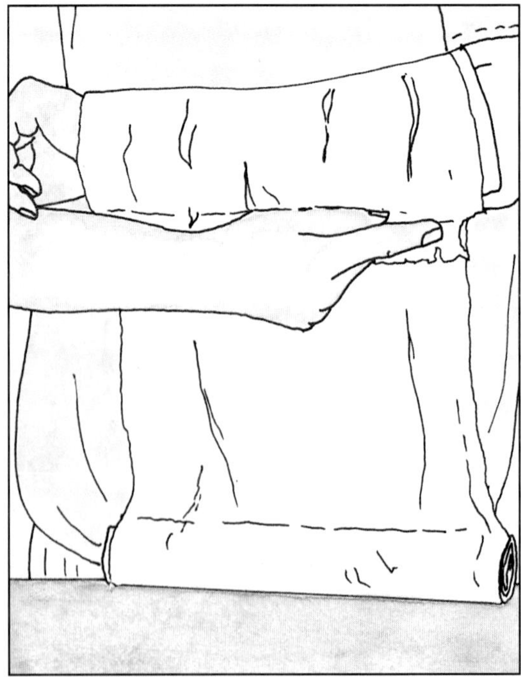

Covering the poultice with plastic wrap to prevent leaks

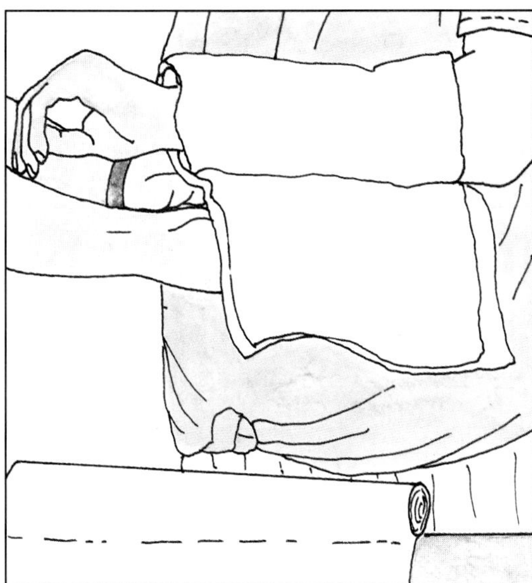

Wrapping a towel around to keep the heat in

Reheating the poultice over a pan of boiling water

FOMENTATIONS

Fomentations have similar uses to poultices but are not as powerful. They may be used where a condition is not so severe or where it would be too uncomfortable to use a poultice.

To make a fomentation

Soak a piece of soft cloth in a hot 3x infusion or decoction. Wring out the excess liquid, test on your wrist for temperature and apply as hot as is comfortable. Cover

Soaking a cloth in the hot fomentation liquid

Wringing excess liquid from the fomentation cloth

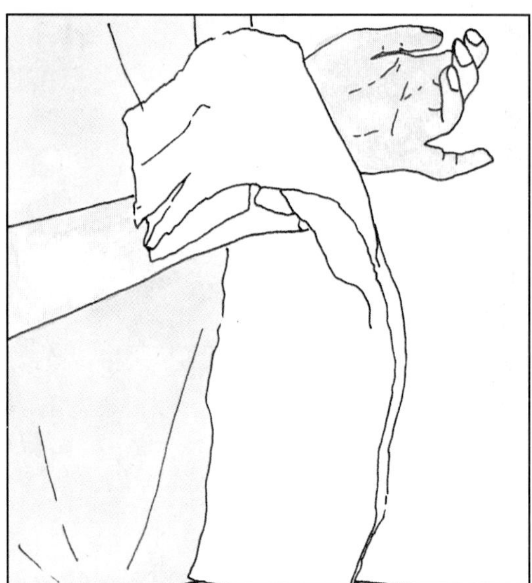

Testing on your wrist for excessive heat

with plastic wrap and a towel. Repeat often in the first two hours or until relief is obtained.

Compresses

Compresses are made in the same way as fomentations but cold liquid is used instead of hot. They need to be changed as soon as they become warm. Compresses are used to reduce inflammation and ease the pain of sprains.

Powdered herbs

To make powdered herbs you need either a mortar and pestle or a coffee grinder. Grind herbs very finely, pass through a very fine mesh sieve and store in a jar marked with the name of the mixture, e.g. Haemorrhoid Mixture, Wound Mixture. Include a list of the herbs in the mixture and the expiry date (see Storage p125). The grinding and sieving need to be very well done, to avoid irritation to the affected parts. I store these herbs in my refrigerator for maximum protection of their properties, as finely ground herbs and spices lose their quality far more quickly than coarse material.

Packs (nose)

To stop nosebleeds it's sometimes necessary to pack the nose. There are two ways of doing this:

1. Roll a small piece of cotton wool into a cylinder and soak it in one of the tinctures or juices suggested in Chart 6. Gently insert it into the nose and leave for as long as possible. Be very careful when removing it to avoid starting the bleeding again.
2. Bruise the leaf of a herb suggested in Chart 6 until it's juicy, roll into a cylinder and push very gently into the nose. Remove carefully to avoid starting the bleeding again.

Keep the hands of the patient above the head or in a bowl of very cold water. Either of these treatments will help.

Suppositories

This is a preparation made with a low melting point base, mixed with healing agents. It is used in the rectum, vagina or nostrils. My favourite base is cocoa butter. This is available through pharmacies or direct from pharmaceutical suppliers. Cocoa butter is the fat extracted from the crushed,

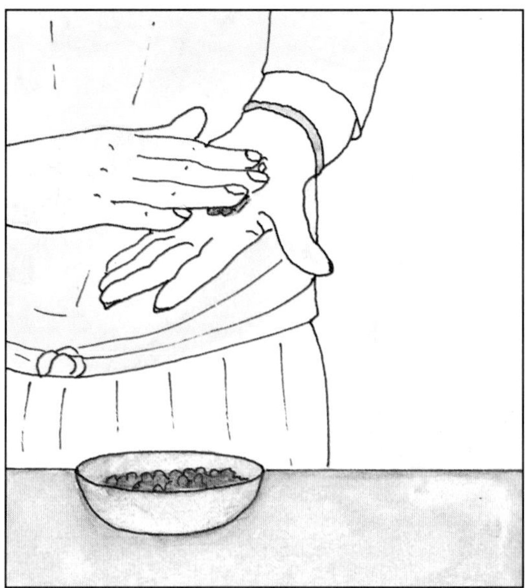

The way to roll a suppository

roasted seeds of the cocoa plant (*Theobroma cacao*). Cocoa butter is useful in both medicinal and skin care preparations. It is a fine emollient with a very low melting point so it liquifies easily on contact with the skin. The other thing in its favour is that it smells really good. Never put cocoa butter in a pan directly on the heat source. Its melting point is so low that it burns really easily. Melt in a bowl over a pan of hot water or a double boiler.

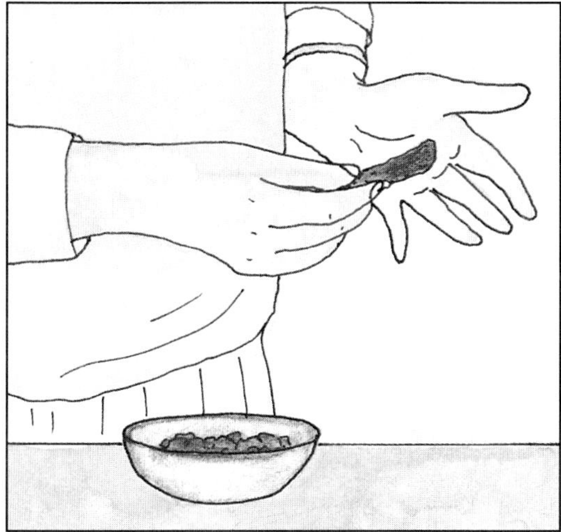

This is the approximate shape and size of a suppository

To make suppositories

Melt 60 g (2 oz) of cocoa butter as described above. Mix in powdered dried herbs until the mixture is the consistency of very thick gravy. You can add 5-10 drops of tincture to strengthen the effect of the preparation. If you want to use more tincture than I suggest, add a *little* melted beeswax as well as the cocoa butter to get a better 'set'.

Take the pan off the heat and stir until the mixture is a consistency which can be moulded. Rectal suppositories should be about 5 cm (2 in) long, about as thick as the middle finger and slightly conical. The thickness can be adapted to your own requirements. Vaginal suppositories (also known as pessaries) need to be shorter and more conical. Cotton pads can be used to protect underwear from staining.

Wound washes

Dirt is a factor to contend with in some injuries. An attempt must be made to wash this dirt away before any further treatment takes place. The water used to wash the wound must first have been boiled and cooled. Add any of the following to the water:

- Powdered vulnerary and/or antiseptic herbs, made into an infusion and strained.
- A few drops of suitable essential oil.
- Tinctures: 10 drops to every 250 ml (1 cup) of water.

If the injury is to a foot or hand, the part can be immersed in a bowl. If it is a limb which is wounded, cotton wool used as a gentle swab will be effective.

Garlic oil

Garlic cloves	*250 g (8 oz)*	Peel, chop finely. Put in a jar and
Olive oil		cover completely with warm olive oil.

Leave in a warm place for one week. Strain through four layers of fine cheesecloth or muslin. Bottle in amber glass, store in a cool dark place.

Horseradish vinegar

Finely grate fresh horseradish root.
Cover with cider vinegar. Stand for two weeks. Strain.

Medicinal properties

Chart 5 is called 'Medicinal Properties' and will give you some insight into the functional effects of the many constituents in each herb. I have included only those terms which seem relevant to this book and this century. The terminology may be unfamiliar so I include a glossary which you should study. This will make for greater understanding of why the herbs are used for certain problems.

Glossary of medical terms

Alterative	A substance which changes a condition.
Anodyne	Pain-easing and soothing.
Anthelmintic	Causing expulsion or death of worms.
Antibilious	Relieves a bilious condition.
Antiseptic	An agent which prevents sepsis.
Antispasmodic	Prevents or eases spasms.
Aperient	Opening, laxative.
Aromatic	Having an agreeable smell and taste.
Astringent	Causing contraction of soft tissue.
Bitter	Bitter herbs which stimulate appetite.
Carminative	Expelling wind and easing griping pains.
Cholagogue	Stimulating a flow of bile.
Demulcent	Softening and lubricating internally.
Depurative	A cleansing and purifying agent.
Diaphoretic	Promoting perspiration.
Digestive	Aiding digestion.
Diuretic	Increasing the flow of urine.
Emmenagogue	Promoting menstrual flow.
Emetic	Drugs or agents which cause vomiting.
Emollient	Softening externally.
Expectorant	Helping to expel mucus.
Haemostatic	Having the power to stop bleeding.
Hepatic	Having an effect on the liver.
Nephritic	Having an action on the kidneys.
Nervine	Strengthens and calms the nerves.
Refrigerant	Heat-lowering.
Sedative	Soothing and calming.
Stimulant	Energy-producing.
Stomachic	Given for disorders of the stomach.
Tonic	A strengthening agent.
Vulnerary	Wound-healing.

Chart 5 Medicinal Properties

	Alterative	Anodyne	Antibilious	Anti-inflammatory	Antiseptic	Antispasmodic	Aperient	Aromatic	Astringent	Bitter	Carminative	Cholagogue	Demulcent	Depurative	Diaphoretic	Digestive	Diuretic	Emmenagogue	Emollient	Expectorant	Haemostatic	Hepatic	Nephritic	Nervine	Refrigerant	Sedative	Stimulant	Stomachic	Tonic	Vulnerary
Alfalfa																					X		X						X	
Aloe																														X
Angelica						X		X								X	X			X										
Anise					X						X									X										
Basil						X		X			X																	X		
Bay									X							X												X		
Bergamot											X																X			
Borage													X						X						X					
Calendula				X	X				X			X									X									X
Caraway											X									X										
Catnep		X				X					X														X	X				
Cayenne															X												X			
Chamomiles		X				X				X																X				X
Chives																X													X	
Comfrey				X					X				X							X										X
Coriander						X		X			X																	X		
Dandelion				X			X					X		X			X					X								
Dill						X					X						X											X		
Elder															X		X										X			X
Fennel								X			X																	X		
Feverfew											X							X									X		X	X
Garlic					X									X						X										
Ginger			X					X			X				X	X				X							X			
Horseradish																	X											X		
Hyssop															X					X							X			
Lavender						X						X												X						X
Lemon Balm						X									X			X								X		X		
Lemon Grass																									X					
Liquorice				X			X	X					X						X	X										

Chart 5 (cont) Medicinal Properties

	Alterative	Anodyne	Antibilious	Anti-inflammatory	Antiseptic	Antispasmodic	Aperient	Aromatic	Astringent	Bitter	Carminative	Cholagogue	Demulcent	Depurative	Diaphoretic	Digestive	Diuretic	Emmenagogue	Emollient	Expectorant	Haemostatic	Hepatic	Nephritic	Nervine	Refrigerant	Sedative	Stimulant	Stomachic	Tonic	Vulnerary
Mallow													X						X											X
Marjoram																		X											X	
Peppermint						X		X			X					X	X										X	X		
Spearmint		X	X			X		X			X				X										X			X	X	
Mullein		X				X							X							X										
Nasturtium					X															X										
Nettle	X								X					X			X				X								X	X
Oregano						X					X				X					X								X	X	
Parsley																X	X													
Pennyroyal											X				X			X								X				
Plantain	X								X				X							X										X
Red Clover	X													X			X			X										
Raspberry									X																		X			
Rosemary						X						X			X									X					X	X
Rue						X					X							X									X	X		
Sage				X					X			X										X								X
Savory, summer									X		X									X							X	X		
Savory, winter									X		X									X							X	X		
Shepherd's Purse					X																X						X			X
Southernwood										X						X											X		X	
Tansy																		X												
Tarragon																	X	X										X		
Thyme				X		X										X				X									X	X
Valerian		X				X																		X		X				X
Violet	X			X											X					X										X
Water/Landcress																	X			X							X	X	X	
Wormwood										X																		X		
Yarrow	X														X	X					X						X		X	X
Yellow Dock	X								X			X																	X	

Using herbs for healing

Chart 6 is provided to help you begin to learn about the best herbs to use for a particular problem. I talk later about the combinations that will gain the best results from the herbs. These combinations take a long time to learn and frequently need to be mixed individually for each person. We are all unique and often need a remedy which is tailor-made for our own body.

Using herbs in the treatment of a problem is not just a matter of looking at the chart and choosing all or some of the herbs which are mentioned for the ailment. In fact, this could be quite a dangerous thing to do, rather like using a sledgehammer to tap a piece of glass into position! A problem can be created by many things and it's important to search for the cause before starting treatment. For example, a headache can be the result of faulty eyesight, tight shoes, stress, cervical problems, acidosis, anaemia, upset stomach, bad teeth, onset of influenza or cold, hepatitis, hypertension and lots more. Diarrhoea can be a symptom of gastroenteritis, worms, giardiasis, dysentery or amoebiasis.

If a problem is severe or of long duration, you should first seek the help of a qualified practitioner. After establishing the nature of the problem it would then be in order to tell your naturopath or doctor that you would like to use herbs as part of your healing process.

Many people who are ignorant of the properties of herbs consider them to be harmless. This is a dangerous misconception. To be of use, any herb needs pharmacological activity. This is the property which alters the physiological state of the body and, if used correctly, promotes healing. Conversely, if used for extended periods or in excessive doses, it can cause problems. I have said elsewhere in this book that the dose recommendations must be adhered to and that no medicines should be taken for more than six days of the week, the seventh day being for rest. It's good to eat very simply on this day, soups, salads or juices, and to have pleasant exercise and relaxation.

Before you begin to treat your acid stomach, bowel cramps or pain in the neck it's good to sit quietly with a piece of paper and a pencil and make lists for every aspect of your life — parenthood, spirituality, sex, recreation (maybe these last two should be bracketed together!), the quality of the food you eat, communication with your partner or friends, and any other area which you feel is relevant. Give each a mark out of ten, ten being the best and one the worst. If any aspect scores less than six your life is out of balance and your health will also be unbalanced.

At some time or other we have all used such expressions as "you're a pain in the neck" or "you make me sick", and this actually happens. In conflict situations muscles become so tense that they can't relax, and excess adrenalin creates complex conditions in the body which, if not resolved, may lead to physical and emotional problems.

Help is sometimes needed to make changes in areas which have been unbalanced for a long time, but these days we are fortunate that there are professional therapists who use many techniques to help us release our tensions. Methods such as Rajneesh rebalancing work on the body, treating it in a very sensitive way with connective tissue massage to release muscular tension patterns and the underlying emotional causes. Others use breath therapy to allow us to reach those hidden angers and griefs which can distort our lives. Voice dialogue is a method which helps us to 'get in touch' with the various vulnerable inner aspects of ourselves. Newsagents and health centres usually carry directories which contain lists of therapists who could be of help to you.

There are several ways to use your chosen herbs. The easiest is called a 'simple', meaning that only one herb is used. For instance, a cup of chamomile tea at bedtime to ensure a good night's sleep or ginger tea to settle a queasy stomach are examples of this method. If you want to use simples, refer to Charts 5 and 14 to help you choose the most suitable herb.

The more professional and possibly safer way to use the herbs is as a 'compound', using several herbs in a mixture. The reasons for this are:

1. Some problems need a variety of actions for relief to be gained; e.g. sluggish liver would require the use of hepatic and possibly digestive, antispasmodic and aperient herbs. This is because a disorder can result in other organs becoming involved and needing treatment. A herb used in such a way to address a problem directly is known as an 'active botanical'.
2. Where there is inflammation or irritation present it is necessary to use demulcent herbs to buffer the action of the other ingredients and to soothe membranes.
3. Some herbal mixtures taste pretty terrible and the use of aromatics helps to make them more acceptable.
4. An aperient, unless diarrhoea is a problem, is always helpful; having the bowels functioning well helps the system rid itself of toxins.

A formula for a herbal compound, therefore, could be:

- 3 parts active botanical (see 1 above)
- 1 part demulcent (see 2 above)
- 1 part aromatic (see 3 above)
- 1 part aperient, unless diarrhoea is present (see 4 above)

A typical formula for arthritis could be:

- 1 part nettle: diuretic, alterative, alkalising and calcium-rich.
- 1 part dandelion: diuretic, laxative, tonic.
- 1 part elder: anti-inflammatory, alterative, diaphoretic.
- 1 part mullein: demulcent, analgesic, alterative, antispasmodic.
- 1 part angelica: aromatic, diaphoretic, antispasmodic, tonic.
- 1 part liquorice: laxative, anti-inflammatory, demulcent.

You will see that this formula is aimed at excreting waste products through the kidneys, bowel and skin, reducing inflammation, easing pain and giving necessary nutrients to the body.

For urinary tract infections you could choose:

- diuretic herbs, to increase the flow of urine
- antiseptic herbs, to deal with the infection
- demulcent herbs, to soothe inflamed tissue.

Every complaint should be approached in this manner but the psychological aspects must be taken into account as well as the physical. A lot of problems which manifest in a physical way disappear when stress is brought under control. When I was irritable, tired and 'headachy' as a child, my mother's first treatment for me was a dose of Syrup of Figs and a long ride on my bike. She was a very uncomplicated and intuitive lady who believed that if your bowels were functioning well, you had plenty to occupy you and were happy, everything would sort itself out! These days it's often an aspirin and a day in bed for children with similar afflictions. I wonder who recovered the most quickly?

KEY to Chart 6

E	Eat raw as sprouts in salads, dips, sandwiches, casseroles, etc.
J	Apply juice externally.
T	Tincture (see p130).
Ex	Apply tincture externally.
O	Apply ointment (see p134); cover with a dressing.
C	Compress (see p140).
P	Apply powdered herbs (see p140); cover with dressing.
I	Infusion (see p129).
Cp	Capsules, take as directed on container.
X	Only raw root is of value. See p141 for vinegar recipe. 1 teaspoon juice may be added to syrup or oxymel (see p132).
A	Extract. Even though it's only marked in a few places on the chart, it may be used anywhere to disguise taste of compounds.
S	Syrup or oxymel (see p132).
M	Mouthwash: make infusion (see p129).
∅	Suppositories (see p140).
W	Eyewash (see p132).
Fb	Foot bath (see p133).
D	Make powdered mix and use as talcum, or mix tinctures to dab or spray.
R	Nose pack (see p140).
F	Fomentation (see p139).
★	⅛ teaspoon in glass of warm water.
G	Gargle (see p133).
B	Bath (see p177).
In	Inhalation (see p133).
Pl	Poultice (see p135).
Z	See 'Cautions' after individual herbs in Chapter One.

Note: If tinctures are not available then it's perfectly all right to use infusions or decoctions.

Chart 6 Herbs that Heal

	Abrasions	Adrenals	Allergies	Anaemia	Appetite, depress	Appetite, stimulate	Arthritis	Asthma	Bacterial infection	Bites	Bed wetting	Bladder problems	Bleeding, external	Bleeding, internal	Blood cleanser	Body building	Boils	Bowel problems	Breath sweetener	Bronchial problems	Bruises	Burns, minor	Cancer prevention	Catarrh	Chills	Chilblains	Childbirth	Circulation	Colds	Colic
Alfalfa Z		E		E		E	E								E	E		E												
Aloe Vera																						J								
Angelica						T														T					T	T				T
Anise					T														T											T
Basil										Ex		T																T		T
Borage Z																				T			T							T
Calendula	O			T									E								C		T							
Caraway					T																									T
Catnep				T																T									T	T
Cayenne													P	T											T	O		T		
Chamomile Z						T														T										
Comfrey Z						T														T										
Dandelion				T			T								T															
Elderflower																				T					T				T	
Fennel					T														T											T
Feverfew Z						T																								T
Garlic			Cp	Cp			Cp	Cp	Cp											Cp			Cp	Cp					Cp	
Ginger																				T					T	T		T	T	T
Horseradish Z						X		X												X				X				X		
Hyssop								T																T						
Landcress		E				E									E								E							
Lavender																														T
Liquorice Z							A								A					A								A		
Mallow	O																O			S		O		T						
Marjoram								T			T																			T
Mullein Z				T				T										T		T									T	
Nettle Z	O			T			T						T			T				T				T				T		
Parsley Z			T				T	T				T			T				E				T							
Peppermint							T												M										T	T
Plantain	O									O	T	T	T		T						C									
Red Clover						E									E		E			T			T							
Raspberry																		T		T							T		T	
Rosemary Z																			M									T		
Rue Z																														T
Sage												T			T										T	T			T	
Shepherd's Purse													T	T				T												
Tansy Z																														
Thyme Z						T			T									T	M	T	C		T	In						T
Valerian																				T										
Violet																				T			T		T					
Watercress		E				E										E							E							
Witch Hazel													C								C	C								
Wormwood Z						T																								
Yarrow Z	O					T						T			T						C	C	T		T	T			T	
Yellow Dock				T								T			T					T			T							

Chart 6 (cont) Herbs that Heal

	Constipation	Convulsions	Coughs	Cramps, stomach	Cystitis	Deodorant	Diarrhoea	Digestion	Diuretic	Dizziness	Dysentery	Earache	Eczema	Epidemics	Eyes, inflamed	Exhaustion	Fatigue	Fever reducers	Fractures	Gall bladder	Gas	Glands, swollen	Gout	Haemorrhoids	Heartburn	Heart strengthener	Hay fever	Headaches	High blood pressure	Indigestion
Alfalfa Z									E				E				E						E							
Aloe Vera																								O						
Angelica			S	T										T		T					T				T					
Anise			S					T													T									T
Basil				T																								T		T
Borage Z															W											T				
Calendula							T								W									∅						
Caraway						D		T													T									
Catnep		T					T	T													T									
Cayenne																T	T				T					T			T	
Chamomile Z					T													T										T		
Comfrey Z																			Pl								T			
Dandelion					T				T				T							T			T							
Elderflower																														
Fennel			S					T							W						T	F								T
Feverfew Z																		T			T							T		T
Garlic								Cp				Cp						Cp											Cp	
Ginger								T										I			I							I		T
Horseradish Z			X																											
Hyssop			S																											
Landcress													E	E												E				
Lavender						D				T						Fb	Fb													
Liquorice Z	A		A																							A	A			
Mallow			S		T																						T			
Marjoram			S																		T				T			T		T
Mullein Z			S				T				T										T						T			
Nettle Z							T				T		T											∅					T	
Parsley Z					T				T											T			T				T			
Peppermint	T	T		T				T		T											T							T		
Plantain			S				T				T										T			∅						
Red Clover																				E										
Raspberry	T							T																						
Rosemary Z								T													T					T			T	
Rue Z			S																											
Sage			S				T	T										T										T		
Shepherd's Purse	T						T				T													∅		T				
Tansy Z															W															
Thyme Z						D		T													T				T			T		
Valerian			S																											
Violet													T															T		
Watercress													E													E				
Witch Hazel							T				T													C						
Wormwood Z	T			T				T										T												
Yarrow Z				T			T											T						∅				T		
Yellow Dock	T							T					T										T							

Chart 6 (cont) Herbs that Heal

	Infection	Influenza	Infertility	Inflammation	Insect bites	Insomnia	Intestinal purifier	Irritable bowel	Jaundice	Kidney cleanser	Lactation	Liver	Lung problems	Menstrual cramps	Menstrual problems	Menses, delayed	Migraine	Mucus	Nausea	Nerves	Nosebleeds	Oral hygiene	Pain	Pancreas	Pituitary	Prostate problems	Psoriasis	Pyorrhoea	Radiation burns	Rashes
Alfalfa Z										E									E		E				E		E			E
Aloe Vera					O																								J	O
Angelica				C																										
Anise							T				T							T				M								
Basil					O																									
Borage Z											T									T										T
Calendula									T						T													M		
Caraway														T																
Catnep		T	T			T														T			T							
Cayenne										T														T						
Chamomile Z						T								T						T			T							
Comfrey Z	O				O								T																	
Dandelion									T			T															T			
Elderflower		T																T												
Fennel							T				T											M								
Feverfew Z									T								T													
Garlic	Cp	Cp					Cp						Cp					Cp						Cp						
Ginger		T																												
Horseradish Z								X		X								X												
Hyssop	T									T		T																		
Landcress										E		E								E							E			E
Lavender																				T										
Liquorice Z												A	A																	
Mallow								T		T		T	S																	Ex
Marjoram																			T			M								
Mullein Z						T							S					T		T			T							
Nettle Z										T																				
Parsley Z									T	T		T				T									T	T	T			
Peppermint		T																	T	T		M								
Plantain	T				O				T	T											R									
Red Clover									E			E								E							E			E
Raspberry		T									T				T				T	T										
Rosemary Z												T			T					T		M								
Rue Z																				T										
Sage													S						T	T		M						M		
Shepherd's Purse																					R									
Tansy Z																														
Thyme Z													In									M						M		Ex
Valerian						T														T			T							Ex
Violet													T																	Ex
Watercress										E		E								E							E			E
Witch Hazel				C	C																									C
Wormwood Z									T			T				T			T											
Yarrow Z		T							T																					
Yellow Dock									T			T															T			

Chart 6 (cont) Herbs that Heal

	Raynaud's disease	Respiratory infection	Restlessness	Rheumatism	Ringworm	Scabies	Scalds	Scar tissue	Shock	Sinusitis	Sores	Spasms	Spleen	Stomach cramps	Stress	Stroke	Sunburn	Swelling	Tonic	Toothache	Throat, sore	Ulcerated sores	Urinary problems	Vomiting, excessive	Varicose veins	Warts	Whooping cough	Worms	Wounds	Yeast problems
Alfalfa Z																			E											
Aloe Vera							J	O									J												O	
Angelica				T			C												T				T							
Anise																											S			
Basil																											S			
Borage Z					J																									
Calendula					T	Ex					O											O			C			T	O	
Caraway												T																		
Catnep			T						T			T			T															
Cayenne	T			T					T							★														
Chamomile Z			T						T			T			T			C												
Comfrey Z											O							C												
Dandelion				T																		O				J				
Elderflower		T																			G								O	
Fennel												T																		
Feverfew Z				T										T					T											
Garlic	Cp																										Cp	Cp		Cp
Ginger	T													T	T				T	M				T			S			
Horseradish Z				X						X																		X		
Hyssop													T								G							T		
Landcress				E															E											
Lavender											O				T		B													
Liquorice Z		A													A															
Mallow											O										G	O	T				S		O	
Marjoram		T																									S			
Mullein Z		T									O										G								O	
Nettle Z		T		T							O								T											
Parsley Z				T									T						E						T					
Peppermint		T	T						T					T										T				T		
Plantain							O				O						C	C											O	
Red Clover				T								T																		
Raspberry																							T	T						
Rosemary Z	T										O	T		T															O	
Rue Z	T																								T			T		
Sage		T																			G									T
Shepherd's Purse																														
Tansy Z																									C			T		
Thyme Z		T				Ex					O										G	O					In	T	O	
Valerian			T						T			T			T							O							O	
Violet											O								T		G						S		O	
Watercress				E															E											
Witch Hazel							C				C						C	C							C				C	
Wormwood Z				T															T									T		
Yarrow Z				T													C													
Yellow Dock				T									T																	

Chart 7 Children's Problems

	Alfalfa sprouts	Angelica	Anise	Catnep	Cider vinegar	Chamomile	Dill	Elderflower	Fennel	Garlic	Ginger	Honey	Hyssop	Lemon balm	Lemon grass	Lemon juice	Liquorice extract	Mallow	Mullein	Plantain	Red clover sprouts	Red raspberry	Sage	Spearmint	Thyme	Violet	Yarrow
Bedwetting	R											X		T					T	T	R						
Catarrh	R		T		A	T			T			X	T	T			E		T		R						
Chickenpox	R			T								X				X					R	T		T			O
Colds		T		T	A	T						X	T		T	X								T		T	
Colic ★			T	T		T	T		T						T									T			
Constipation	R					T		T				X					E	T	T								
Cradle Cap ★						O																					
Croup				T		T						X						T							I	T	
Cough		M	M		A							X	M				E	M	M				M		M	M	
Delicate Children	R	T	T			T						X	T			X					R	T					
Diarrhoea											T	X										T					
Earache										L																	
Fevers ★		T		T		T	T	T				X	T		T	X	E							T			T
German Measles	R			T		T								T							R	T				T	T
Glands & Mumps	R			T	F	F					T	X							F		R	T				F	
Headache						T						X		T	T	X								T		T	
Haemorrhage, Cuts																			C	C							C
Insect Bites				T	C	T										C				J							
Insomnia				T		T						X		T													
Measles	R			T		T		T			T	X		T		X	E									T	
Mouth Ulcers												X						G					G	G	G		
Nappy Rash ★						W		W							W												
Nerves	R			T		T						X		T										T			
Nosebleed																			S	S							S
Restlessness				T		T						X		T													
Scabies																									To		
Stomach Upsets				T		T					T							T									
Teething				T		T			T			X		T								T					
Tonsillitis				T		T						X	G			X						T	G			T	
Vomiting			T								T				T							T		T			
Whooping Cough					A							X						T			R	T			I	T	

KEY to Chart 7

★ See recipes following Chart 7.

L Pour a few drops garlic oil (see p141) into a warm, sterile teaspoon. Draw up into an ear dropper, squeeze *gently* into the ear. Plug the outside opening of the ear with cotton wool. NB: The pure oil from garlic oil capsules must never be used in the ears of children. It is far too strong and could cause intense pain and damage to the eardrum.

O Use a cool 2x infusion. Dab on affected area, leave to dry.

T Give infusion in recommended dose (see below).

A Add 2 drops to each teaspoon of infusion.

R Add to food daily.

F Fomentation on swollen glands.

I Thyme oil inhalation (for inhalation method see p133).

E Add 1 or 2 drops to each teaspoon of infusion to improve taste and for its medicinal properties.

X Add to infusions to improve taste.

J Squeeze juice directly onto sting or bite.

G Gargle/mouthwash (see p133).

C Compress (see p140).

S Pack nose with cotton wool plug soaked in a cold 3x infusion and hold the arms above the head or put the hands in a bowl of cold water. Witch hazel from the first aid box can also be used to soak the plug.

To Thyme oil, diluted 50/50 with castor oil. Use as a compress; change four times daily.

M Administer herbs in oxymel (see p132).

W Ointment.

Dose: Six days a week only, resting on the seventh. The adult dose is 125ml (½ cup) 3 times daily, ½ hr before food.

Children:	30 kg (66 lb) and over	½ adult dose
	15-30 kg (33-66 lb)	¼ adult dose
	7-15 kg (15½-33 lb)	⅛ adult dose

Note: Discontinue treatment with the chosen herb after three weeks. Resume after a further week if the treatment is working or change to another herb if no improvement is seen.

Children's problems

When treating children we need to be very careful to use only the most gentle remedies. The herbs in Chart 7 have all been shown over centuries to be suitable for children but, even so, we must never forget that everything on this planet will be an allergen to someone. If your child suffers from allergies, be aware that chamomile, for instance, could cause a problem. A 'patch' test can be helpful for both children and adults. To do this, make a very strong infusion of the suspected herb, dab it thoroughly on the inside skin of the elbow, cover and leave for 24 hours. If there is any redness or soreness at the end of this time the herb should be avoided.

It's good to encourage children to drink mild herbal teas, mixed with fresh fruit juices, from an early age. If they develop a taste for these drinks it will have twofold benefits: drinking the teas is a preventive act, and the children won't be resistant to the teas if they are sick. Herbs which are good to use for these drinks are lemon grass, spearmint or red raspberry leaf or fruit, mixed with apple, orange or lemon juice, water and honey. Fruit juices should always be diluted with water or herb tea before being given to children; the undiluted juice is too strong for small, immature digestive systems to cope with. Avoid giving the same herb over long periods of time. Vary the drinks from day to day.

Recipes for children

COLIC

It's very convenient to make powdered mixtures, stored in glass jars and marked with the mixture number. You might find that one blend is more effective for your baby than another. If the problem persists seek professional help.

Colic mixture 1
- Anise seed
- Fennel seed
- Dill seed

Colic mixture 2
- Catnep, dried
- Spearmint, dried
- Dill seed

Colic mixture 3
- Chamomile, dried
- Lemon grass, dried
- Fennel seed

Make all the above as described on page 129. Give in doses of 1 to 2 teaspoons as needed.

CRADLE CAP

Chamomile flowers
Elder flowers
Calendula petals
Nettle, dried
Almond oil

Make a herbal oil (see p170) and massage gently into the scalp. This is a lovely oil to use all over the body of your baby.

NAPPY RASH

Make an ointment using the recipe on page 134. Use chamomile, elder, lemon grass and mallow root to make the herb oil and substitute cod liver oil for 10 ml (2 teaspoons) of the herb oil. This recipe makes a really effective soothing and healing ointment which acts as a barrier cream as well. The ointment may stain, so use a nappy liner.

Babies should be allowed to crawl around with their bare bottoms exposed to the sun and fresh air for some part of every day (not at the hottest time of the day) as a good preventive measure. Small babies love being in a pram under a tree, no nappy, legs waving in the air, watching the leaves and the clouds moving. Keeps them, and you, happy for hours. A strong net (cat and mosquito proof) fastened firmly over the pram is a safety precaution.

The first aid box

Everyone, at some time has been — or will be — faced with a major or minor injury to themselves or others: cuts, burns and stings, and more serious things such as heart attacks and broken bones. Knowing what to do in these situations can prevent excessive trauma or pain and in some instances can save a life.

It should be noted that this section deals with *first* aid. Many injuries need professional help as soon as possible. The dirt in a seemingly innocent cut can carry infections such as tetanus. The pain of earache may be a symptom of middle ear infection, a potentially serious condition.

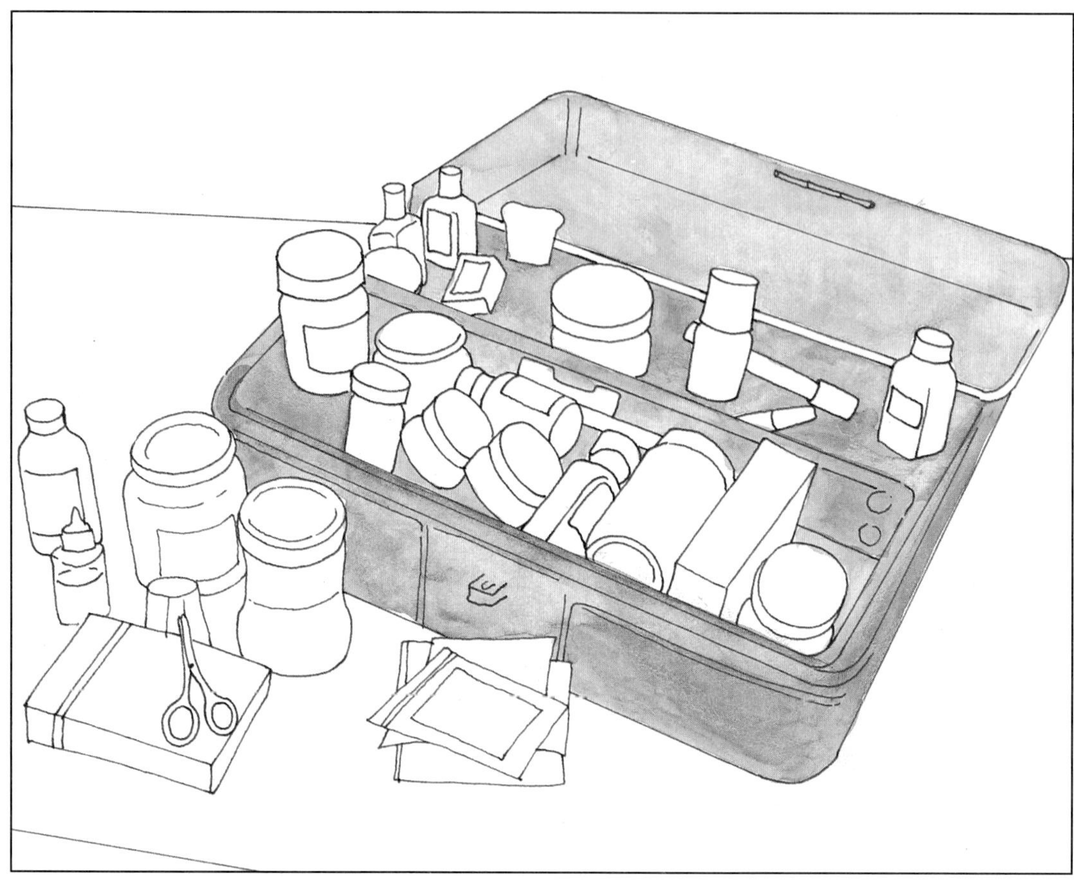

CONTENTS OF FIRST AID BOX

H Aloe vera gel*
H Charcoal tablets
H Garlic oil capsules or garlic oil (p141)
P Ipecac (ipecacuanha) syrup
H Linseeds
P Menthol crystals
H Oils: castor, lavender*, rosemary, tea-tree*

KEY

M Make yourself

P Buy from a pharmacy

H Buy from a health food store

* Keep in both house and car first aid boxes

M Healing ointments of your choice* (see p134).
M Dried, mixed powdered herbs in small jars (see p140).
H Dr Bach rescue remedy*
H Slippery elm tablets and powder
M Tinctures (p130): calendula*, chamomile, cayenne, ginger, shepherd's purse*
P Witch hazel extract*
* Bandages, slings, clean cloth, plasters, eye patch
* Scissors, tweezers
Steel or enamel dish
Small funnel
Thermometer
Two or three eye droppers
Glass or plastic 25ml medicine measure
* Cotton buds and wool

There are two things needed in order to be an effective helper:

- Take a short first aid course with St John Ambulance or similar organisation.
- Provide your car and house with well equipped and maintained first aid boxes.

My medicine box is a bright red, metal toolbox and is kept in a conspicuous place in our home. It is checked regularly and re-stocked as supplies run low. A metal box is robust, weatherproof and, if you have children, lockable.

There is an excellent book on the market called *The Johnson and Johnson First Aid Book*, published by Grafton. I highly recommend it and feel that every household would benefit from having a copy in their first aid box.

Description of First Aid Box Contents

Many of the items in the first aid list are not made from your home-grown herbs. Sometimes this is because of the difficulty of preparing items such as charcoal tablets. In other cases it's because the remedy suggested is the best to use in an *emergency* situation and won't necessarily be used on a continuing basis.

Aloe vera gel

It's possible to use the fresh gel from your garden plants but if you use this often you may build up an allergy. The cure for the allergic rash is either aloe cream or stabilised aloe gel. The reaction seems to be caused by the yellow juice between the skin and the flesh of the plant.

Charcoal tablets

Charcoal is an antacid remedy used as far back as the ancient Egyptians. It is a powerful absorbent in the stomach and intestinal tract, acting like a sponge. The charcoal we use today is 'activated', which means it's been treated with steam to make it even more absorbent. It disinfects and deodorises, picks up harmful bacteria and passes them from the body. It has a reputation for being helpful in curing a hangover but I haven't tried this. Charcoal can have a constipating effect if overused. This effect is useful, however, for helping to cure simple diarrhoea.

Garlic oil capsules

Garlic oil contains a very powerful antibacterial agent called allicin. The antiseptic action prevents the formation of bacteria as well as healing infections. This makes it an ideal preventive herb.

Ipecacuanha syrup

This is a Brazilian herb which, used in small doses, is an expectorant and in large doses becomes an emetic. Its main use in the first aid box is its emetic properties in cases of poisoning. It must never be used if kerosene (paraffin), bleach, acid or alkaline liquids have been swallowed (i.e. if the liquids are corrosive or have strong fumes which can suffocate) or if the patient is under the age of one year.

Caution Always follow the instructions on the manufacturer's label.

Linseeds

These are the seeds of the flax plant. They are brown in colour with a smooth, silky husk which is so shiny it looks as though it has been polished. Placed under the lower eyelid, the seed swells up into a gelatinous mass and attaches itself to foreign bodies in the eye. It then moves to the corner of the eye and can be lifted out.

Menthol crystals

Menthol is the chief constituent of peppermint oil. The oil is treated by cooling to a low temperature, when crystallisation begins. It has many uses but in the medicine box it's used as an inhalation.

Oils

Castor oil comes from the seed of the castor oil plant. Castor oil was once used internally as an aperient, but this is a brutal way of dealing with sluggish bowels as it causes severe griping. Keep your castor oil for use as an external remedy. It has amazing drawing power, reputed to be as much as 10 cm (4 in) in depth. It soothes as it's drawing, whether it is a splinter in flesh or a foreign body in the eye.

Lavender oil is distilled from the flower head. It acts as a sedative.

Rosemary oil is distilled from the leaf of the plant. It is a first-rate treatment for muscular tension.

Tea-tree oil is distilled from leaves of some of the Malaleuca family of plants, the main one being *Malaleuca alternifolia.* It is almost a first aid kit on its own. It has powerful antibacterial and antiseptic properties.

Ointments

Make these by following the method on page 134.

Powdered herbs

As the name implies, these are vulnerary herbs which have been dried and ground to a powder. Use where a wound needs to be kept dry. For the method see p140.

Rescue remedy

This is a mixture of the homeopathic flower tinctures cherry plum, clematis, impatiens, rock rose, and star of Bethlehem. This tincture is useful in any minor or major situation where there is shock and nerves need to be calmed. It is taken 4 drops at a time onto the tongue. Use as often as every 15 minutes if the situation warrants it. It can be rubbed on the pulse points if the patient is unconscious.

Slippery elm

A North American tree from which the bark is stripped for its medicinal value. I try to use this remedy in emergencies only as the tree population is being decimated. Instead of taking a small amount of bark from each tree, the whole tree is debarked and so dies. The powdered bark is a specific for soothing inflamed membranes both internally and externally.

Tinctures

Read the relevant information on Chart 5 to find more uses for these tinctures.

Witch hazel extract

This tincture is one of the finest and gentlest astringents there is. It is available from pharmacies.

KEY to Chart 8

M Massage on temples, back of neck or afflicted area.

S Sniff straight from bottle.

C Apply compress two-hourly.

D Put three drops in eye; keep covered.

E Squeeze oil from capsule in ear or use homemade (see p141). For children use only homemade oil.

X Use as directed on container for purchased items. Homemade items have instructions for use with recipes.

Ø Put one seed under lower eyelid.

O 15 drops in 2 tablespoons water to drink.

N Drop in cavity and rub on gum.

I Inhalation (see p133).

T Add 1 teaspoon to 1 cup of yarrow or sage tea; drink hot.

W Add 1 tablespoon to 1 cup boiled water; cool and use as wash.

B Add 10 drops to a lukewarm bath; soak until condition is eased.

A Sprinkle on wound; apply dry dressing.

P Use for poultice (see p135).

H Take internally.

Chart 8 First Aid and Medicine Box

	Aloe vera gel	Charcoal tablets	Garlic oil capsules	Ipecac syrup	Linseeds	Menthol crystals	Oil, castor	Oil, lavender	Oil, rosemary	Oil, tea tree	Ointment, comfrey	Ointment, general	Ointment, plantain	Powdered herbs	Rescue remedy	Slippery elm tablets	Slippery elm powder	Tincture of calendula	Tincture of chamomile	Tincture of cayenne	Tincture of ginger	Tincture of shepherd's purse	Witch hazel extract
Anti-Infection		H	H							X		X		A				X					
Bleeding, External													X					X				X	C
Bleeding, Internal																				O		O	
Bruises	X										X						P						
Burns, Minor	X									X					X		P						
Chills, Colds						I														T	T		
Cold Sores										X													
Cuts										X				A				X				X	
Earache			E																				
Eyes, Foreign Bodies					Ø		D																
Fainting								S							X								
Fever																				T	T		
Flatulence		X														X			X	T	T		
Headaches						I		M	M						X								
Head Lice										X													
Heartburn		X																					
Infections							C					X					P					W	C
Insect bites							C			X			X									C	C
Nausea																X					T		
Pain															X	X			X				
Poisoning		X		X																			
Shock								S							X								
Sores												X		A									
Splinters							C					X											
Sprains									M		X												
Sunburn	X							B							X								C
Swelling											X				C								C
Toothache																		N		N			
Trauma															X				X				
Weeping Sores														A									
Wounds												X		A			P	X					

CHAPTER FOUR

THE BODY BEAUTIFUL

To make a bath for melancholy.
Take Mallowes, pellitory of the wall, of each three handfuls,
Camomell flowers, Mellilot flowers, of each one handfull,
Hollyhocks, two handfuls, Isop one greate handfull,
Senerick seed one ounce,
and boil them in nine gallons of water until they come to three,
then put in a quart of new milke
and go into it bloude warme or something warmer.

Mary Fairfax, *Still-room Book,* 1630

Twenty years ago I worked as a cosmetician for one of the most famous cosmetic houses in the world. I believed that the products I was using and selling were good quality and value even though they were expensive. Then I attended a seminar held by one of the directors of the company where he told us that a new lipstick being launched cost the company 3 cents to make and retailed for $4.90. This was considered very smart business and merited a round of applause. He went on to tell us of a 'miraculous' new cream about to be released in which the vital ingredient was the urine from pregnant mares! These and other 'insights' led me to give up my job and return to herbs, my first love.

After we had been living at the farm called 'Rivendell' for about four years the herb gardens were bursting with life and vigour. I was using herbal remedies to treat people with problems and we were selling the herbs potted and dried, but still had a huge surplus. At this time it became apparent there was a need for skin and hair care products which would fulfil certain criteria: not tested on animals, as free from chemicals as possible and full of skin and hair nutrients.

As I was hopeless at chemistry during my schooldays I didn't know how to begin converting the plants into marketable products. After several months of trial and error I made a friend called Fred, a pharmacist who taught me how to make a stable emulsion and who has been my mentor from that day on for all things to do with chemistry. After this meeting things began to happen very fast and we soon had a small number of skin and hair products (tested on people of all ages) which shops seemed eager to sell.

Friends moved from Perth to work in the gardens, the laboratory, the kitchen and office. We had fun, fights, triumphs and traumas. There can have been no more beautiful or unlikely place to have a 'factory'. When it was time to make healing cream, shampoo or moisture lotions, you stepped out of the lab door, basket and secateurs in hand, to collect herbs in the terraced gardens. This could take some time as you breathed the early morning herb-scented air, paused to pick a handful of sun-ripened fruit and took a few minutes to sit on a log, eating and looking at the hills patterned with long morning shadows from the gum trees. These stolen moments with the sun on your face and warm juice running down your chin are what memories are made of.

We had several exciting years running the business, priding ourselves on the high quality of the products: always the freshest herbs, the most expensive, natural and pure essential and non-essential oils. We no longer own the business but it still thrives in Bunbury, making beautiful, cruelty-free skin and hair care products called 'Rivendell Farm'.

These days people are faced with massive advertising, expensive packaging and extravagant claims for skin care products. In the main these are synthetic, costly and have been tested in an unnecessarily cruel way on animals. Creams, lotions and shampoos sold in shops have to fulfil a number of requirements. They need to have a long shelf life which means the addition of quite strong preservatives. (My friend Fred made a very good point when he said: "Nature makes nothing which is not biodegradable. If it doesn't rot, it's not natural.") These products must never separate, so the emulsifying waxes are usually made from chemical ingredients. They rarely have natural essential oils to perfume them as cost is a big factor and these oils are expensive. The synthetic perfumes used are an irritant to many skins and most certainly don't add any goodness even if they don't affect you in a deleterious way. I'm not saying that all bought cosmetics are bad. Your local health food shops and some pharmacies will carry products like 'Rivendell Farm' which are full of good things; but if you don't want *any* unknown ingredients on your skin or hair then it is safest to make your own. It is also much, much, cheaper!

The recipes in this chapter will pamper your skin and hair, are easy and fun to make and a pleasure to use. Many of them won't feel or look like the shop-bought variety but you will quickly become used to the difference. Don't feel intimidated by the thought of making your own cosmetics — it's no different to cooking a meal (much easier in some cases) and the quantities are not usually too critical. Many will need to be refrigerated but I have found that some of these recipes freeze really well and the remainder keep refrigerated for a few weeks.

Note: See page 10 for suggestions on record keeping.

Glossary of cosmetic terms and ingredients

Acid/alkaline Skin has an acid mantle ranging between 5.5 and 6.2. This protects the skin from invasion by bacteria. Most soaps leave the skin alkaline; the skin will readjust the balance in 1 - 2 hours but in order to restore the acid mantle quickly it's good to use an acidic tonic (see recipes on p190).

Agar agar A jelly prepared from various types of seaweed. It may be used to thicken recipes and is a non-animal substitute for gelatine.

Almond *(Prunus dulcis)* Ground sweet almonds are used cosmetically in a variety of ways. The meal may be used as a cleansing, refining, emollient scrub and the milk (see p166) is cleansing, refining and moisturising. The oil is a useful non-drying cosmetic ingredient.

Aromatherapy The treatment of mental and physical complaints through the inhalation of volatile essential oils. The method frequently employed is massage.

Arrowroot A white powdered starch obtainable from the root of several plants. This powder is soothing to the skin used either as a powder or mixed to a paste or gell (see p166).

Astringent An agent which has the power to contract tissues.

Beeswax A wax, secreted by bees, used to make the cell walls of the honeycomb. It is used as an emulsifier and binder in ointments, creams and salves (see p 166 for treatment of this wax).

Benzoin tincture This tincture is made from alcohol and the aromatic and resinous juice of *Styrax benzoin,* a tree from Java and Sumatra. It has antiseptic, astringent, antifungal and protective properties and can be used as an aid in preserving creams and lotions.

Note: Your pharmacist may offer you either simple or compound tincture of benzoin. It's most important that you use only *simple tincture of benzoin.* The compound has additives which can be toxic and harmful to the body.

Borax (sodium tetraborate) A mineral found on alkaline lake shores, borax is mildly alkaline and softening. It can be used effectively in most cosmetic products but must never be used internally or on broken skin. It can be combined with beeswax to form a stable emulsion. I wouldn't recommend its use in baby products.

Castile A soap made from olive oil and other ingredients. Try to find one with at least 50% olive oil. It's sometimes quite difficult to get the hard white soap but the liquid is easy to find and lovely to use. My favourite liquid soap is a mixture of coconut, olive and peppermint oils.

Castor oil or **Red turkey oil** Castor oil has many cosmetic and medicinal uses (see p158). When the oil is first expressed from the plant it contains many poisonous alkaloids which have to be removed before it's sold as 'medicinal' castor oil. There is another process used which produces water-missible oil called 'sulphonated', 'treated' or 'red turkey oil'. This treatment makes the oil very suitable for bath oils as it mixes with the water. It's quite likely you will only be able to get red turkey oil from pharmaceutical wholesale suppliers as it's now considered 'old-fashioned'.

Cetomacrogol wax This is an emulsifying wax which begins its life as coconut oil and then undergoes various laboratory processes. This wax or similar ones are needed if you want to make an oil in water emulsion (see p164). You will end up with a less natural product but emulsions are fun to make and it's possible to pack them with goodies.

Cocoa butter *(Theobroma cacoa)* A solid fat extracted from the roasted, crushed seed of the cocoa plant. This fine emollient has a very low melting point and liquifies on contact with the skin. It is used in creams, ointments and lotions where its properties help to prevent and/or soften wrinkles and stretch marks and aid in the treatment of skin rashes, and it has the added advantage of smelling deliciously of chocolate. If you have problems obtaining it from your pharmacy I suggest you try a pharmaceutical wholesale house. They are usually quite happy to supply on a cash basis. For ease of measuring small amounts, it may be treated in the same way as beeswax (see p166).

Coconut oil A white saturated fat with a very low melting point, extracted from the white meat of the coconut. Coconut oil is beneficial to the skin and hair.

Deodorant A substance used to inhibit or disguise odour.

Emollient Used to sooth external inflammation or dryness.

Emulsion A mixture of oil and water which, when combined, doesn't separate. There are two types of emulsion:
1. *Water in oil:* In this emulsion the oil is the continuous phase and has water packed into it as microscopically small droplets. This type of emulsion forms a cream or lotion which feels oily when first applied to the skin. Almost all creams and lotions made from ingredients such as coconut oil, beeswax and cocoa butter are water in oil emulsions and as such feel greasy when first applied to the skin. This needn't put you off as the greasiness is usually quickly absorbed.
2. *Oil in water:* This emulsion is the reverse of the above with the tiny droplets of oil being surrounded by water. This creates creams and lotions which feel moist but not greasy when first applied to the skin and are absorbed into the skin without leaving much or any oily residue. A 'vanishing cream' is an example of this type of emulsion. To make creams and lotions of this type it's necessary to use emulsifying waxes. These come from various natural sources (e.g. animal or vegetable fats, petroleum) or may be completely synthesised in a laboratory. The wax which I occasionally use if I want a vanishing cream is cetomacrogol emulsifying wax (described above). If you don't feel good about using any synthetically treated products at all, you will have to settle for water in oil emulsions. I feel fine about using emulsifying wax for some of the things I make — the proportion is sometimes as low as 5% and the wax is an inert, non-allergenic ingredient which started off life as a nut on a tree. The final choice has to be yours, so I offer recipes for both types of creams and lotions.

Essence A mixture of 30 ml (1 oz) essential oils with 500 ml (2 cups) vodka (high-proof).

Essential oil The concentrated perfume of a plant usually obtained as an oil by steam distillation.

Exfoliant An agent used as a gentle peeling agent to rid the skin of dead cells.

Gelatine A powdered glue-like substance, made from animal bones, hoofs and skin. Used as a thickening agent. See **agar agar** if you are vegetarian and don't want to use any animal products.

Glycerine A substance found in animal and vegetable fats. It is sweet, colourless, odourless and transparent, with the consistency of syrup. As a humectant it is useful in cosmetics and also serves as an antibacterial agent, softener, lubricant and preservative. In order to preserve effectively, it needs to be 20% of the total formula, which would be far too much for the average cream or lotion, but, if smaller amounts are combined with 4% tincture benzoin, together they make a good natural preservative.

Honey Honey cleanses, heals, softens, moisturises, hydrates and acts as a humectant. You will see from this impressive list why honey is an ingredient in so many cosmetics.

Humectant A substance with the capacity for attracting and holding moisture in the skin, e.g. glycerine and honey.

Hydrate To keep the normal fluid balance in the skin.

Kaolin — A fine earth clay used for making porcelain, soap, paint and paper. Cosmetically, it is used as a binder in packs and scrubs. Kaolin is particularly useful for oily/combination skins as it can absorb a large amount of grease.

Lanolin, anhydrous — Also known as wool fat. This is the fat in the wool of sheep which is extracted by boiling the wool after the sheep has been shorn. This fat is very close in composition to the sebum in human skin and, because of this compatibility, lanolin is a valuable lubricant and moisturiser. There is now some controversy regarding the use of wool fat (see p135).

Lecithin — An internal and external emulsifier, usually made from the soya bean. It's available in health food shops in powder, granule or liquid form. It leaves the skin with a soft sheen and a smooth texture.

Loofah — Those of you who haven't come across this wonderful bath aid have a treat in store. A loofah is a tropical member of the gourd family. It grows in a similar fashion to marrows and looks very similar. The sponge is the fibrous skeleton which emerges when the flesh has rotted away. The texture is quite coarse but not unpleasantly so. Used before or during a shower or bath it gets rid of dead skin and whips up the circulation to leave you glowing.

Lotion — A liquid preparation applied to the skin.

Milk — Milk is inexpensive, healing, softening and nourishing. It may be used fresh or dried and will be found useful in facials, baths, face packs and lotions. Use skimmed milk for oily skin, whole milk for dry or normal skin.

Moisturiser — See **Humectant.**

Mucilage — Gummy, jelly-like substance obtained from certain plants (see also **tragacanth**).

Oats *(Avena sativa)* — To most people the word 'oats' probably conjures up a picture of bowls of steaming porridge on cold mornings; it's unlikely they would think of soft, silky skin. Oats are rich in iron, protein, potassium, magnesium and silicon and this makes them wonderfully nutritious, both internally and externally. They can be used as a bath additive, cleanser, nourisher, skin softener and exfoliant.

Salve — A soothing, softening and healing ointment.

Tonic — A mild astringent.

Tragacanth *(Astralagus gummifer)* — Powdered, dried gum obtained from the plant. An excellent, softening emollient which swells to a mucilage when liquid is added. It's very expensive but you need only use a little and it's a very useful thickener for creams and lotions.

Vinegar — The word 'vinegar' is a derivation from the French *vin aigre* which means sour wine. Cider vinegar is made from apples and seems to be the best to use for cosmetic purposes. Skin is naturally acidic and because of this has the capacity to repel infection. If for some reason this acid mantle is destroyed (most soaps are alkaline) a vinegar wash or other acidic treatment (lemon juice) will restore the balance (see **Acid/alkaline** in this glossary).

Methods

To make the recipes in this chapter you will need the equipment listed on page 128.

To avoid the problems of varying systems of measurement I have used the teaspoon as a measure wherever possible. Many books say that 60 drops = 1 teaspoonful = 5 millilitres. We have found that this is not the case. After measuring with various sizes of spoons and droppers, the liquid measurement we came up with was:
18-20 drops = 1 ml; 90-100 drops = 5 ml = 1 teaspoonful.

Wherever infusions, decoctions or oils (both essential and non-essential) are used in a recipe, refer to any of the charts in this chapter to help you make the best choice of herbs.

The strength of herbal oil or liquid to be used is indicated by 1x, 2x, 3x. You will find the method of making these strengths on pages 129 and 170.

Almond Milk or Cream

Milk This is made very simply by pouring 250-375 ml (1-1½ cups) of boiling water over ½ cup of ground almonds. Cover and leave in the refrigerator overnight. Strain well through double cheesecloth or muslin (use the residue as a scrub) and store in the refrigerator. Keeps for only a few days but it freezes well.
Cream Make as above but use less water.

Arrowroot or Cornflour Jelly

(FOR MASK BASE)

Slowly add 6-8 tablespoons cold water to 2 heaped teaspoons of either arrowroot or cornflour. (This jelly can be made to suit your own needs so I suggest adding less water at first and thinning if you find the mixture too thick.) Bring to the boil in a small pan, stirring all the time. Cool to blood heat. You can now add mashed herbs, fruit, vegetables or any other mask ingredient.

Beeswax

Beeswax can be purchased from a pharmacy (expensive) or from a beekeeper (much cheaper). If you go direct to the beekeeper, the wax is likely to be full of strange bits and pieces. Don't worry about this as it's easy to clean. I have often read the instruction: 'Take a tablespoon of beeswax'. Now I've never been quite sure how to do this as beeswax is very hard, sticky and difficult to work with. Here is my method of cleaning and measuring wax.

Buy several ice cube trays. Pour 1 tablespoon of water into one of the hollows and note the level. My trays hold exactly 1 tablespoon in each cube hollow and each cube weighs 12 g (½ oz). You can find trays for very small cubes in which you can make teaspoonful-sized blocks.

Empty the water out, dry the tray and grease it well with oil. Put the beeswax in a pan, cover with cold water and bring slowly to the boil. (Turn the heat down low at this stage as you don't want to boil the wax, just to melt it.) When the wax has melted, turn the heat off and leave the contents to cool and set. Don't let the wax get too cold, just cool enough to hold its shape when you lift it out of the pan.

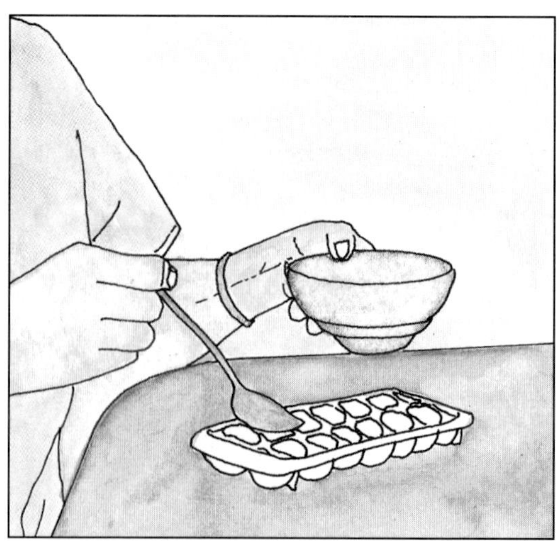

Spooning beeswax or cocoa butter into ice cube trays

Sprinkling chopped herbs onto boiling water

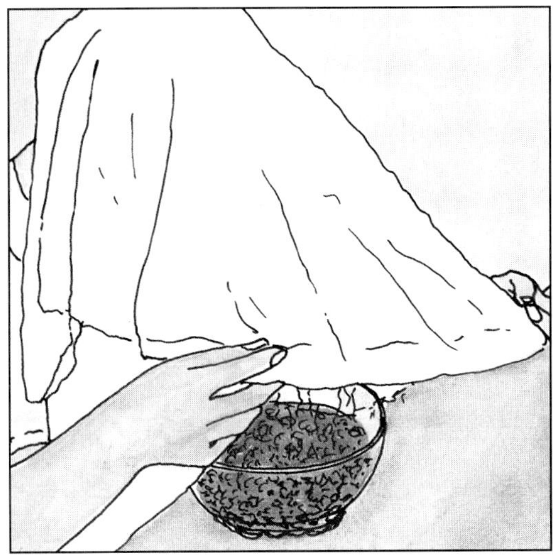

Taking a steam treatment

Drain off the water. Lift out the block of wax and you will see the underside has quite a thick coating of impurities. Scrape this layer off, break up the wax roughly and return to the dry pan.

From this point on this method can also be used for cocoa butter.

Melt the wax or butter *slowly*. Don't let it get too hot or it might burn, or destroy the ice cube tray when you pour it in. When the wax has melted, begin to pour. Fill each hollow in the tray to the predetermined level and leave to set. Turn the cubes out and store in a sealed container. There is a little moth that loves to feed on wax!

A further refinement is to weigh the cubes together before packing and divide the weight by the number of cubes. You will then know how much each cube weighs, so if a recipe specifies an amount by weight you will be able to estimate easily how many cubes to use. Write the weight of a cube on the outside of the storage container.

Decoctions or Infusions

See pages 129 and 130.

Facial Steam

Tie your hair back with a shower cap or head band and cleanse your face in your preferred manner. Chop two handfuls of herbs of your choice, place in a basin and pour 2 litres (3½ pints) of boiling water over the herbs. Holding your face about 20 cm (8 in) away from the steam, cover your head and the basin with a large towel, forming a sort of tent. Keep your eyes closed and let the steam play on your face for about 10 minutes (you can come up for air occasionally if you need to). Finish the steaming session with a lukewarm (not cold) splash.

Steaming is a really 'deep cleanse' for the skin. Skin with broken veins is not suitable for steaming as the heat would aggravate the condition.

Masks or Packs

Cleanse your face and tie the hair back as for steaming. Follow the individual recipes for masks (see p194). Spread on your face, lie down and relax for 15-20 minutes. Wash off with lukewarm water.

Masks can be thickened with all sorts of things from your kitchen cupboard and refrigerator: leftover porridge, dried milk, cooked arrowroot or cornflour (see p166), wheatgerm, ground almonds, banana, cooked pumpkin.

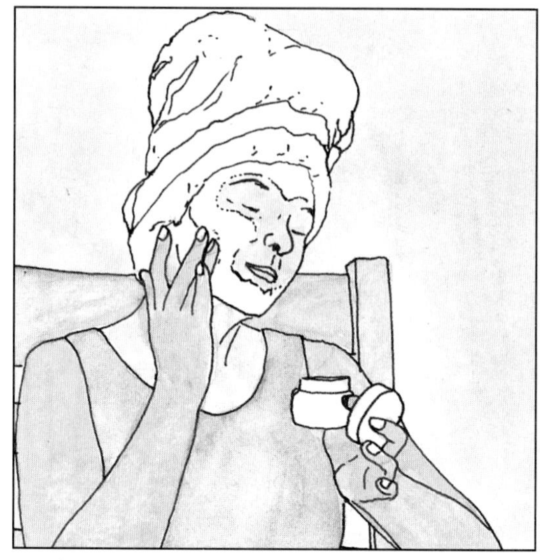

Applying a face pack

Oils

To me, the word 'oils' conjures up a feeling of soft luxury, big fluffy bath towels, perfumed bodies, relaxing massage and time out to do nothing but enjoy.

Scented oils have been used by the Romans, Chinese, Egyptians and Greeks, and I would imagine all the ancient civilisations used perfumed oils in many ways: embalming, anointing, baths, massage, cooking, lighting their homes and polishing furniture.

Today there is a resurgence in the use of oils. It is now recognised that essential oils massaged into the skin are absorbed through the pores and from there disperse rapidly through the system. Aromatherapy is the art of using pure essential oils (usually as massage oil) to treat illness, to relax, to stimulate and to help the body resist disease. Massage has become an accepted treatment for many problems and I find that more and more people are learning the art of massage in order to share with each other a healing, relaxing and communicating experience.

In view of the problems associated with contamination by radioactive fallout, find out as much as you can about the source of your oils and the likelihood of contaminants. Most schools these days are equipped with geiger counters and may be pleased to give the pupils a practical test to conduct.

There are basically two types of oils: fixed oils and volatile oils.

Fixed Oils

Classified as lipids, these are obtained from seeds and are non-evaporative. The most important ones for the purpose of this book are olive, avocado, apricot, castor, safflower, sesame, linseed, peanut, soya and wheatgerm. These are the oils from which you will make creams, lotions, bath and massage oils.

There are two methods of extraction:

1. Cold pressed; as the name suggests, this involves the crushing and pressing of the plant material without the application of heat. This method preserves the properties contained in the oil. Cold pressed oils rarely contain preservatives or anti-oxidants — another point in their favour. The vitamins and minerals are retained in cold pressed oils, which makes the extra cost worthwhile.

2. Solvent or heat extraction; the process involved in this method destroys most of the mineral and vitamin content and the oil is further subjected to the addition of preservatives and anti-oxidants. In comparison with cold pressed oil, this oil is not worth using.

Volatile Oils

These are obtained from the leaves and flowers of some plants and the rind of fruits such as orange, lemon and grapefruit. These oils are frequently called essences, essential oils or ethereal oils. They are non-greasy and evaporative. Volatile oils are extracted mainly by distillation or by using alcohol.

If you are uncertain how to differentiate between volatile and fixed oils, try the following experiment. On a folded paper tissue put a few drops of a fixed oil. In a different area place a few drops of an essential oil and leave overnight. In the morning you will find there is a greasy patch left by the fixed oil but not by the volatile oil.

These essential oils are rarely used alone. They are very powerful and are added to alcohol, water or fixed oils. They must never exceed 2-3% of the total recipe if being used directly on the skin. See Chart 9 'D' for exceptions.

There are a lot of synthetic essential oils on the market. My criterion for buying oils is always: "I don't want the cheapest — I want the best." To obtain the best oils you may have to pay a great deal of money. Rose, jasmine and ylang-ylang are among the most expensive oils and, if they aren't, then they are probably synthetic. They will smell all right but won't have the therapeutic properties of the real thing. In fact, they can be harmful.

It takes enormous amounts of plant material to obtain a small amount of its precious essence. For instance, 100 kg (220 lb) of thyme leaves will yield about 200 g (¾ cup) of essence. This means that if you pick 1 kg (2 lb) of top quality leaves (which is a lot from the average garden) and use a sophisticated extraction method you will obtain only about 2 grams of essence (less than half a teaspoon)! This is not to put you off but to illustrate how precious these oils are.

Compatibility of fixed oils with skin types

Dry skin	*Normal skin*	*Oily skin*
Almond	Corn	Soyabean
Castor	Sesame	Linseed
Cocoa butter	Sunflower	
Olive	Safflower *	
Peanut		
Wheatgerm †		

* Safflower oil is a good 'all-rounder'. It's light, nourishing, almost dispersible in water, quickly absorbed into the skin and altogether very nice to use.
† Wheatgerm oil acts as a preservative, so it's good to include some in all massage oils.

Oils which are easily absorbed into the skin (use for cosmetics)
Corn, safflower, sesame, sunflower, wheatgerm.

Non-absorbent oils (use for massage oils)
Sweet almond, avocado, coconut, olive, apricot, peanut.

Basic Herb Oil

(to use in massage oils, bath oils and creams)

Hot method

1. In a double boiler (not aluminium), place the finely chopped herbs of your choice and cover with a mixture of peanut and safflower oil.

Oils, herbs and cider vinegar in a double boiler on the stove

2. Add 1 tablespoon cider or wine vinegar to each 1 litre (4 cups) oil. Cover with a lid and leave for several hours. The vinegar will begin to extract the properties of the herbs. Heat to no more than 55°C (130°F); if the oil gets any hotter you will lose some of the important volatile qualities of the herbs. Turn off the heat.
3. Repeat the heating several times over a period of 24 hours.
4. Carefully strain the cool oil through a muslin bag, squeezing the bag and herbs to extract as much oil as possible. If you want a super strong oil, you can add more herbs and repeat the process once or even twice more.
5. After a few days you will see some sediment at the bottom of the jar. Carefully decant the oil into a clean jar or bottle, leaving the sediment behind. Refrigerate the oil until needed.
6. Essential oils may be added to this as needed.

Testing that the temperature is no more than 55°C (130°F)

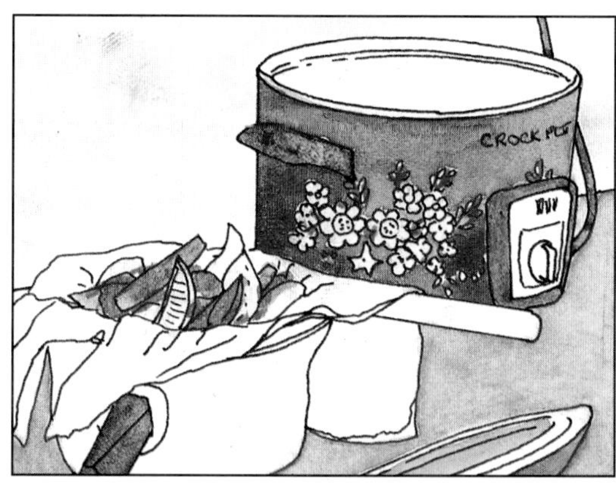

A crock pot

In Australia there is a cooking pot called a crock pot. It's a deep casserole or pot which stands in an electrically heated, metal jacket. It can be controlled to cook *very* slowly. These pots are ideal for herb oils, vinegars, decoctions or for anything which needs long, slow, gentle, heated extraction.

Cold method

To capture the perfume of delicate leaves and flowers you will need to use this method. The resulting oil isn't as strong or as well coloured but it's the only easy way to extract the scent.

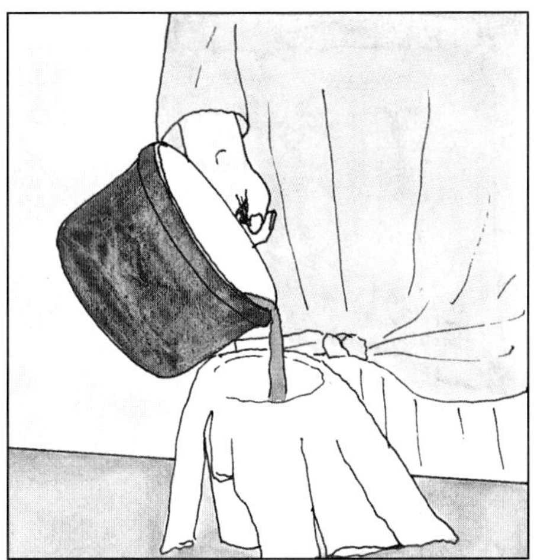
Straining the cool oil into a jug and for leaving sediment to settle to the bottom

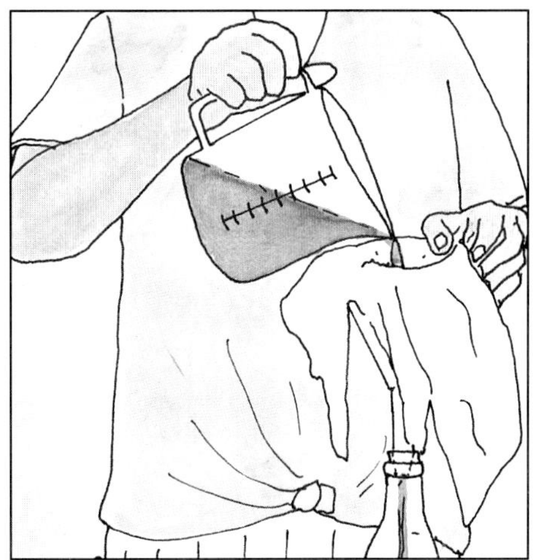
Straining into a storage bottle, taking care not to disturb the sediment at the bottom

1. & 2. As for hot method but with the herbs in a large jar.
3. Cover the herbs with *slightly* warmed oil. Cover.
4. Put in the sun for 1 week. (This oil is best made in the summer. If you don't have strong, hot sunlight the resulting oil may be disappointing.)
5. As 4 above.
6. As 5 above.

Bath Oils

There are two types of bath oils: floating and dispersible.

Floating

I like the floating oil very much because it drifts towards you and settles on your skin where you can gently massage it in. Unfortunately, it doesn't discriminate between your body and the sides of the bath — it drifts that way as well and stays in a ring around the water level. However, I find cleaning the bath a small price to pay for the feeling of silkiness my skin has when I step out of the bath, massage any remaining oil into my skin and blot myself dry with a soft towel.

Dispersible

This oil disappears into the water and doesn't leave a ring around the bath. It needs additives to emulsify the oil to help it to blend with the water or it can be made with a specially treated oil (see castor oil, p158).

It's best to make small quantities of these oils until you find the one you like and then to make lots. It will keep a long time if stored in a dark cupboard in the bathroom.

Floating bath oil

Pour a few tablespoons under the hot water as it's running.

Basic herb oil (see p170)	*2⅓ cups*	Mix together, bottle and shake well.
Essential oil	*3 teaspoons*	

Semi-dispersible bath oil (1)

This is a very luxurious and moisturising bath oil. Add 4-8 teaspoons to the water as the bath is running.

Tragacanth	*2 teaspoons*	Place in a bowl.
Cold infusion 3x **Glycerine**	*2 cups* *6 teaspoons*	Mix together in a jug. Mix *very slowly* with the tragacanth to make a smooth paste.
Basic herb oil	*⅓ cup*	Add, stirring to mix well.
Essential oils	*2 teaspoons*	Add slowly, stirring well. Bottle.

Semi-dispersible bath oil (2)

Bathing in this oil is a lovely, fragrant, aromatherapeutic experience. You might like to choose one of the perfume mixtures from p173 or make a mixture to deal with a specific problem. Sprinkle *one teaspoonful only* into the filled bath.

Vodka, highest proof possible **Essential oils** **Glycerine**	*½ cup* *2 teaspoons* *1 teaspoon*	Bottle and shake well.

Herbal semi-dispersible bath oil

Add as much as you fancy to the bath. Shake before use.

Basic herb oil **Coconut or other good shampoo** **Essential oil**	*1 cup* *2 tablespoons* *3 teaspoons*	Mix all well together.

Dispersible bath oil

Add 1-2 tablespoons as the bath is running.

Red turkey oil (see p158) **Glycerine** **Essential oil**	*1⅓ cup* *⅓ cup* *¼ cup*	Shake all well together.

Massage Oils

When we were making skin care products for sale to the public I devised four aromatherapy massage oils which were called Lovers, Sore and Tired Minds, Sore and Tired Bodies and Stimulant. The first batches were sent out, an equal number of each one. After three months we had discontinued Stimulant and were making eight times as much Lovers as Bodies and Minds. I make no further comment!

Choose your essential oils very carefully for massage oils. The perfume can have a profound effect on the emotions and the body. I have found that the most successful massage oil has 25% of absorbent oils added to the non-absorbent oils. This ensures that even while there is plenty of 'slip', needed for the massage, the oil eventually penetrates the skin and leaves it feeling comfortable and non-greasy.

I pour about 1¼ cm (½ in) of alcohol into the top of the bottle of finished oil. This helps to prevent the oil from going rancid and, like the absorbent oils, assists the penetration of oils into the skin. The proportion of essential oil added to massage oil should never exceed 2.5% in 100%. This means adding ½ teaspoon to each 100 ml (½ cup).

Colognes

Colognes Using Essential Oils

These colognes are fun to make and I hope these recipes will inspire you to make your own personalised perfume. Colognes can be used as perfume, after bath or shower splashes, an aftershave for men or as a light deodorant. They need to mature in a dark place for 2-3 months. Shake them often and keep trying a little on the inside of your wrist. You will be astonished how the perfumes change as they mature.

Sensual

Patchouli	4 drops
Ylang-ylang	5 drops
Clove	1 drop
Vodka	100 ml (3 fl oz)

Fresh and Lemony

Petitgrain	2 drops
Lime	2 drops
Lemon grass	2 drops
Lemon	2 drops
Clove	1 drop
Vodka	100 ml (3 fl oz)

Girl Next Door

Lavender	3 drops
Cinnamon	1 drop
Patchouli	1 drop
Geranium	2 drops
Clove	1 drop
Bergamot	2 drops
Vodka	100 ml (3 fl oz)

Moonlight

Ylang-ylang	5 drops
Rose geranium	3 drops
Patchouli	3 drops
Vodka	100 ml (3 fl oz)

Silk Lady

Lavender	6 drops
Rose geranium	3 drops
Clove	1 drop
Vodka	100 ml (3 fl oz)

Oils

The essential oils in Chart 9 are just a few of the vast number available. I have tried to choose those which are easily obtainable. They must always be kept out of reach of children as some are toxic if swallowed, even in small quantities. To keep the oils potent for as long as possible, store in amber glass away from light and heat.

Chart 9 Oils

	Basil	Bergamot	Cedarwood	Chamomile	Cinnamon	Clove	Coriander	Eucalyptus	Fennel	Geranium	Jasmine	Juniper	Lavender	Lemon grass	Lime	Marjoram	Patchouli	Peppermint	Petitgrain	Pine	Rosemary	Sage	Sandalwood	Sassafras	Tea tree	Thyme	Wintergreen	Ylang Ylang
Air freshener		S						S		S			S	S						S	S				S	S		
Antiseptic	U				U	U		U				U	U	U				U		U	U				U	U		U
Aphrodisiac										M	M						M		M									M
Athlete's foot														W											D			
Brain fag	L/B																				L/M	L/B						
Bronchitis		I			B			I															I					
Burns, minor																									D			
Colds & flu					B			I					B					B									B	
Cold sores								D																	D			
Congested lungs					B			I												I							I	
Cuts & sores	W							W					W												D	W		
Hangover												B									B							
Hayfever																				I								
Headache				M						M			M			M					M					M		
Headlice																								H				
Indigestion									F									F										
Leucorrhoea		E											E										E					
Mouth wash		X							X				X	X														
Mouth ulcers								D																	D			
Muscular strain			B									B					M			B						M	B	
Nerves				B						M	B		B			B	B				M	B						B
Pimples					D			D																	D			
Relaxation				M						B	B					M	M											M
Rheumatism												B									B						I	
Shock				B																	B	B						B
Sinus congestion					I			I												I					I			
Sleeplessness				B							B/M		B		B	B	B											B
Stings & bites								D																	D	D		
Stress				M							B		M			B	B		B			B						B
Sunburn										B			B															
Toothache						J																				J		
Throat condition							G															G			G			
Urinary tract						F						F	B							B			B/D					
Yeast infection																									G/E			

KEY to Chart 9

I Inhalation: 12 drops on water (see p133)

D Dab directly on affected area.

G Use 5 drops in warm water as a gargle.

U Can be used in an inhalation, bath or wash (see p133).

E Douche: 1 teaspoon to 500 ml (2 cups) water.

C Compress (for method see p140).

M Massage: 3 parts essential oil to 97 parts carrier oil (e.g. almond, safflower); massage affected area.

S Spray: Mix several oils together to make 1 teaspoon. Add to 300 ml (1¼ cups) 50/50 vodka and water. Pour into an atomiser or spray bottle and use for spraying the air, carpets and furniture. The spray acts as an antibacteriocide.

W Wash: Mix 25 ml (5 teaspoons) with 75 ml (⅓ cup) warm water. Bottle and use to wash cuts etc (see p141).

X Mouthwash: 4 drops in 1 cup warm water.

L Sniff straight from bottle.

F Take 3 drops in water or fruit juice, three times daily.

H Dilute 50/50 with almond oil. Massage a few drops onto the scalp, cover with shower cap and leave overnight. In the morning, comb hair with fine-tooth comb and shampoo hair. Repeat if necessary.

J Use eye dropper to direct one drop into tooth cavity.

Baths

Poor Marie Antoinette had to clothe herself in a voluminous flannel nightshirt in order to have a bath as the church at that time had decreed that nudity was wicked. We are fortunate to live in an age where bodies are acknowledged as being okay and the taking of a bath can be fun as well as healing, hydrating, relaxing, beautifying or sensual.

Everyone knows the clean, relaxed feeling after a long, leisurely bath but the benefits can be infinitely more in terms of health. Bathing is one of my 'anti-stress' aids. I run a deep bath, pour something pleasant into the water (usually an experiment), light a perfumed candle, spread some 'green gunk' (see p191) on my face, and lie back against a bath pillow sipping a warm drink and listening to soft music. I slip into that wonderful state of 'being nowhere' and remain there for as long as it takes. My stress runs down the drain with the bath water and I leave the bathroom ready to take on the world again.

Skin (which is the largest organ in the body) has been described as the 'third kidney' because of the sweat glands it contains. Like the kidneys, these glands excrete mineral salts, toxins, nitrogenous wastes and water. Given the right conditions, our skin may be responsible for the excretion of one-third of the body's waste products. To do this, the pores have to be free of dead cells, dirt and excess oil. If the sweat glands are unable to function properly an additional load is thrown on the kidneys.

There are many ways of getting the maximum value from your bath such as pre-bath treatments, bath oils, after bath colognes, powders and oils. You will find recipes for all these in the following pages.

Dry Brush Massage

This is a preliminary to the bath. It ensures that all dead skin is removed and the circulation stimulated. You will need a

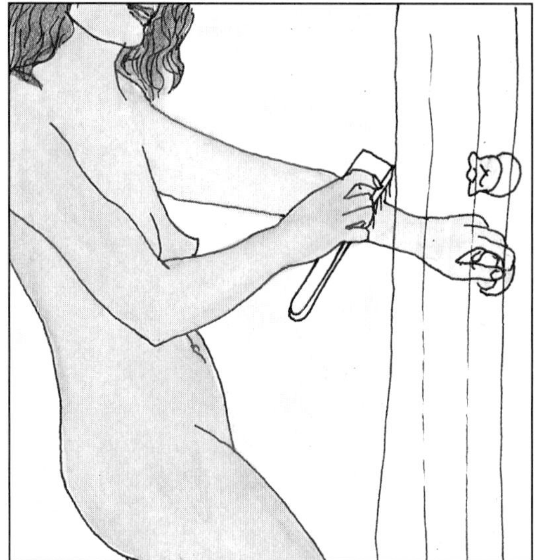

Using a body brush

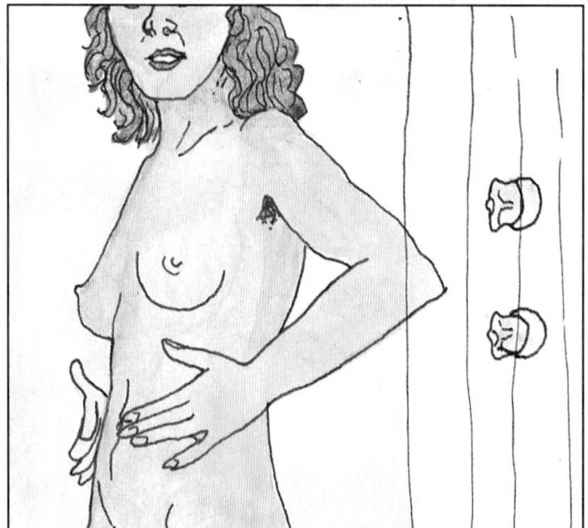

Massaging salt rub onto the body

body brush with a long, preferably removable, handle. These are quite inexpensive and can be bought at health food shops or pharmacies. A long loofah can be used, but I find a brush easier.

Brush the whole body from the neck down, being gentle on delicate areas such as thighs, abdomen and breasts. Pay particular attention to the areas where there are glands, i.e. the groin, armpits and side of the neck. Brush these areas gently but thoroughly with a circular motion.

Salt Rub

This is another pre-shower or bath method for ridding your skin of the dead cells which make it look sallow and dull. It will stimulate the circulation and leave the skin glowing and clean. Stand in the bath or shower recess to use this rub as it's pretty messy. It's even better if you share this with a friend and do each other's backs. *Don't* use the salt scrub on any of the 'tender parts' — they don't like it.

Mix together 1 tablespoon coarse salt and 1 tablespoon basic herb oil. Add 2 drops essential oil for each tablespoon of salt mixture.

Lightly oil your body first and then, using a firm circular motion, rub the mixture onto the skin. You will be astonished to see the amount of dirt that comes off. Shower or bathe and use some herbal massage oil to finish. You will feel and look terrific.

Full Body Bath

Baths which are too hot or too cold are not relaxing. The temperature should be body heat or very slightly higher; 35-38°C (95-100°F) is about right. However, in the case of dry fever, the water temperature can be up to 45°C (115°F); follow by wrapping the patient in blankets to induce sweating. **A patient being treated in this way must never be left alone and shouldn't spend longer than 5-10 minutes in the bath. These hot baths should not be used if the sick person has a heart problem or high blood pressure.**

Special pillows can be bought for use in the bath. Make yourself as comfortable as possible as it's best to stay in the water for about 30 minutes to gain maximum benefit.

If you don't want to use oils in the bath you have the choice of the following recipes. These can also be used if you prefer a shower. The bag containing the herbs or oatmeal mixture may be used as a washcloth; and, instead of putting the infusions in the bathwater, they can be splashed onto your body after a shower.

Oat Cleanser

This cleanser may be used instead of soap. It is also good as a facial scrub if a small amount is mixed to a paste with water, gently massaged into the skin and rinsed off with cool water. When used in the bath it is very soothing to itchy, sore skin. It's excellent for babies' baths but only the gentlest herbs should be used. I make large quantities of this mixture as it keeps indefinitely if well stored.

To use: Put 1 cupful in a muslin bag (see p128) and tie the top securely. Put the bag into a saucepan and cover with 2 litres (3½ pints) water. Bring to just below the boil and barely simmer, covered, for 15 minutes. Pour the liquid into the bath and use the bag as a washcloth.

Oat cleanser

Powdered bran	*1 part*
Powdered oats	*2 parts*
Powdered milk (skim)	*1 part*
Powdered soap (optional)	*3 parts*
Powdered herbs	*3 parts*

Mix all together and store in an airtight jar.

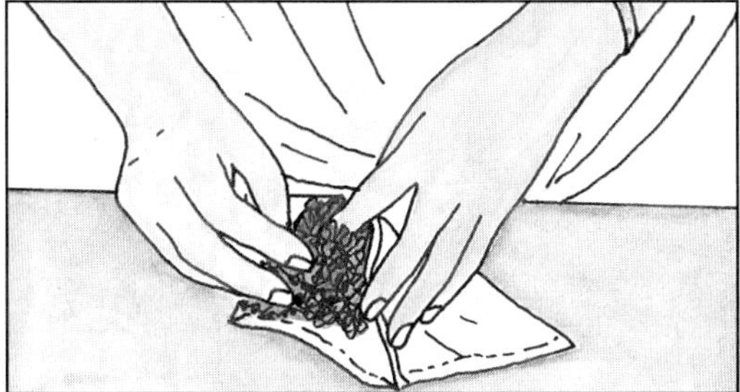

Putting herbs into a little bag for use in the bath

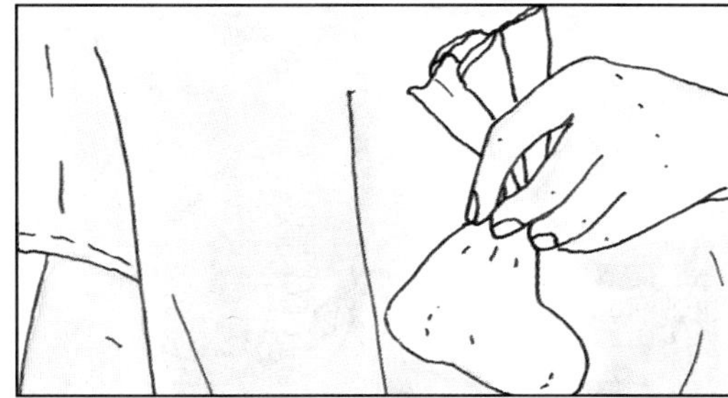

The bag needs to be tied at the neck

Herb Bath

Use Chart 10 to choose the most suitable herbs. Make either a 3x infusion and pour the strained liquid into the bath, or make it as the oatmeal recipe above but with herbs as the only ingredient. I like the bag method best as I enjoy scrubbing myself with the bagful of herbs.

After a bath or shower you may enjoy a herbal vinegar splash to restore tone and acid balance (see p190). To use the vinegar, add 1 teaspoon to a cup of water and pat it all over the body. The undiluted vinegar may be used on underarms as a mild deodorant. The vinegar smell vanishes very quickly.

Body Powder

If you enjoy using powder after a bath or shower, here is a recipe for a natural one. A word of caution though: powder used excessively can block the pores of the skin.

Arrowroot powder *or*
Conflour (cornstarch) *or*
Talc (available from pharmaceutical suppliers)

Mix one of the above with an equal quantity of powdered dried herbs, citrus peel and spices. You may add a few drops of essential oil (not too much or the powder will go lumpy). Mix all the ingredients well and rub through a sieve. Store in a flat bowl with a lid and apply with a piece of cotton wool.

Herbs which blend well together are:

For Babies	**Deodorant**	**For Men**
Chamomile*	Rosemary	Liquorice
Lemon balm	Thyme	Rosemary
	Sage	Lavender
	Lavender	Coriander seed
	Orange peel	

* See caution p33.

Chart 10 Baths

	Borage	Bran	Calendula	Chamomile	Comfrey root	Dried milk	Epsom salts	Lavender	Lemon balm	Mallow root	Mustard	Nettle	Oats, rolled	Pennyroyal	Rosemary	Sage	Savories	Thyme	Valerian	Yarrow
Arthritis							E											X		
Bruises							E											X		
Chills	X		X	X							M	X		X		X	X			
Colds	X		X	X							M	X		X		X	X			
Cramps															X			X		
Debility		B				B							B							
Digestion															X	X				
Dry skin			X		★	O				★			B							
Eczema		B								★			B							X
Fibrositis							E											X		
Flu	X		X	X							M									
Headaches								X			M									
Insomnia				X					X										X	
Itchy skin		B	X		★	O				★			B							X
Lumbago							E											X		
Muscles, sore							E								X	X		X		
Nervous exhaustion				X					X		M							X	X	
Psoriasis		B						X		★			B					X		X
Respiratory problems											M							X		
Skin problems				X	X					★			B		X			X		X
Sprains							E								X			X		
Stimulate circulation											M	X		X	X		X			
Swellings								X							X			X		
Tension				X					X										X	
Varicose veins											M									
Wounds				X	X			X							X			X	X	X

KEY to Chart 10

X 3x infusion (see p129)

E Add 1 cup Epsom salts as the bath is running and make sure the salts are dissolved. Stay in the bath for 30 minutes, massaging affected parts of your body while in the bath. Essential oils and/or herbs may be used in conjunction with the salts.

B Use method described for oat cleanser (p177).

M Dissolve 2 tablespoons mustard and add to a foot bath of hot water. Keep the feet immersed for 15-30 minutes, topping up with more hot water as needed. See p133 for more details on foot baths.

★ 3x decoction (see p130).

O Dried full-cream milk. Mix 2 cups to a liquid with water and add to the bath. Use in conjunction with herbs and oils.

Baths

Use Chart 10 in conjunction with the recipes to create the best combination of herbs to help cure individual problems. Check Charts 5 and 12 for extra help in choosing herbs.

A footbath

Hair

When I was a child we washed our hair with soap and rainwater, finishing off with a herbal vinegar rinse. I have photographs of myself with strong, glossy brown hair (totally straight and *not* blonde, which was the great grief of my life) and I remember brushing my mother's hair, so black and shiny that it looked polished. Conditioners, permanent waves, hair colorants from a bottle and even 'bought' shampoos weren't heard of and yet most people, unless they were sick, had a good head of hair.

These days, shampoos and conditioners are (like cosmetics) big business, making millions for the companies who produce them. The average commercial shampoo is so damaging to your hair that you have to use a conditioner to make your hair behave. The cheaper shampoos are made to formulae very similar to dishwashing liquid or carpet shampoo (I know this for a fact as I have seen the formulae). They strip the hair of all the natural oils and weaken it. Conditioners add a wax or similar coating to the hair, giving a false illusion of thickness, gloss and health.

It takes a little perseverance to get your hair back to its natural state. It could be as long as three weeks before the wax coating is completely removed from the hair shaft and the herbs can begin to show what they can do.

Hair care, like skin care, starts from the inside. Our hair is one of the first indications if all is not well. Stress, inadequate nutrition, lack of sleep and illness are some of the conditions which cause hair to fall out or to become dull and lustreless. The following suggestions could help you to retain or regain a fine head of hair.

1. The food you eat and your inner health are the main factors governing the strength and appearance of your hair. It's best to get the following nutrients on a regular basis, some of each, every day:

Nutrient	Some sources
• Pantothenic acid	Peanuts, wheatgerm, brewer's yeast, brown rice
• PABA	Yeast and wheatgerm
• Vitamin F	Brown rice, wheatgerm, oatmeal, almonds, peanuts
• Silicon	Sunflower seeds, oats, dark lettuce leaves, parsnips
• Phosphorus	Seeds, grains, beans, nuts, oats, wheatgerm

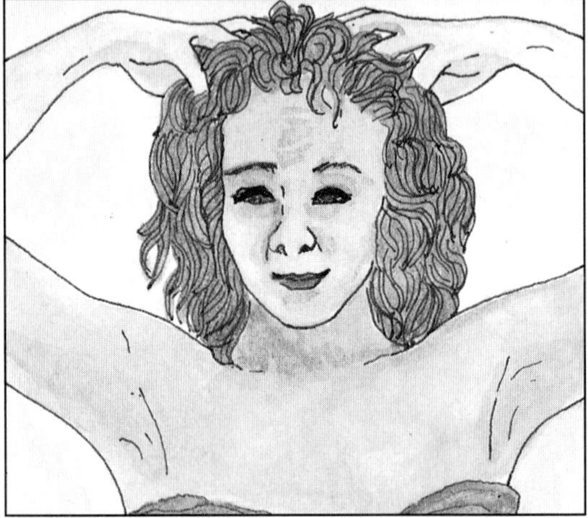
Using the fingertips to massage the scalp

2. Use the best bristle brush you can afford — nylon and plastic are very hard on the hair, causing it to split.
3. Resist the urge to shampoo more than once a week. Oiliness is made worse by frequent shampooing as it stimulates the oil glands.
4. Use a natural, homemade shampoo (see recipe below) or, failing this, use the best health food store shampoo that you can afford.
5. Follow your shampoo with a herbal rinse. The use of a 'non-oily' herb oil will add a sheen and enhance the appearance, smell and health of your hair (see p184).
6. Don't do anything rough to your hair while it is wet. After shampooing, lightly towel (or rub with a piece of silk for high sheen) and run your fingers through to arrange it. Wait until it is much drier before doing anything else. Wet hair is very elastic and can be badly stretched and weakened by rough treatment.

Use hair dryers as infrequently as possible and never on a high heat. This can cause weakening and damage by making the hair brittle, dull and lifeless.
7. Pay special attention to your hair in summer. The sea and sun can wreak havoc and you can end the season with dry,

The way to use a herbal rinse

brittle, lifeless hair. Rinse well after swimming and wear a hat or scarf if you are out of doors for long periods of time. Use a pre-shampoo oil treatment at least once a fortnight.

Recipes for hair treatments

Pre-shampoo Treatments

Unless your hair is terribly dry, lustreless or sunburnt you won't need to use these treatments more than once a month or so. The appearance of your hair will tell you when it's time.

Basic Directions

1. Massage the treatment into the scalp as well as the hair.
2. Cover the hair with a shower cap or plastic bag.
3. Wrap your head in a hot towel or sit in the sun for an hour or so.
4. Shampoo, rinse, shampoo again, rinse again.

Protein treatment

Use lukewarm water for shampoo or you will end up with scrambled egg in your hair.

Beaten egg	*1*	Mix all well together.
Glycerine	*1 teaspoon*	Follow basic directions above.
Safflower oil	*4 teaspoons*	

Oil Treatment

Basic herb oil (see p170). Choose herbs from Chart 11. Warm the oil slightly and follow basic directions above.

Green Gunk

My favourite pre-shampoo treatment is 'green gunk' (in fact, it's one of my favourite treatments for almost everything!) — see page 191 for recipe.

Shampoos

First, get to know Chart 11 and decide which heading best fits your hair or problem. You can use more than one line. For instance, you might have fair hair which is in poor condition and which is also very dry. In this case you would choose herbs from those categories. You don't have to use every herb that I mention, just as many as you have. Even one herb is better than no herbs at all.

Now choose a method from the three given below.

Dry Shampoo

Cornmeal, oatmeal, orris root, bran — 1 teaspoon of any of these may be sprinkled through the hair and massaged into the scalp. Brush out well. The more you wash your hair, the oilier it will become as you over-stimulate the sebaceous glands. You can use a dry shampoo to remove the excess oil or if, for some reason, you can't wash your hair.

Health Food Store Shampoo

You will need the bottle of shampoo you have bought plus an empty bottle. Empty one-quarter of the shampoo into the empty bottle. Save for another time.

Put 4 heaped teaspoons dried (or 8 teaspoons fresh) herbs into a pan with 250ml (1 cup) water. Cover and simmer very gently for 10 minutes. Allow to stand for 30 minutes.

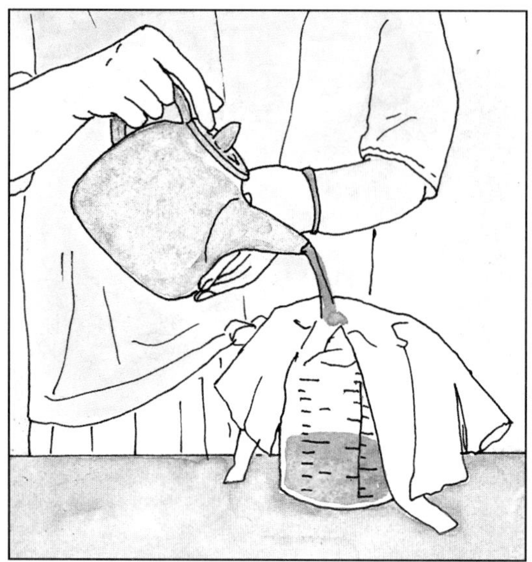

Straining an infusion to make a shampoo

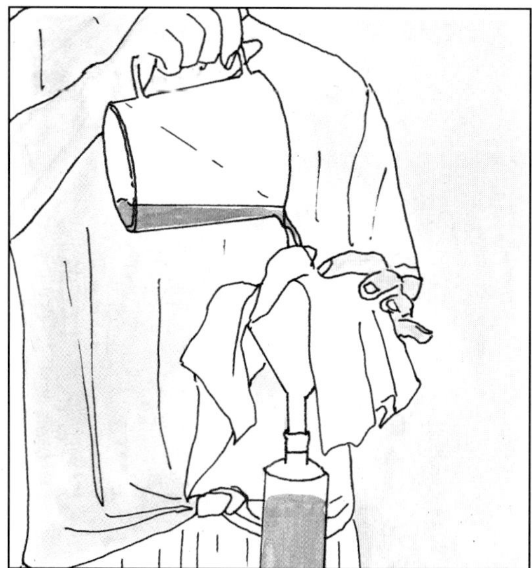

Straining the infusion again as it's added to the shampoo

Strain, pour back in pan and simmer until enough remains to top up the three-quarters full bottle. Cool before adding. Shake very gently to mix well.

I use a mixture of 50/50 herbs and shampoo because I don't mind a thin consistency and want as much herbal content as possible. Try for yourself and see which you like best.

CASTILE SHAMPOO

Make a herbal infusion as for the above recipe, 'Health food store shampoo'. Add to liquid Castile soap (available from health food stores) in the proportion ¼ infusion to ¾ soap. Bottle your *real* herbal soap and enjoy!

If you choose to make and use this shampoo it will be necessary to use a vinegar rinse to restore the acid balance to the hair. I feel that Castile soap shampoos are the best for your hair, but they will take a bit of getting used to as they don't feel at all like conventional shampoos. Give them a month's trial and your patience will be rewarded.

Rinses

Choose the herbs from Chart 11. They can be the same as the ones used in the shampoo.

Make 1 litre (4 cups) of a 3x infusion or decoction (see p129). Strain and cool to useable heat. Add 4 teaspoons cider vinegar or herbal vinegar.

Put a bowl in the washbasin and pour the rinse over your hair, catching the surplus in the bowl. Empty back into the jug and repeat as long as you have the energy or the rinse.

Using the palms of the hands to stroke herb oil through the hair

Chart 11 Healthy Hair

	Acid balance	Antiseptic	Cleansing	Conditioning	Dandruff	Dark hair	Dry hair	Dry scalp	Falling hair	Fragrance	Growth	Fair hair	Normal hair	Oily hair	Pre-shampoo	Scalp irritation	Shiny hair	Softening	Tonic
Basil										R	X		S						X
Bay			S										S			X			
Calendula												R					R		
Castor oil															P				
Catnep											R								
Chamomile							R					S				S	R		
Cider vinegar	Ø			Ø	X	Ø	Ø					Ø		Ø		Ø	Ø		
Comfrey root					S		S	X					S			S		S	
Clover			S				R						S						X
Elderflower							R					R				X			
Lavender		S		R			R			R			S						X
Lemon balm			S							R			S						
Lemon grass			S	R						R				R					X
Lemon peel										R				R			R		
Mallow root					S		S	X								D		R	
Nettle				R	X	R		X	X		X		S				R		X
Olive oil							P								P			P	
Orange peel							S			R								S	
Parsley				R							X					X			
Rosemary		S		R	X	R			X	R	X					X	R		X
Sage						R			X								R		
Southernwood						R			X		X		S			X			X
Thyme		S	S						X	R									X
Willow bark					S									R			R		
Witch hazel					S									R					
Wormwood						R			X		X		S			X			X

KEY to Chart 11

R Rinse (see p182)

S Shampoo (see p184)

D 1x decoction (see p129)

X Tonic (see p184)

P Pre-shampoo treatment (see p181)

Ø Add to herbs being used for the same condition.

Tonic

Choose herbs from Chart 11.

3x hot infusion (p 129)	*2 cups*	Strain into a jug.
Borax	*3 teaspoons*	Dissolve into the infusion.
Essential oil	*1 teaspoon*	Add, bottle, shake well.

This tonic will keep for 3 - 4 weeks in the refrigerator but I make this quite large quantity and freeze the remainder in small containers. This tonic should be applied to the scalp at least once a day. Sprinkle it on and, using the pads of the fingers, massage the scalp briskly with a zig-zag movement. This will have the triple benefit of bringing blood to the surface (excellent for hair growth), improving the skin on the scalp and giving the hair the benefit of the herbs.

Hair Oil

This oil will give health and sheen to hair without making it greasy. It also gives your hair a wonderful, natural fragrance.

Mix together equal parts of rosemary, lavender and basil, juniper or jojoba oils. Put a few drops on the palm of your hand and rub your hands together. Now rub the oil from your palms through your hair. This can be done as little or as often as you like.

Natural skin care

As with the hair, your skin usually shows the condition of your health. Stress, lack of sleep, poor diet and illness are some of the conditions which can be reflected in the skin. It's a very complex organ acting as an efficient envelope, a temperature regulator, a toxin excretor and a sensory connector between the nervous system and outside stimuli. Our skin is made up of three layers: the epidermis, the dermis and subcutaneous tissue.

Epidermis

This is the outer layer which is visible. It is made up of dead and dying cells which are flattened and overlap to form an elastic, partially waterproof surface. These cells are constantly being replaced by new cells from beneath. This layer is renewed every month. All layers are gradually replaced over a period of seven years. This is very heartening as it means it's never too late to improve the condition of the skin, though it doesn't mean we will ever get back the skin we had in childhood. With age, the skin gradually loses elasticity. We can, however, slow the aging process to a considerable degree. Friction or exfoliant treatments help to rid the skin of dead cells more quickly, allowing the new cells to move up.

Dermis

This layer produces the new cells which make their way up to the epidermis. The dermis contains the sebaceous glands, blood vessels, hair follicles and nerves and is connected to the epidermis by collagen fibres.

Subcutaneous Tissue

This is the fatty layer which gives a protective pad to underlying bone and organs. This layer contains sweat glands.

Skin isn't just a layer to 'stop us fraying round the edge' but a complex structure which serves us well and deserves the best treatment we can give it. There are a few simple steps you can take to make sure you have done the best you can — the rest is up to nature! These steps are:

The Layers of the Skin

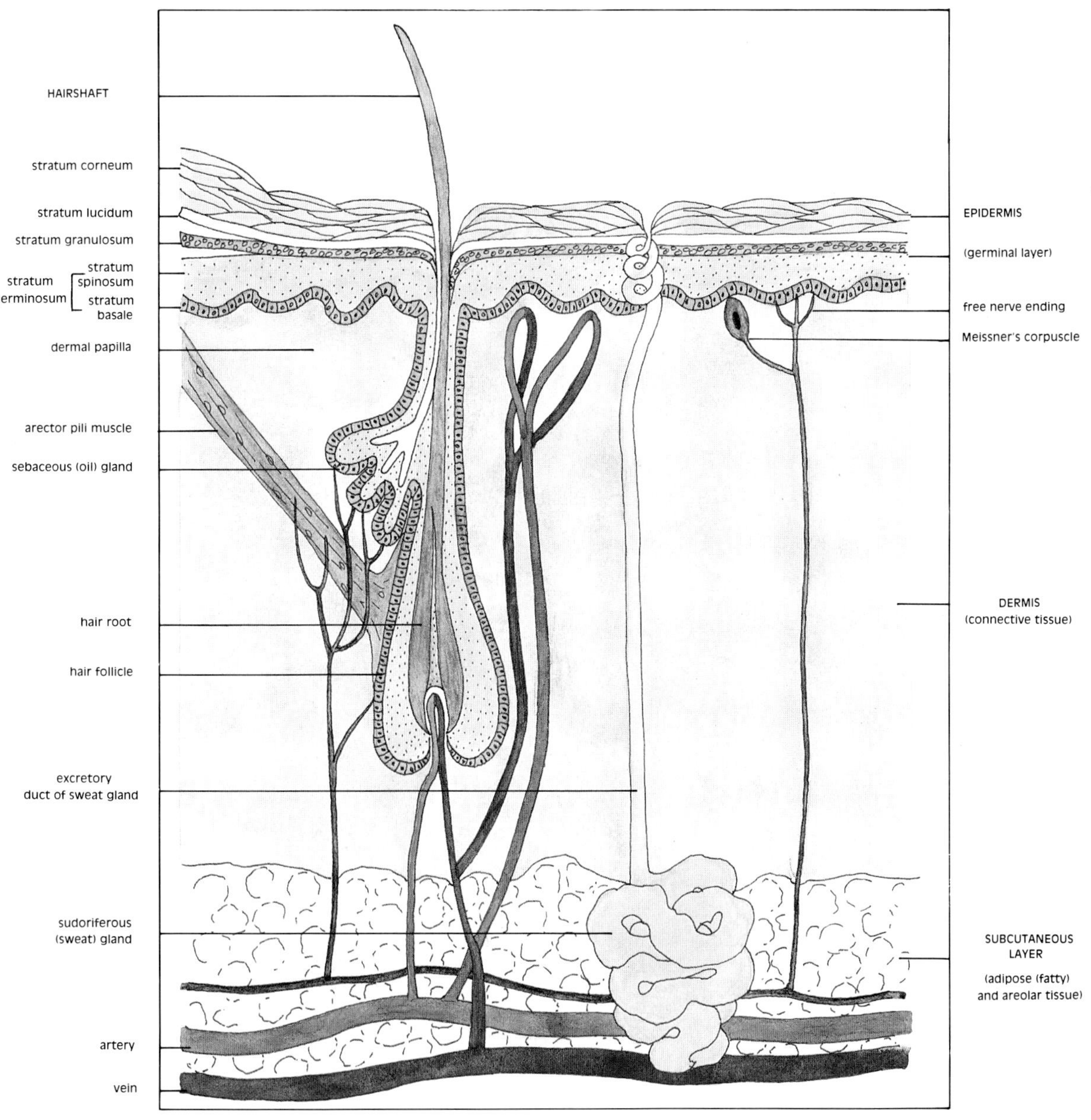

1. Eat lots of fruit and vegetables.
2. Drink 6 - 8 glasses of water daily.
3. Get 6 - 8 hours sleep a night.
4. Do some form of exercise daily, whatever you enjoy.
5. Use the purest skin preparations that you can make or buy.
6. Keep out of the sun during the hottest part of the day and use a good sunblock whenever you are outside in the summer.
7. If you play sport or are out of doors a lot make sure you use plenty of moisturiser to protect the skin.
8. Cultivate a positive attitude. Stress is about the worst thing for skin, giving that lined, drawn look. I teach meditation and always notice the astonishing difference in people's faces after a class — they look several years younger and softer.

Skin Types

There are four main skin types:

Normal skin Alas, rarely seen; it is fine-textured, smooth, supple and soft, with no blackheads or spots. This skin should be cherished and maintained with light cleansers, lotions and tonics or fresheners.

Oily skin The texture is usually thick, coarse and shiny. Large pores are a characteristic of this type of skin. There is a tendency to blackheads and spots due to the over-excretion of oil with its clogging tendencies. Take heart if you have oily skin; it wrinkles less and later than any other type. This skin needs plenty of moisture and little oil except on the throat and lips and round the eyes. Use astringent face packs, tonics and treatments to give a good acid mantle.

Combination skin As the name suggests, this is a combination of normal/dry and oily skin. The oily areas are usually across the forehead and down the nose to the chin; sometimes there are small areas on the jawline. This skin needs two different programs, oily/normal or oily/dry.

Dry skin This skin is fine-textured, thin and delicate. It has a tendency to line easily. If neglected the skin flakes and feels tight and uncomfortable. Hot packs and steams need to be avoided as they encourage the broken veins to which this type of skin is prone.

1

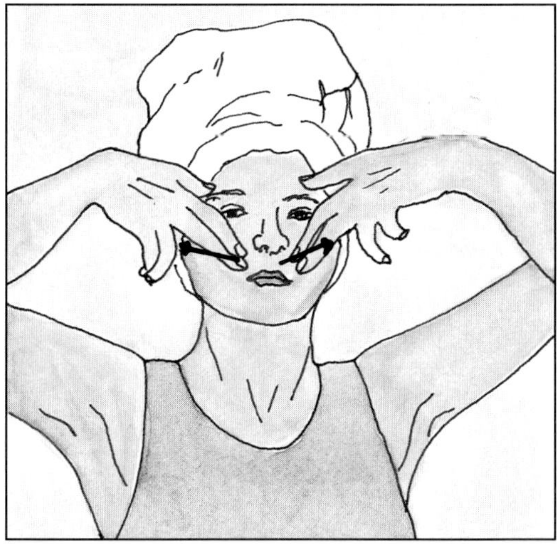

2

Facial massage

It's good to develop a skin care routine to keep the skin in good condition. This needn't be time-consuming but is as necessary as cleaning your teeth. Two factors determine the number of times a day you need to follow this routine: the work

Using two fingers and an upward direction to give yourself a facial massage

you do (whether dusty or clean), and whether you live in the city with polluted air or in the country. If you spend much time in air-conditioned rooms your skin will need more moisturising.

The way you apply treatments to your skin and throat is very important. Remember that skin loses its elasticity as it gets older so use two fingers only, in gentle, non-stretching movements. Gravity is working against us as well, in an effort to pull everything towards the ground, so always use upward movements in an effort to counteract this. The diagram will demonstrate the directions.

Daily Routine

1. Cleansing

If you have oily skin or work in a dirty environment you will need to cleanse at least twice a day. If your skin is normal or dry, then once a day should be sufficient. The evening is the best time to cleanse, to rid the skin of the grime and oil accumulated during the day. The aim of cleansing is to rid the skin of excess grease, dead skin cells and dirt. Some people don't feel clean unless they have used soap and water on their face. This is fine if you are careful to use good quality soap and then follow with a rinse designed to restore the acid balance (see glossary). For those who don't like soap (I haven't used soap on my face for about 30 years except to experiment with herbal soaps, and even these make my skin feel uncomfortably tight and dry), there is a choice of using oil, cleansing cream or lotion. You will find a selection of suitable cleansers in the recipe section which follows.

2. **Toning**

Toning helps to refine skin texture. It's also essential where heavy cleansers have been used, in order to rid the pores of excess grease which could clog and cause blackheads. The type of toner you use is determined by the method you have used to cleanse. This will be indicated in the recipe section following.

3. **Moisturising**

All skin needs water as well as oil in order to remain soft and supple. If water is just splashed onto the skin it evaporates off before it can be absorbed, so it needs an additional agent to hold it on the skin until absorption takes place. Some of these agents are oil, glycerine or honey. Moisturising can be done as often as you like; you will be able to tell by the feel of your skin if it's time for more. See the section which follows for moisturiser recipes.

Steam Treatments

In addition to the daily program it's nice to use a mask or facial steam occasionally. Steaming whips up the circulation, adds moisture and softens the grease in clogged pores, making blackheads easier to remove. Facial steaming should never be used if you have broken capillary or 'thread' veins as the heat would aggravate the condition. All other skins will benefit from this treatment and it can be used monthly for dry or sensitive skin, once a fortnight for normal skin and once or twice weekly for skin with very clogged pores or excessive grease. See page 167 for how to give yourself a steam treatment.

Scrubs

These are used to peel or exfoliate the outer, dead layer of skin. This needs to be done gently and not too often. It can leave your skin silky soft, glowing and looking much younger. Scrubs should be applied to a previously cleansed and wet face. Avoid the delicate area around the eyes.

Masks

Masks can cleanse, tone, moisturise, exfoliate, refine, heal and nourish. They are fun to make and use, leave your skin feeling and looking years younger and give you an excuse to lie down for a while. Before you use a mask you need to cleanse the face thoroughly. If you find the mixture too sloppy you can make a poultice (p135) the size of your face and throat to contain the ingredients. Don't apply mask mixture to the delicate area around the eyes.

Skin care recipes

It's easy to personalise a range of skin care items by using the same essential oils as perfume. Try to find really pretty jars and bottles in which to put your 'lotions and potions' and make beautiful labels; they will then feel and look very exclusive and special. All preparations need to be tightly covered to exclude air.

When water is used in a recipe it's very important that it is purified or distilled, as water is a first-class medium for growing bacteria.

Cleansers

Soaps

There are many good books available on the art of soap-making so I'm not going to include any basic recipes here. Soap-making is quite tricky as you need to use caustic which can burn badly if it is splashed onto skin. The recipes below use ready-made soap as the base. I buy the cheapest soap in my supermarket, which is called 'Velvet'. It comes in packets of six, is unperfumed and has no fancy additives. I find it the ideal base to make a range of soaps which are inexpensive, cleansing, moisturising, sweetly scented and a pleasure to use.

The amount of infusion/decoction needed in these recipes is a variable because the soap you buy can contain varying amounts of water.

Lemon and corn soap		Oily and combination skin
3x hot infusion/decoction	*½ - 1 cup*	Strain well.
Soap, finely grated **Glycerine**	*4 cups* *4 teaspoons*	Melt with infusion/decoction. Cool to blood heat.
Polenta **Lemon essential oil**	*¼ cup* *½ teaspoon*	Add, work in well.

When you have made the soap, form it into balls or press into greased moulds or baskets lined with cheesecloth. If lots of air can reach the soap, it will dry more quickly. Drying time will be about 6 weeks.

Honey gel		Good for all skin types
Tragacanth **Purified water**	*1 level teaspoon* *2⅔ cups*	Mix to a thin paste with a little of the water. Heat the remaining water.
Gelatine	*4½ level teaspoons*	Sprinkle on the hot water, dissolve. Slowly add to tragacanth mixture, stirring constantly. Strain.
Honey **Glycerine** **Vodka** **Liquid Castile soap** **Essential oil** **Tincture benzoin**	*5 level teaspoons* *½ cup* *5 teaspoons* *4 teaspoons* *16 drops* *5 drops*	Add all these ingredients. Stir well, bottle. Invert occasionally while cooling to mix in oil. Will keep in refrigerator for several weeks.

To use, wet the face first. Squeeze a little of the mixture into the palm of your hand and massage gently onto the face, working up a lather. Splash cool water on your face to remove the cleanser. Blot dry. This cleanser doesn't really need a toner to follow but you could follow with a vinegar splash if you like (see 'Toners' below). If you want a real 'zing', then use peppermint oil as the essential oil.

Honey and glycerine soap — All skins

I have very fine, dry skin so I make this soap for use on my body. I use orange peel, comfrey and mallow root decoction. I add orange oil to finish. The soap smells and feels wonderful on my skin.

3x hot infusion/decoction	*½ - 1 cup*	Strain.
Soap, finely grated **Glycerine** **Honey**	*4 cups* *2 teaspoons* *2 teaspoons*	Melt in a double boiler with the infusion or decoction. Cool to blood heat.
Essential oil	*½ teaspoon*	Add, mix in very well.

Cleansing balm — Normal/dry/combination skins

A rich cleanser which leaves the skin feeling very soft. Use a skin tonic after this cream.

Beeswax	*12g/½ oz (1 cube)*	Melt in small pan over a low heat.
Coconut oil	*1 tablespoon*	Add, melt gently.
Basic herb oil	*¼ cup*	Add slowly, stirring. Remove from the heat when all melted. Cool to blood heat, don't allow to begin to set.
Herb infusion **Borax**	*4 teaspoons* *½ teaspoon*	Dissolve together. Beat into above.
Tincture benzoin **Essential oil**	*10 drops* *10 drops*	Add, beat until well mixed. Spoon into jar. Keeps well with refrigeration except in very hot weather.

Toners

Cosmetic vinegar

I choose a variety of herbs that will be useful for many functions as I use this vinegar as a deodorant, hair rinse, skin tonic, wound wash and bath additive. The dilution rate is a matter of personal preference. I would never use more than 2 teaspoons in a cup of water as a facial rinse or after shower splash, but would use it neat as a deodorant. Your skin type also determines the dilution, oily skins being able to tolerate a much stronger mix.

Cider vinegar	*2 cups*	Heat *half* to just below boiling point.
Herbs	*60 g (2 oz)*	Chop or mash very finely. Add to the hot vinegar. Pour into a jar and leave for a week. Strain through double cheesecloth. Add remaining vinegar.
Glycerine	*4 teaspoons*	Add, bottle. Keeps well without refrigeration except in very hot weather.

Cucumber tonic — All skins

If your skin is oily you should peel the cucumber. If dry or normal, leave unpeeled. The main astringent content is in the flesh. This is a lovely, light, refreshing toner. I keep cubes in the freezer and wipe one over my face when the weather is hot; it gets rid of that awful sticky feeling.

Cucumber	*1 medium*	Blend to a pulp, strain twice through double cheesecloth.
Witch hazel **Distilled water** **Essential oil**	*6 teaspoons* *3 teaspoons* *1 teaspoon*	Add to above, strain once more. Bottle. Needs refrigeration and will keep for only a few days. Freezes well.

Herbal tonic — All skin types depending on herbs used

This tonic can be made using the same herbs and essential oils as your cleanser and moisture lotion.

2x infusion/decoction	*¼ cup*	Double strain the infusion through coffee filter paper.
Witch hazel extract **Glycerine** **Tincture benzoin** **Essential oil**	*¼ cup* *½ teaspoon* *5 drops* *5 drops*	Mix all well with above. Bottle. Shake well before using. Needs refrigeration and will keep for only a few days.

MOISTURISERS

Most of the recipes in this section are emulsions. Some are oil in water, others are water in oil. See glossary (p164) for descriptions of these two types of emulsions. Try both types before making up your mind. You'll certainly have fun with them.

This first one isn't an emulsion. It's very simple to make, is nourishing for all skins and is one of my favourites. It is suitable for men, women and children. The skin of a child needs protection as much as an adult if the climate is harsh, but this protection needs to be very light and non-clogging to those fine pores.

Green gunk — A water in oil emulsion

Use as a pre-shampoo treatment, moisture cream, bath oil, after shower skin oil, hand cream, etc. My grandchildren named this preparation! It's basically a mayonnaise, though the taste isn't as good as the action.

Egg yolks **Herb vinegar**	*2* *1 tablespoon*	Beat in blender until well mixed.
Herb oil	*2 cups*	Add *slowly* until the mixture is very thick
Yoghurt **Essential oil**	*2 tablespoons* *1 teaspoon*	Mix in very well. Store in refrigerator where it will keep for several weeks.

Almond and glycerine moisture lotion

Apply a little of this lotion after cleansing. Smooth into the skin until absorbed. It needs refrigeration and will keep for only a few days, but freezes well.

Purified water **Ground almonds**	*½ cup* *2 tablespoons*	Boil the water and pour over the almonds. Cover, leave for 2 hours.
Cucumber **Water**	*¼ medium* *¾ cup*	Blend together, bring to the boil, turn the heat off, cool. Add to almond mix. Strain all through double cheesecloth.
Tincture benzoin **Glycerine**	*10 drops* *2 teaspoons*	Add, mix well. Store in a bottle in the refrigerator.

Orange moisture lotion/night cream — Dry, normal and combination skins

This is a water in oil emulsion. Use orange peel in the infusion and basic oil mix. This is a lovely moisturiser, rich and creamy. Very little is needed. Massage gently into the skin until absorbed. It's greasier than an oil in water emulsion but feels very soothing and feeds dry skin very well. The emulsion holds well without refrigeration unless the weather is very hot. If it should separate, shake well until blended again.

Beeswax	*1 cube (12g/½ oz)*	Melt in a small pan, using a double boiler.
Coconut oil **Cocoa butter**	*1 tablespoon* *½ cube (6g/¼ oz)*	Add and dissolve.
Basic oil (p 170)	*½ cup*	Add slowly, stirring. Take off heat.
3x infusion **Borax**	*½ cup* *½ teaspoon*	Dissolve together, strain. Add slowly to above, stirring, to 45°C (115°F).
Orange oil	*15 drops*	Stir in well. Bottle. Shake the bottle occasionally until the mixture is cold.

Note on oil in water emulsions

The use of a little more of the water phase (infusion) will give you a lotion rather than a cream. Experiment until you find which is the best for your skin. It's possible to preserve these creams for longer 'shelf life'. Ask your pharmaceutical supplier which is the safest preservative to use.

Lemon cream		Oily/combination skins

An oil in water emulsion. Those of you with oily or combination skins will realise there are parts of your face and throat which need oil as well as water. This is a lovely moisturiser which won't make your skin feel greasy. Use lemon peel and/or lemon grass in the infusion and the basic herb oil.

Cetomacrogol wax **Basic herb oil**	*30g (1 oz)* *2 teaspoons*	Melt together in small double boiler. Heat to 65°C (150°F).
Infusion/decoction **Glycerine**	*¾ cup* *3 teaspoons*	Heat together in separate pan to 70°C (160°F). Pour onto wax and oil. Stir *continuously* to 45°C (115°F).
Tincture benzoin **Essential oil**	*1 teaspoon* *18 drops*	Add, mix in well, pour into jars. Will keep in refrigerator for several weeks.

Aloe and comfrey moisture cream		Dry/normal/combination skins

An oil in water emulsion. This cream is also very good to use as a burn soother. It will keep in the refrigerator for several weeks.

To make aloe juice, chop several leaves and put into a blender. Blend to a juicy pulp, adding a little distilled water if necessary. The pulp will be very glutinous. Put into a pan, heat to boiling point, taking care not to burn the pulp. Cool and strain. This juice is then ready to use.

Cetomacrogol wax **Basic herb oil (comfrey)**	*30g (1 oz)* *4 teaspoons*	Melt together in small double boiler. Heat to 65°C (150°F).
Aloe juice (see above) **Glycerine**	*¾ cup* *4 teaspoons*	Heat together in separate pan to 70°C (160°F) Pour onto wax and oil. Stir *continuously* to 45°C (115°F).
Tincture benzoin **Essential oil**	*1 teaspoon* *15-18 drops*	Add, mix in well, pour into jars.

Other skin care preparations

Facial Scrubs

Herb scrub

Ground rice **Ground herbs**	*1 part* *2 parts*	Mix well. Store in a closed jar.

To use: Add a little milk and mix to a soft paste. Put a little in the palm of your hand and, with gentle circular motions, massage the mixture onto your moistened skin. Splash off with cool water.

Mealy scrub		
Oatmeal **Cornmeal, fine** **Ground almonds** **Kaolin** **Raw brown sugar**	*4 parts* *1 part* *2 parts* *½ part* *½ part*	Mix well together. It can be made up in bulk and stored in an airtight container until you need it.
Honey **Glycerine** **Essential oil**	*1 teaspoon* *1 teaspoon* *2 drops*	Mix together in a small bowl. Add 1-2 tablespoons of the dry mix, blend together.
Water	*To mix*	Add enough to make a soft paste.

To use: Wet your face. Put a little of the mixture into the palm of your hand and, with the fingers, massage the scrub onto your skin in a gentle circular motion. Splash off with cool water.

Masks

After applying a mask lie down for the length of time specified. The mask will stay in place better if you are horizontal and will work better if you are relaxed. (See page 167 for more information about masks.)

Green herb mask		All skins depending on herbs chosen
Fresh herb, chopped finely **Purified water** **Honey**	*2 handfuls* *2 tablespoons* *1 teaspoon*	Blend or mash together until pulpy and very fine.
Wheatgerm		Add enough to make a soft paste.

Pat onto face and throat. Lie down for 10-20 minutes.

Oily skin mask		
Lemon grass, dried and powdered **Brewer's yeast** **Yoghurt**	*1 tablespoon* *¼ teaspoon* *1 tablespoon*	Mix together.
Kaolin or oat flour		Add enough to form a soft paste.

Pat onto face and throat and leave for 10-20 minutes. Rinse off with lukewarm water and apply moisturiser.

Mask for dry/delicate skin

Aloe pulp **Honey, melted**	*3 tablespoons* *1 teaspoon*	Scrape the pulp from the inside of aloe leaves. Blend with the honey.
Almond meal		Add enough to make a soft paste.

Smooth over face and neck and leave for 10-20 minutes. Rinse off with warm water and apply moisturiser.

Arrowroot mask — All skin types

This is a very useful mask as the honey and glycerine attract and hold moisture in the skin. By using the charts this recipe can be adapted for any skin type/problem. For a thicker or thinner mask vary the amount of arrowroot. The mixture thickens as it cools.

Arrowroot **Honey** **2x infusion or decoction**	*2 teaspoons* *2 teaspoons* *¾ cup*	Mix to a paste with a little of the liquid. Mix in remaining liquid. Cook, stirring until thickened. Cool.
Basic herb oil	*1 teaspoon*	Add. Keeps well without refrigeration except in very hot weather.

Smooth over face and neck and leave for 15 minutes. Rinse off and apply moisturiser.

A few more recipes

Lip salve

This salve will heal and soothe chapped lips and used regularly will keep lips soft and unlined even in harsh weather conditions. It keeps well without refrigeration except in very hot weather.

To make the camphor oil for this recipe, dissolve 3 level teaspoons of camphor crystals in ¼ cup of safflower oil. Leave to dissolve. This will need to be made a few days before making the lip salve.

Beeswax	*1 cube (12g/½ oz)*	Melt in a small pan over a low heat.
Cocoa butter	*½ cube (6g/¼ oz)*	Add and melt *very gently*.
Lanolin or petroleum jelly	*1 teaspoon*	Add and melt, stirring.
Camphor oil	*¼ cup*	Add, mix in well. Take off heat. Cool to blood heat.
Glycerine	*1 teaspoon*	Mix in *well*. Pot in tiny jars.

Hand lotion

This lotion keeps well without refrigeration except in very hot weather.

Witch hazel	*1 teaspoon*	Mix all together. Apply a few drops and massage well in.
Glycerine	*2 teaspoons*	
Cologne (see p173)	*5 teaspoons*	

'Green gunk' (see p191) is a very good hand cream. It moisturises, feeds, balances and leaves your skin soft. You can put it on thickly, cover with cotton gloves and then with plastic ones and go to bed. Or you can massage it in gently while you listen to music or watch television.

For very dirty hands

Powdered oatmeal	*4 parts*	Mix together and store in a sprinkler jar. Shake some on to wet hands, massage till clean. Rinse.
Raw sugar	*1 part*	

Breath sweetener

Use as a delicious mouthwash. Use fresh herbs if possible.

Sherry	*2 cups*	Pour into a very clean jug.
Spearmint	*1 teaspoon*	Put all the finely chopped herbs and spices into an empty bottle; top up with the wine. Cork and store in a dark, cool place for 2 weeks. Strain, filter and re-bottle.
Peppermint	*1 teaspoon*	
Lemon thyme	*1 teaspoon*	
Sage	*1 teaspoon*	
Cloves, bruised	*4*	
Cinnamon, powdered	*1 teaspoon*	

KEY to Chart 12

A Mix 2 teaspoons with 1 cup water as gentle toner.

E Eyewash (see p 132).

X 3x infusion/decoction (see p 129).

C Cleanser (see p 189).

S Steam (see p 167).

D Apply direct.

P Pack (see p 167).

T Tonic (see p 191).

N Nourishing and moisturising (see p 191).

V Cool compress (see p 140).

I Infusion (see p 129); drink at night to cleanse system.

SC Scrub (see p 193).

B Brush on eyebrows and lashes every night.

Z Overuse on skin can cause photosensitivity, leading to pigmentation.

Chart 12 Natural Skin Care

		Blackheads	Blemishes & spots	Cleansing, dry	Cleansing, normal	Cleansing, oily	Cleansing, sensitive	Eyebrows & lashes	Eyes, tired	Nourishing, dry	Nourishing, normal	Nourishing, oily	Nourishing, sensitive	Packs, dry/normal	Packs, oily	Steam, dry	Steam, normal	Steam, oily	Toning, dry	Toning, normal	Toning, oily	Toning, sensitive	Veins, broken
Aloe vera			X							N	N	N	N	P								T	
Anise														P				S					
Bay		S	X																		T		
Bergamot			X												P						T		
Borage						C													T				V
Calendula			X																	T	T		V
Caraway														P									
Castor oil			D					B						P									
Catnep									V						P								
Chamomiles			P	C	C		C							P		S	S		T	T		T	V
Cider vinegar																			A	A	A		
Comfrey root										N	N	N	N			S	S			T		T	
Dandelion			I	C	C										P					T			
Elderflower			X	C	C	C	C		E					P		S			T	T			
Fennel		S							E					P	P		S	S			T		
Honey			D	C	C	C	C			N	N	N	N	P	P								
Horseradish			X																				
Lavender	Z		X						E					P				S		T	T		
Lemon balm			X	C																T	T		
Lemon grass		S		C											P			S		T	T		
Lemon juice			T												P					T	T		
Mallow root									E				X			S						T	
Marjoram						C									P			S	T				
Milk, dried				C	C		C							P	P								
Nasturtium		S	X																				
Oatmeal		SC		C	C	C	C							P	P								
Parsley						C								P	P								
Peppermint			I			C									P								
Plantain															P			S					
Red clover																S	S						
Red raspberry						C												S					
Rosemary		P	P																				
Sage			I		C	C									P			P					
Thyme			X																		T		
Witch hazel tincture						X														T	T		
Yarrow	Z					X									P			S		T	T		

CHAPTER FIVE

Eating Your Way To Health

Outside the courtyard, near the entrance gates, is a great garden of four acres with a fence running round on either side. Here grow tall flourishing fruit trees: pears, pomegranates and shining apples, sweet figs and luxuriant olives. The fruit of these trees never falls off or fails, but is there winter and summer, all the year round; for the west wind, always blowing, forms new fruit while it ripens others. Pear after pear comes to maturity and apple after apple, one bunch of grapes after another and fig after fig. There, too, a fruitful vineyard has been planted, of which one part, in a warm level spot exposed to the sun, is a drying ground, and elsewhere some grapes are being gathered and others trodden. In front there are unripe grapes only now shedding their blossom, while others are already turning colour. There too, beyond the furthest row of vines are well kept beds of herbs which are fresh all the year round, and there are two springs, one of which sprinkles the whole garden, while the other is channelled under the entrance of the courtyard to issue by the lofty palace and here the townsfolk draw their water. These were the splendid gifts of the gods in the house of Alcinous.

Homer, *The Odyssey,* Book VII

When we sold the 'Rivendell Skincare' business I was left with time on my hands. I cast around for something to do and an old ambition of mine surfaced — to run a restaurant. This seemed an unrealistic thing to do as we were 30 kilometres from the nearest town but, as ever, the prospect of a challenge was exciting. We rebuilt the kitchen, enlarged a room overlooking the valley, bought quantities of crockery and cutlery and indulged in moments of blind panic. In a few weeks 'The Prancing Pony' restaurant was open. We learnt a whole new way of using herbs. The emphasis in the past had been on their medicinal and skin care properties, and the cooking aspect, while acknowledged, had never been really explored.

To many people the word 'herb' means a sprig of parsley decorating a plate of food, sage used in poultry stuffing, or a pinch of mixed dried herbs in a stew. We found excitement in discovering innovative ways of using herbs and our restaurant was often something of a food revelation to visitors. Even the 'after-dinner mints' were peppermint leaves dipped in chocolate!

We provided each table with a small dish of fennel seeds for guests to nibble after their meal and the floral decorations on the tables were small delicate bunches of herbs. The view from the windows was always changing: placid black cows in the valley, heads down in the rain, grazing before darkness fell; a crescent moon rising above the gum trees and kangaroos venturing out on the hills to feed in the safety of the coming night. Sometimes there was mist in the valley and the farmhouse would seem to float on an island surrounded by grey swirling sea. It was always different, always lovely.

The old saying 'You are what you eat' is only partly true. As discussed in other parts of this book, it needs a great deal more than just food to create a healthy body, but it does form a good foundation on which to build. Herbs used in cooking and in drinks can have many benefits.

1. They can add vitamins and minerals to the diet. Unless you grow your own unsprayed vegetables or buy them direct from an organic grower you are likely to be getting a good dose of chemicals and not many of the vitamins. By the time the vegetables have been through the hands of the grower, retailer and wholesaler and finally yours, enough time has elapsed for them to be little more than a good source of fibre.
2. Herbs can be used to replace salt as a flavouring agent; this is good for everyone but particularly those on salt-restricted diets. Later, you will find a basic recipe for a herb salt (see p246) which you can adapt to suit your family. Most of the so-called 'herb salts' on sale consist of salt with a few ground herbs added. Other herbs such as angelica can help to sweeten food, making it easier to reduce our intake of sugar. Or they can be used as a sugar substitute for those on a sugar-free diet.
3. By adding herbs to your cooking you are using them in a preventive way. For instance, caraway added to cabbage, or coriander to beans, during cooking helps to prevent flatulence as well as giving the dish a delicious flavour. This seems to make more sense than drinking a cup of caraway tea after the meal to cure the discomfort.

When choosing herbs to cook with, you can cross-reference Charts 5 and 6 with Charts 13-16 to check if a herb is the best one to use for your family. Vitamins and minerals are not the only active substances to be found in herbs. Other constituents work on the body in a very subtle way, improving and strengthening every function.

4. The use of herbs can transform a 'good plain meal' into a gastronomic delight. Roast potatoes are enjoyed by most people but are taken for granted. Sprinkle them with chopped rosemary before roasting, sit back and wait for the compliments. Such simple things can transform you from an 'average' cook to an excellent and innovative one.

Vitamins and minerals

Vitamins are organic substances present in minute amounts in food. They are essential for health, and are also responsible for the assimilation of some minerals. Minerals, in their turn, are a necessary aid to the assimilation and functioning of vitamins as well as providing the body with necessary elements. The way in which vitamins and minerals function is extremely complex; for instance, iron is assimilated more easily from meat, but a high protein diet (such as one including a lot of meat) would increase the need for this mineral. Vitamin C increases the assimilation of iron from vegetables but decreases its availability in meat and also decreases the assimilation of copper.

Some people take vitamin and mineral supplements in the mistaken idea that this enables them to eat any amount of rubbish, because the pills will take care of them. But vitamins and minerals are not substitutes for proteins, carbohydrates and fats; in fact, they

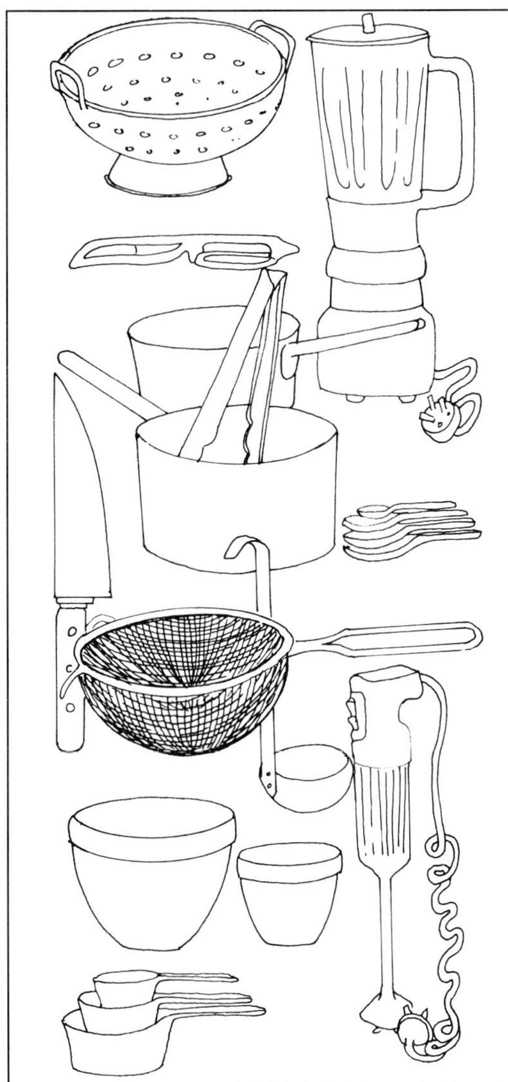

Equipment needed in the kitchen

Wooden spoons
Grater
Selection of very sharp knives
Bowls
Mixing bowls
Pans, different sizes, non-aluminium
Scales
Double boiler
Wok
Measuring cups and spoons
Pestle and mortar
Vegetable peeler
Soup ladle
Slotted spoon
Funnel
Tongs
Fish slice
Sieves, 2 sizes
Colander
Cake rack
2 chopping boards — one for 'clean' food, (e.g. bread, cheese), one for foods that stain (e.g. vegetables)
Tea strainer
Pot for herbal teas, non-metal
Rolling pin
Baking trays and casseroles
Blender
Electric coffee grinder — optional

need these nutrients in order to be assimilated into the body. Without a balanced diet the most assiduous taking of supplements will not give you good health. A balanced wholesome diet, however, is becoming very difficult to achieve in these days of fast foods, preserved meats, pre-packaged foods, sprayed and stale vegetables and, in most cities, terrible water.

Thankfully, there is a growing awareness of these problems and we are now able to find (sometimes after a long search) free range eggs, 'organically' grown vegetables, unsprayed wheat and other foods which we can trust.

The illustrator of this book, Dhenu, and I run classes on wholefood and vegetarian cooking and try to emphasise that food should be fun to cook and delicious to the whole family. If you are eating brown rice and vegetables every day of the week your chances of keeping well (and sane) are poor. You would soon drive your family from the dining table to the nearest pizza parlour. In order to receive maximum nutrition you need to eat a wide variety of foods. Varying your foods has the additional benefit of preventing the build-up of some allergies.

I have already talked about the possible lack of vitamins in the vegetables we eat due to the length of time they are stored. A further loss takes place when they are cooked; for instance, if cabbage is boiled in a lot of water, the amount of vitamin C remaining can be as low as 22%. On the other hand, if the vegetable is steamed or pressure cooked the amount retained becomes 70-80%. If vegetables are soaked before cooking, the resulting loss of some vitamins and minerals can be 100%. Even uncooked fruit can lose its vitamin C content if stored for too long. Apple juice stored in a refrigerator for 16 days (if the bottle has been opened and is only partially full) loses 95% of its vitamin C.

Not all vitamins are as fragile as this but most suffer to some degree when subjected to heat. This makes it important that we eat as much uncooked food as we find palatable and that it is as fresh as we can get it. Minerals tend to leach out into the cooking water rather than be destroyed by cooking, so it's very important to use the water for soups and stocks or, flavoured with tomato juice, as a drink.

Stress, cigarette smoking and air and water pollution are a few of the factors which can cause further depletion in the body so, even if all the above criteria are fulfilled, we might still find ourselves at risk from lack of essential nutrients.

Vitamins

In the list of vitamins which follows, the term 'fat soluble' means that the vitamin in question needs fat as well as minerals to be absorbed into the body. These vitamins are stored in the body and if too much is taken toxic symptoms can occur from the build-up. 'Water soluble' means that the vitamin is excreted and not stored in the body. Ideally, water soluble vitamins need replacing each day.

Vitamin A Oil soluble

Some benefits:
- Counteracts night blindness.
- Improves poor eyesight.
- Needed for growth and reproduction.
- Aids recovery from illness.
- Keeps the mucous tissue lining the mouth, respiratory and urinary tracts in normal condition.

Results of deficiency:
- Can cause problems seeing at night or dry eyes.
- Stunting of growth in children.
- Increased infections of respiratory tract, mucous membranes and skin.

Vitamin B1 (thiamine) Water soluble

Some benefits:
- Helps digestion of carbohydrates.
- Improves mental outlook.
- Useful to combat air and sea sickness.
- Helps promote normal functioning of heart, muscles and nerves.
- Prevents accumulation of fat in the arteries.
- Useful to diabetics, elderly people (especially after operations), alcoholics and those who eat a lot of 'junk' food.

Results of deficiency:
- Can cause lack of initiative, depression, inability to concentrate, memory deterioration.
- Numbness of hands and feet, tender calf muscles.
- Disturbed sleep, night sweats.

Vitamin B2 (riboflavin) Water soluble

Some benefits:
- Essential for cell growth.
- Maintains healthy mucous membrane, skin and eyes.
- Assists digestion.
- Needed for good eyesight, healthy skin and cellular growth.

Results of deficiency:
- Arthritic conditions, Parkinson's disease.
- Stomach ulcers, acne, diabetes.
- 'Teary' eyes, 'burning' feet and sore tongue.

Vitamin B3 (nicotinic acid and nicotinamide) Water soluble

Some benefits:
- Aids all aspects of digestion.
- Helps promote sleep.
- Assists the body to produce energy reactions from all cells.
- Helps create good circulation.

Results of deficiency:
- Vomiting, diarrhoea, constipation.
- Emotional instability.
- Sore, painfully fissured tongue.

Definciency of vitamin B3 is rarely seen. It is most likely in alcoholics with a poor protein intake.

Vitamin B5 (pantothenic acid) Water soluble

Some benefits:
- Health of adrenal glands.
- Improves poor memory.
- Helps reduce cholesterol build-up.
- Prevents onset of premature aging, including baldness.
- Treats post-operative shock.

Results of deficiency:
- Balding.
- Muscular weakness.
- 'Burning' feet; numbness and tingling.
- Reduces resistance to stress.

Vitamin B6 (pyridoxine thydioloride) Water soluble

Some benefits:
- Protects against kidney stones, harmful effects of radiation and X-rays.
- Protects mother and child from the effects of anaesthesia.
- Helps prevent nausea in pregnancy.
- Reduces night cramps.
- Reduces symptoms of pre-menstrual stress syndrome.

Results of deficiency:
- Irritability, nervousness, insomnia.
- Dermatitis.
- Sore tongue with prominent taste buds.
- No memory of dreams.

Vitamin B12 Water soluble, but only needed in very small doses

Some benefits:
- Forms and regenerates red blood cells.
- Increases energy.
- Helps utilise fats, carbohydrates and protein.

Results of deficiency:
- Pernicious anaemia.
- Brain damage.
- Numbness of hands and feet.
- Depression, confusion, deterioration of mental functions.

Vitamin K (menadione) Fat soluble

Some benefits:
- Produces prothrombin, a blood-clotting factor.
- Needed for the conversion of carbohydrates.
- Protects the liver from lead pollution.

Results of deficiency:
- Bleeding disorders.
- Coeliac disease.
- Colitis.
- Excessive diarrhoea.

Biotin (vitamin H)

Some benefits:
- Helps to prevent greying of hair and baldness.
- Helps to heal eczema and dermatitis.
- Eases muscular pain.

Results of deficiency:
- Eczema.
- Exhaustion.
- Severe cradle cap.

Choline Water soluble

Some benefits:
- Regulation of cholesterol levels.
- Health of nervous system.
- Helps liver and gall bladder to function.
- Soothes the nerves.

Results of deficiency:
- Cirrhosis.
- Possible onset of Alzheimer's disease.
- High blood pressure.
- Excessive weight loss.

Vitamin C (ascorbic acid) Water soluble

Some benefits:
- Maintenance of healthy connective tissue and bone.
- Helps absorption of iron.
- Heals wounds.
- Helps prevent many viral and bacterial infections.
- Lowers incidence of blood clots in veins.

Results of deficiency:
- Hardening of the arteries.
- Bruising, sore gums.
- Decreased immunity.
- Hypochondria.

Vitamin P (bioflavinoids, rutin, hesperidin) Water soluble

Some benefits:
- Increases capillary strength.
- Helps build resistance to infection.
- Helps prevent and heal bleeding gums.
- Aids treatment of rheumatism and arthritis.

Results of deficiency:
- Weak capillaries.

Vitamin D (calciferol) Fat soluble

Some benefits:
- Health of glandular and nervous system.
- Needed for development of bone, muscles and teeth in children.
- Aids assimilation of vitamin A.
- In combination with vitamins A and C can help prevent colds.

Results of deficiency:
- Rickets in children.
- Severe tooth decay.

Vitamin E (alpha tocopherol) Fat soluble

Some benefits:
- Supplies oxygen to the body.
- Helps prevent thrombosis.
- Improves fertility.
- Retards aging of cells.
- Helps prevent miscarriage.

Results of deficiency:
- Some reproductive disorders.
- Some anaemias.

Minerals

Calcium The body contains more calcium than any other mineral, making it the most important mineral in our diet.

Some benefits:
- Strong bones and teeth.
- Maintains a healthy heartbeat.
- Helps insomnia.
- Improves the acid/alkaline balance of the body.

Results of deficiency:
- Lung disease.
- Asthma.
- Loss of appetite.
- Varicose veins.
- Rickets.

Chlorine

Some benefits:
- Production of gastric juices.
- Regulates heart and blood pressure.
- Cleanses the blood.
- Assists hormone distribution.
- Helps rejuvenate skin tissue.

Results of deficiency:
- Loss of teeth and hair.
- Infertility.

Iodine (iodide)

Some benefits:
- Helps regulate metabolism and 'burn' fat.
- Regulates the thyroid gland.
- Gives energy and mental clarity.
- Benefits hair, skin, teeth and nails.

Results of deficiency:
- Goitre.
- Weight problems.
- Nervousness and irritability.
- Poor mental abilities.
- Irregular heartbeat.
- Hardening of the arteries.

Iron

Some benefits:
- Improves oxygen transfer in the body.
- Helps the body resist disease.
- Prevents fatigue.
- Prevents and cures iron-deficiency anaemia.

Results of deficiency:
- Anaemia (iron deficiency).
- Muscle fatigue.
- Difficulty in breathing.
- Obvious heartbeat on exertion.

Magnesium

Some benefits:
- Helps conquer depression.
- Aids digestion and relieves indigestion.
- Helps create a healthy heart.
- Needed for formation of new tissue.

Results of deficiency:
- Pre-menstrual stress syndrome.
- Hypoglycaemia.
- Muscle cramps.
- Learning disabilities.
- Eye 'tics'.

Manganese

Some benefits:
- Assists hormone production.
- Helps eliminate fatigue.
- Improves memory.
- Assists maintenance of blood sugar levels.

Results of deficiency:
- Difficulty in co-ordinating movement.

Phosphorus

Some benefits:
- Lessens arthritic pains.
- Improves circulation and normalises blood pressure.
- Promotes health of hair, teeth, skin, nails, brain.
- Maintenance and repair of the nervous system.

Results of deficiency:
- Rickets.
- Bleeding gums.
- Low resistance to infections.

Potassium

Some benefits:
- Sends oxygen to the brain.
- Helps prevent hardening of the arteries.

- Assists repair of liver function.
- Helps in repair and health of muscles.

Results of deficiency:
- Irritability and weariness.
- Poor appetite, constipation.
- Irregular heartbeat.

Sulphur

Some benefits:
- Needed for health of hair, skin, teeth, nails.
- Purifies blood.
- Antiseptic and cleansing for digestive system.
- Clears the body of acid mucus.

Results of deficiency:
- Signs of dandruff.
- Poor digestion.
- Lessening of 'well-being'.

Zinc

Some benefits:
- Helps decrease cholesterol deposits.
- Helps cure 'loss of taste'.
- Helps increase fertility.
- Helps keep prostate gland healthy.

Results of deficiency:
- Infertility.
- Susceptibility to infection.
- Behavioural and sleep disturbances.
- White spots on nails.
- Slow wound healing.

VITAMINS AND MINERALS

Herbs used fresh or correctly gathered, dried and stored can help to 'bridge the gap' between what our bodies need and what they are in fact getting. Chart 13 will help you choose herbs for table salts and cooking that will give you the widest variety of nutrients.

Chart 13 Vitamins and Minerals

	Vit. A	Vit. B1 (Thiamine)	Vit. B2 (Riboflavine)	Vit. B3 (Niacine)	Vit. B5 (Pantothenic acid)	Vit. B6 (Pyridoxine)	Vit. B12 (Cobalmine)	Biotin	Choline	Vit. C	Vit. D (Ergocalciferol)	Vit. E (Tocopherol)	Vit. K (Quinones)	Vit. P (Rutin)	Calcium	Chlorine	Fluorine	Iodine	Iron	Magnesium	Manganese	Phosphorus	Potassium	Sulphur	Zinc
Alfalfa	X						X	X	X	X	X	X	X		X	X						X	X		
Angelica								X				X			X	X									
Anise		X	X	X		X			X						X				X	X			X		
Catnep	X	X	X	X	X	X		X		X					X	X				X		X			
Calendula	X							X		X						X						X			
Cayenne	X									X					X			X	X	X		X		X	
Chamomile	X														X	X			X	X					
Comfrey	X						X	X		X					X	X						X	X		X
Dandelion leaf	X	X	X	X	X	X		X	X	X		X			X	X			X	X		X	X		X
Fennel																							X	X	
Garlic	X	X								X		X			X		X		X			X	X	X	X
Landcress	X			X				X		X	X	X				X	X		X	X	X	X	X	X	
Lemon balm								X								X									
Lemon peel						X								X		X									
Mallow leaf	X	X	X		X	X		X							X	X			X						X
Marjoram								X								X									
Mullein	X	X	X		X	X		X			X					X			X	X			X	X	
Nasturtium								X								X									
Nettle	X				X					X	X	X		X	X	X			X		X		X	X	X
Oregano								X		X						X									
Paprika	X									X															
Parsley	X	X	X		X	X		X		X					X	X			X	X			X	X	
Peppermint	X									X						X		X	X	X			X	X	
Plantain	X							X					X		X	X							X		
Red clover	X	X	X		X	X		X		X				X	X	X				X	X				
Red raspberry	X	X	X		X	X				X	X	X			X	X			X		X	X			
Rosemary	X							X		X						X	X		X	X					X
Rue								X						X		X									
Sage	X	X	X		X	X		X		X						X	X					X	X	X	
Thyme		X	X		X	X		X		X	X					X								X	
Watercress	X							X		X	X	X				X	X		X	X	X	X	X	X	
Yarrow	X							X		X		X	X			X			X		X		X		

Using a small infuser to brew a cup of herb tea

Herb teas

We drink for many reasons: to quench thirst, to warm or cool ourselves, to share companionship with friends and to comfort ourselves. In the case of herb teas, there is the additional benefit of the therapeutic properties to be gained. Tea and coffee have a valuable role as stimulants but, unfortunately, we often drink them to excess and the stimulating properties can become destructive to the nerves and body, leaving us feeling 'jumpy' and with an 'acid' stomach. If we try to limit the intake of tea and coffee to about three cups a day, drinking herbal infusions or decoctions the rest of the time, we are getting the best from both types of drinks.

Using Chart 14 will enable you to make blends of tea to suit your own palate and needs. Try small amounts at first; when you find a mix you like, then you can make it in bulk. The drinks may be made using fresh or dried herbs but, if you want a specific mix, dried herbs will ensure that you have the same blend throughout the year.

The herbs should be chopped or crushed until the pieces resemble Indian tea in size. Store the mixtures in glass jars away from the light, keeping out only enough for immediate use. In this way you will preserve the flavour, colour and goodness for as long as a year. Keep a separate teapot or infuser for herbal drinks as tannin residue can alter the delicate flavour of the herbs.

Instructions for both infusions and decoctions may be found on page 129.

Much of the therapeutic value of herb teas is in the essential oils which will evaporate off in steam. It's important to cover the mug or pot to prevent loss of these oils.

It can be unwise to stick to one single herb or blend of herbs until you are absolutely sure of what you are doing. If you don't thoroughly understand the properties of the herbs you are using, you may unwittingly overstimulate certain organs or functions of the body. Try to vary the types of drinks and always check with the other charts to see what function your chosen herbs perform.

Continual use of one herb may aggravate the very symptoms which you are trying to alleviate. For instance, a young woman came to see me complaining of

Chart 14 Herb Teas

		Acidity	Antidepressant	Appetite depressant	Appetite stimulant	Bad breath	Blood cleanser	Bowels	Cold & shivery	Coughs	Digestion aid	Flatulence	Hangover	Headaches	Hysterics	Insomnia	Irritability	Low energy	Menstrual pain	Morning sickness	Mouth sores	Nausea	Nerve tonic	Nightmares	Refreshing	Relaxing	Stomach upsets	Thirst-quenching	Tonic	Toxicity	Vitamin/mineral
Alfalfa		D			D		D															D					D		D	D	D
Angelica	X										A																A		A		
Anise	X			S		S			S		S	S					S		S	S									S		S
Basil	X																			L		L						A	L	L	
Bergamot	X						L		L											L					L				L		
Borage	Z																M	M							M			A			
Calendula					F			F	F								F														
Caraway	X										S	S					S		S	S							S			S	
Catnep																L			L												L
Chamomiles			F									F	F		F	F	F		F	F			F	F		F					
Coriander	X					S						S																			
Dill	X					S		S				S																			
Elder							L		F														F			F				F	
Fennel	X			S		S		S																						S	
Ginger	X				R			R	R			R		R					R	R		R								R	
Lemon balm	X								L					L	L		L		L	L			L		L	L					
Lemon grass	X																								L			L			L
Lemon rind	X				O	O	O	O	O	O															O			O			O
Lemon juice	X	O			O	O	O	O	O	O	O						O								O			O			O
Mallow root											R	R									R						R		R		R
Marjoram											L			L					L	L				L		L					
Peppermint	Z					L	L		L			L		L					L	L		L	L						L		
Mullein	Z									L																					
Nettle	Z	L			L		L												L										L	L	L
Orange peel	X					O						O					O								O		O		O		O
Oregano	X																							M		L					
Parsley	Z			L										L															L		L
Raspberry								L		L									L	L	L	L							L		L
Red clover		D			D		D	D		D																			D		D
Rosemary	Z					L								L				L					L						L		
Sage	X		L			L			L	L				L		L					L					L			L		L
Savories											L																L		L		
Tarragon					L											L										L					L
Thyme, cm					L	L						L	L						L		L		L				L				L
Thyme, lem	X				L							L							L												L
Valerian	Z														R		R						R								
Yarrow	Z						L		M																						L

KEY to Chart 14

Z Herbs marked Z carry the following cautions:

Borage/mullein The hairs on the leaves of these plants can cause contact dermatitis and also stomach problems. Use gloves to pick the leaves if you are sensitive. Always strain the tea through a fine sieve to avoid ingesting the hairs.

Nettle Old plants need to be well cooked as they contain a principle which could cause kidney damage if eaten raw.

Parsley Avoid using as tea if pregnant. The amount normally used in cooking and salads is safe.

Rosemary/sage Not to be used in large quantities or for an extended period.

Thyme Not to be used on a regular basis or in large amounts.

Yarrow Extended use may make skin light-sensitive, resulting in pigmentation.

Valerian Extended use may have a depressant effect. Take no more than twice a day for six days.

X An aromatic herb that will disguise unpleasant flavours.

O Add to drinks to improve flavour and to increase vitamin and mineral content.

D Use chopped, whole, sprouted herb.

A Use either leaf or root.

S Crushed seeds.

L Leaf.

M Leaf or flower.

F Flower.

R Root.

headaches. During our conversation she said, 'I've been drinking eight to ten cups of peppermint tea each day for weeks, but my headaches seem to get worse, not better.' Of course the condition would worsen as peppermint contains powerful constituents and her body was reacting to an overdose of these properties. Making mixtures of the herbs overcomes (to a large degree) the potential danger of ingesting too much of one constituent and creates the excitement of discovery as you make and taste a new and unique blend.

You can use honey to sweeten the teas if you like. Honey rots teeth in the same way as sugar but it contains many valuable minerals, enzymes and organic acids. It also acts as a disinfectant, protecting against bacterial and fungal infections. With such valuable attributes, cleaning your teeth after eating or drinking is a small price to pay. Try to buy honey direct from an apiarist or, failing this, ask your health food store where the honey comes from and whether or not it has been heated or treated in any way. It is best to get the least 'messed about with' honey.

Making Your Own Herb Tea Blends

Refer to page 10 for suggestions on record keeping.

To create herbal mixtures you will need to know the individual taste of each herb. In your record book make a list down the side of the page of the herbs which you have available and put headings across the top. These could be: Bland, Lemony, Bitter, Sweet, Full-bodied etc. The last column should be for comments. Fill in the columns using a pencil so that you can rub out easily. Note successes and disasters, to guide your future efforts.

First, try making a tea using one herb (noting name and amount in your book) with maybe a bland or a lemony flavour. If this is not very exciting, try adding another herb, perhaps a full-bodied or bitter one. You will quickly get the 'feel' of blending after making a few mixes.

I work in a fairly haphazard way using a quarter of a cup of boiling water and adding pinches of herbs until the taste is to my liking. You can be more scientific if you like. The important thing is the end result.

As I have mentioned before, it's not good to drink a particular blend or individual herb tea for more than six days a week or for longer than three weeks. Some of the following recipes are teas for particular conditions, others for pleasure. You may like to try each tea and then add or substitute your own flavours. If you have a source of unsprayed oranges and lemons, you can grate and dry the rind (zest) for use in drinks, cakes and desserts. All these teas are made using the infusion method on p129.

Some Good Combinations

Pregnancy

Ginger root — 1 part
Liquorice — 1 part
Nettle — 2 parts
Mallow, root or leaf — 1 part
Yellow dock — 1 part
Raspberry — 4 parts

Sleepy Time

Chamomile — 2 parts
Lemon balm — 2 parts
Nettle — 2 parts
Liquorice — 2 parts
Catnep — 1 part
Elderflower — 1 part

Comforter

Peppermint — 2 parts
Lemon balm — 1 part
Chamomile — 2 parts

Post-Natal

Raspberry — 4 parts
Fennel — 2 parts
Borage — 1 part
Dandelion, root or leaf — ½ part
Nettle — 1 part
Dill — 1 part
Mallow, root or leaf — ½ part

Summer Quencher

Lemon grass — 3 parts
Lemon balm — 2 parts
Borage leaf — 2 parts
Lemon peel — 2 parts
Dill seed — 1 part

Strain after 10 minutes. Leave to cool. Add lemon juice and ice cubes if liked.

Elder Tisane

Elderflowers — 6 parts
Caraway — 1 part
Red clover — 2 parts
Dried orange peel — 1 part
Lemon balm — 1 part

The gourmet herbalist

I like to use fresh herbs whenever I can but this isn't always possible as herbs such as tarragon are winter dormant and others have specific times when they are at their best. If you have been very careful about the gathering, drying and storing, the dried herbs will be a good second best. A general rule is to use two or three times more fresh herb than dried.

Try using herbs in your favourite recipes. For instance, if you are making cheese scones, look at Chart 15 to see which are the best herbs to use with cheese and add a finely chopped teaspoonful. Note what you have done and the result. In this way you don't need to use new recipes but can improve those which your family already enjoys. It's easy to go overboard in the beginning, mixing too many herbs into too many dishes, leaving your taste buds totally confused. When we were running the skin care business at the farm there were about fifteen people involved. We lived communally, taking turns at the chores. One lass who was new to cooking decided to make a very unusual soup for our lunch so she added two tablespoons of liquorice powder as flavouring to the pot! We ended up eating herb omelettes and salad for lunch.

'Easy does it' until you are familiar with the herbs and the way their flavours change or deepen when they are cooked. Many herbs need to be added towards the end of cooking as they can become bitter and/or lose vitamin and mineral content if cooked for too long. When you begin to use Charts 15 and 16 remember to keep an eye on the 'Amount to Use' column. This will guide you until you are more at home with the herbs. A safe way to learn the amounts which suit your family is to add a little, taste, add more if you like and so on (and keep notes).

After the recipes you will find suggestions for mixtures of herbs (p246). These are useful when you are in a hurry or when it's not convenient to use fresh. The recipes in this chapter are some of the ones which proved popular at 'The Prancing Pony' restaurant or were devised and used by my colleague, Dhenu, when she worked in 'Zorba the Buddha' restaurants in Australia.

KEY to Charts 15 and 16

N	Add sparingly	**L**	Use leaf
M	Add in moderate amounts	**F**	Add flower or petals as garnish when dish is cold
G	May be used generously	**Sd**	Use seed
X	Use in the appropriate dishes	**P**	Use petals
S	Crushed seed	**O**	Sprouts
E	Add towards the end of cooking	**R**	Root

Chart 15 Hot Dishes

	Amount to use	Beans, all	Beef	Cabbage family	Carrots	Cauliflower	Celery	Cheese dishes	Chicken	Curries	Eggplant dishes	Egg dishes	Fish	Lamb	Marrow, squash etc	Mushrooms	Natural sweetener	Omelettes	Peas	Potatoes	Rice	Salt-reduced diets	Sauces	Shellfish	Soups	Stewed fruit	Stews	Tomato dishes	Vegetable hotpots	Zucchini
Alfalfa sprouts	G							E			E	E						E			E				E		E		E	
Angelica stem	M																X					X				X				
Anise	N			S	S																					S				
Basil	M							E		E	E		E		E				E							E	E	E	E	E
Bay	N		X						X				X	X									X	X	X		X	X	X	
Bergamot	N																									X				
Borage	G										X											X			X	F			X	
Calendula	M																				F									
Caraway	N			S	S																					S				
Cayenne	N	C		C				C		C	C	C	C	C	C			C			C	C	C		C		C		C	
Chives	G							X										X		X		X	X	X	X		X		X	
Coriander	M	L	S					L		S			L											L	L					
Dill	M			S		S							S	S				L	L	L			L		S					L
Fennel	M			S		S			L				S	S				L							S					
Garlic	M	X	X						X	X	X		X	X							X	X	X	X	X		X	X	X	X
Ginger	M		X		X				X	X																X			X	
Horseradish	M		X									X											X				X		X	
Hyssop	M		X										X	X											X		X		X	
Lemon balm	G								X				X	X		X										X				
Lemon grass	G								X	X																				
Marjoram	M														E	E								E			E	E		
Mints	M				E								E	E					X	E						X				
Nasturtium	M							L				L											F		F	F				
Nettle, young	G			X																		X			X		X		X	
Oregano	M	E	E						E		E		X	E				X	X	X		X	E		E		E	E		E
Parsley	G	X	X		X	X	X	X	X		X	X	X	X	X	X		X	X	X	X	X	X	X			X	X	X	
Red clover sprouts	G							E			E	E						E			E				E		E		E	
Rosemary	M								X					X				X		X	X		X						X	
Sage	N	X														X			X				X		X		E	X	E	
Savories	M	X		X				X				X	X						X			X					X		X	
Tarragon	M							X	X				E			E							E	E	E		E			E
Thyme, common	M	X	X		X			X			X	X	X	X	X		X					X	X	X	X		X	X	X	X
Thyme, lemon	M								X			X	X										X	X	X				X	X
Water/landcress	G								E		E	E	E									X					X	X	X	

Chart 16 Cold Dishes

	Alfalfa sprouts	Angelica	Anise	Basil	Bergamot	Borage	Calendula	Caraway	Cayenne	Chives	Cress, water & land	Dandelion	Dill	Fennel	Garlic	Ginger	Horseradish	Lemon balm	Mints, both	Nasturtium	Oregano	Parsley	Red clover sprouts	Rosemary	Sage	Savory, summer	Tarragon	Thyme, common	Thyme, lemon
Amount to use	G	G	N	M	G	G	G	N	A	G	G	M	M	M	A	A	A	M	M	M	N	G	G	N	N	N	N	N	M
Apples			S	L	L			S										L											
Avocado				L					X						C		R					L					L		
Baked custard																R		L											
Bean salad															C							L				L		L	
Biscuits			Sd					Sd								R								L					
Cakes								Sd								R													
Chicken																						L		L		L	L		
Cottage cheese	O			L			P	S		L			L				R			L		L	O		L	L	L		
Crystallising		S			P	F	P									R			L										F
Drinks		L				F										R		L	L										
Eggs, stuffed										L							R			L		L				L			
Flower salads					P	F	P					P								F									F
French dressing				L						L												L				L			
Fruit juices		S				F												L	L										
Fruit salads						F	P									R		L	L					L				L	
Garnishes	O	S			P	F	P			L	L							L		F		L	O					L/F	F
German potato salad										L			L									L							
Herb butter										L	L				C							L		L		L	L	L	
Herb salad	O		L	L		L	P			L	L	L		L	C		L	L	L	L/F		L	O			L	L		L
Jellies		S																L	L										
Liqueurs		S	S													R		L	L					L	L				
Mayonnaise				L					X		L				C		R				L						L		L
Mushroom salad				L				S		L												L							
Pickles									X				S											L					
Potato salad				L		L/F		S		L				L							L						L		
Punch		S				L/F													L					L					
Rice salad	O						P		X	L			L		C							L	O	L		L			
Salads	O			L	L/F		P	L		L		L	L	S			L		L	L		L	O			L		L	
Sandwiches	O			L			P			L	L						R			L			O						
Seafood cocktail										L											L	L							
Soup, chilled						L		S	X	L	L									L/F	L	L				L			
Tomato juice			L						X	L				L							L	L		L			L		
Tomato salad	O		L							L				L							L	L	O				L		
Tuna	O								X	L			L	S			R					L	O						
Vegetable juice			L						X					L			R				L	L		L			L		
Vinegars				L					X	X			L		R		R		L		L			L			L	L	L

Methods

Brown rice, to cook		
Brown rice, long grain	*1 cup*	Dry roast in a heavy pan until brown and toasty. Take off the heat.
Boiling water	*2 cups*	Pour over *very carefully*, using a lid as a shield. It will splatter and steam so take care not to burn yourself. Return to the boil, put a tight lid on the pan. Cook on the lowest heat *without stirring or poking* it until 'dimples' appear on the top of the rice (30-40 minutes).

This method can be used for wheat, buckwheat etc. as well as rice and results in fluffy, delicious, separated grains.

Eggplant in a colander being 'degorged'

Protecting your hand from the steam by using a lid as a shield

Degorging

Degorging is a process used to prepare eggplant (aubergine) for cooking. Eggplants contain a bitter principle which is not desirable, particularly if you eat this vegetable often. Removing this bitter juice is called 'degorging' and the whole process takes about 1 hour, so you need to plan your cooking accordingly.

The initial preparation depends on the recipe. Sometimes you will cube or slice the eggplant, or you might have to cut it in half and slice through the flesh in criss-cross fashion (not cutting through the skin). After the chopping or cutting, rub or mix the flesh with plenty of coarse cooking salt. Put the cubes/slices in a sieve or colander to drain. If cut in half, place flesh down on draining rack. Leave for 1 hour. Rinse well (you will see that a lot of brown juice has seeped from the flesh). Squeeze to remove excess water.

The other benefit gained from degorging is that the flesh will absorb more juice from the cooking. Degorging is sometimes used for other 'wet' vegetables like cucumber and zucchini (courgette).

Honeys

I like to use honey in herbal drinks and as often as possible in cooking. Flavoured honeys are delicious and healthy, and they also make attractive gifts. To make them, heat the honey gently until it's runny, add 2 teaspoons of chopped herbs to each cup of honey and leave for a couple of weeks. Reheat, strain and pour into a jar.

To make a ginger honey for cooking or for a hot herb and lemon drink (for use when you are cold and shivery or are coming down with a cold): peel and chop 1 cup of ginger, put in a small strong pan and cover with honey. Bring to the boil and *just* simmer for about 1 hour. Strain and pour into a clean jar. I use this honey more than any other as it's useful for desserts, marinades and many other dishes.

These honeys need refrigerating as the heating seems to destroy some of the natural keeping properties.

Garlic Puree

This will keep in the refrigerator for several weeks. The flavour is 'nutty' and not as overpowering as fresh garlic.

Put the unpeeled cloves of garlic on an oiled tray and paint all over with oil. Bake at 180°C (350°F) until soft (10-15 minutes). Cool, squeeze the pulp into a small jar. Cover with olive oil.

Sprouting

Sprouting seeds and grains is a way of growing fresh greens even if you live in a one-room apartment. Sprouts are full of vitamins and minerals. They taste good and are cheap, easy and fun to grow. Even if you have a large garden it's not practical to grow some herbs, notably alfalfa, red clover, mung, lentils and fenugreek. The alternative is to sprout the seeds and use the sprouts either dried or fresh in the ways suggested in other chapters.

A word of warning before you begin. Seeds bought from a farm or garden supplier have most likely been sprayed to protect them from insect attack. These sprays are most poisonous and the seeds shouldn't be used. Get your supplies from a health food shop or a supplier who can guarantee the seeds and grains haven't been treated in any way.

It's always a temptation to sprout too much seed when you first begin. The seeds look so small that it's impossible to imagine the size they will grow to. As a guide to quantities, remember that ¼ cup of seeds becomes 2 cups of sprouts, and it's better to maintain a steady supply of fresh sprouts than to have bowls full of sprouts losing goodness in the refrigerator.

It's not necessary to buy expensive equipment to do your sprouting; chances are that you already have everything you need in your home.

General Instructions

1. For all methods, remove any debris or broken seeds before you begin sprouting. If these bits are left in, they may rot and spoil the whole batch.
2. Rinse the seeds and soak in warm water overnight. Drain, pouring the drained water on indoor plants or using it for stock in cooking. Put the seeds in your chosen container (see below).
3. The sprouts need to be kept in moist (not wet), dark and warm conditions. They need rinsing each day or they will begin to rot or dry out.
4. When alfalfa and red clover sprouts are about 2 cm (1 in) long and the little leaves appear (after 3-5 days) they can be exposed to sunlight for a time until the leaves turn green. Mung, lentils and fenugreek can be eaten as soon as the little roots are ¾ cm

Soaking the seeds before sprouting

Sprouts ready to be exposed to the light for 'greening'

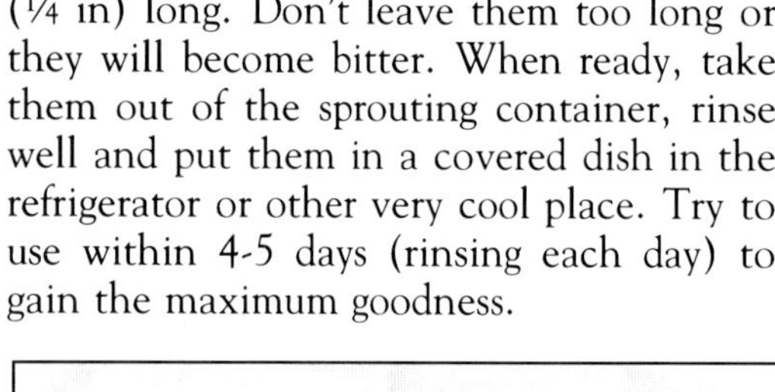

(¼ in) long. Don't leave them too long or they will become bitter. When ready, take them out of the sprouting container, rinse well and put them in a covered dish in the refrigerator or other very cool place. Try to use within 4-5 days (rinsing each day) to gain the maximum goodness.

Containers and Methods

Unglazed flowerpot saucers

These are inexpensive, easily available, aesthetically pleasing to have around the kitchen and they work well. I have two sizes: one pair 3cm deep and 15cm in diameter (1 x 6 in) and one pair 5 x 20 cm

Unglazed flowerpot saucers standing in a dish of water

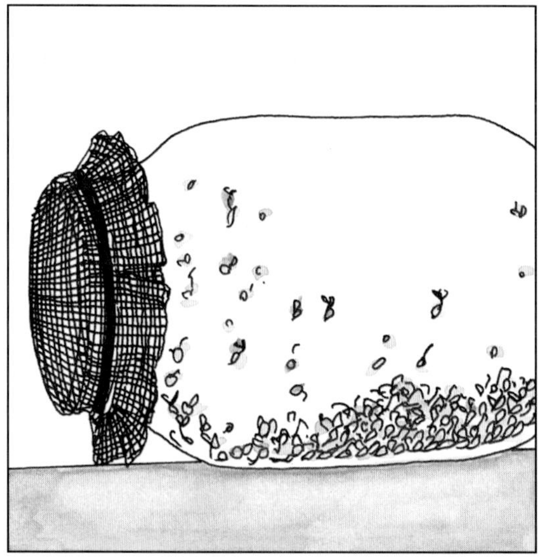

Position of jar as the sprouts are growing

(2 x 8 in). These different sizes allow for different sized sprouts.

Wash and soak the containers in water to prepare them, before starting the sprouting. Sprinkle the soaked and drained seeds evenly in the bottom of one saucer and invert the other saucer to cover it. Stand them in a dish of water, which will be absorbed through the unglazed saucers. Keep them near the stove or in a kitchen cupboard. Another good place is on top of the refrigerator towards the back where the heat escapes. Top up the dish of water as needed.

When the plants are as tall as you want, take the top saucer off, leave them standing in the container of water and put near a window for a day or so. They will grow a little more during this time and develop their green leaves. Store as suggested in 4 above.

Sprouts ready for use

Ice cream containers
Square or round 2 litre (3½ pint) ice cream containers make excellent sprouting trays. They don't look pretty, but they don't cost anything and are very efficient. To prepare them, punch a lot of holes in the bottom with a skewer. I use these for big seeds like mung beans, lentils and fenugreek, but you can make them suitable for small seed by laying blotting paper, cheesecloth, nylon fly netting or similar in the base. Spread the soaked and strained seeds evenly over the bottom of the container and put the lid on. Twice a day stand the container in enough water to come up through the holes and just cover the seeds, then lift it out and let it drain. The treatment is the same as saucers from this point on.

Glass jars
Any size glass jar can be used. You will need some sort of cover for the jar: a piece of nylon fly netting, coarse cheescloth, net curtaining or old pantihose, the main factor being that the sprouts inside the jar must get enough air or they will rot. Use an elastic band to hold the cover on. Remember the eventual size of the plants, for it becomes difficult to rinse them properly if they are too closely packed. Follow the general instructions for growing. The jar needs to be kept on its side. If I use a jar, I cover all but the mouth with a folded cloth to keep out as much light as possible, or place in a cupboard.

You will see from the above that all sorts of containers can be used for sprouting. Look around your house and you will find many things that can be used: colanders, sink tidies, sieves, tea strainers (sprouts for one person!). I'll leave the rest to your imagination.

Stock

Keep a stock pot 'on the go' all the time. If the stock is brought to the boil every second day and kept refrigerated it will keep for a long time. This stock is frequently so delicious that it can be served as a soup. It gets richer and stronger each day. While I am in the kitchen cooking I keep the pot simmering on a back burner and throw in all the scraps. After the

meal or cooking session is over I strain the stock, cool it and put it in the refrigerator (the strained scraps go on the compost heap). Each time you cook, repeat this ritual, taking from and replenishing the stock, topping up with more water or vegetable cooking water and scraps. It doesn't take any time at all and the rewards are enormous. If you need very strong stock cubes, reduce the stock to 1/4 by slow simmering, then cool and freeze in blocks.
Note: This stock recipe uses entirely vegetarian ingredients. If you add chicken bones or other meat then the stock should be used within a day or so.

Ingredients

Lots of the following, well washed before throwing in the pot: onion peels, spring onion tops, lettuce leaves, carrot scraps and tops, pumpkin peel, potato peels (not if there is any green on them), mushroom stalks, celery tops, garlic skins, herb stalks and /or leaves, tomato ends.
Not much of: cabbage family, turnips, swedes, parsnips etc.
None of: capsicum (red and green pepper) eggplant (aubergine), beetroot (it makes the stock a most unappealing colour).

Storage of herbs

Herbs in jars on your kitchen shelf may look very attractive but too much light shortens their life so it's better to have small jars near the stove. These can be 'topped up' from the main store, which should be kept in a dark cupboard.

Herb vinegars being made

Dried herbs are at their most effective for 12 months after drying. It's then time to empty your jars onto the garden or compost heap and begin storing the new season's crop.

Garlic and herbs in oil

Storing Herbs in Vinegar

When the annual or winter dormant herbs (such as summer savory, basil and tarragon) are at their best I store large quantities in vinegar and oil to last through the winter. Make the vinegar in the same way as the tincture described on page 130 (don't use any water, just cider vinegar) and dilute it with fresh cider vinegar to taste.

Chopped fresh ginger and horseradish root store really well in vinegar or sherry and the resulting liquid is delicious to use in cooking.

Layering herbs in salt to store

Storing Herbs in Oil

Drizzle some best quality olive oil in the bottom of a wide-mouthed crock or jar. Put in a layer of fresh, dry herb leaves. Drizzle more oil. Carry on in this way until all your leaves are stored. The last layer should be oil. The herbs will keep through winter and the oil may be used in cooking. The best herbs to treat in this way are basil and tarragon.

Storing Herbs in Salt

Most herbs store well in salt but I use this method only for herbs which don't dry or freeze well. Basil is an excellent herb to 'salt'. You will need a bag of cooking salt (with no additives) and a very wide-mouthed jar or crock. Put a 2½ cm (1 in) layer of salt in the bottom of the crock, then a 1 cm (½ in) layer of herb leaves and a 1 cm (½ in) layer of salt. Continue until

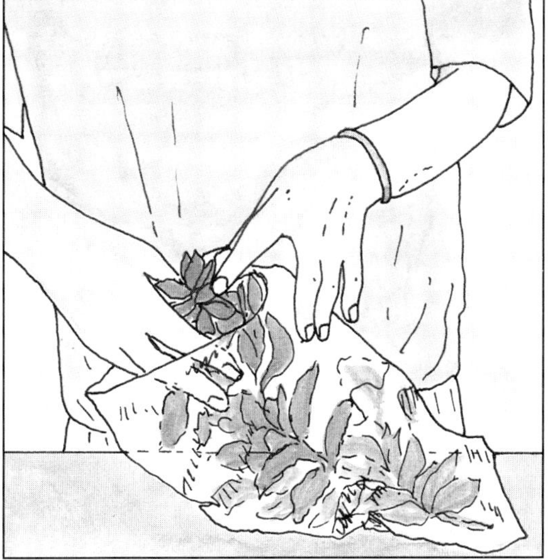

Putting herbs in a plastic bag ready for freezing

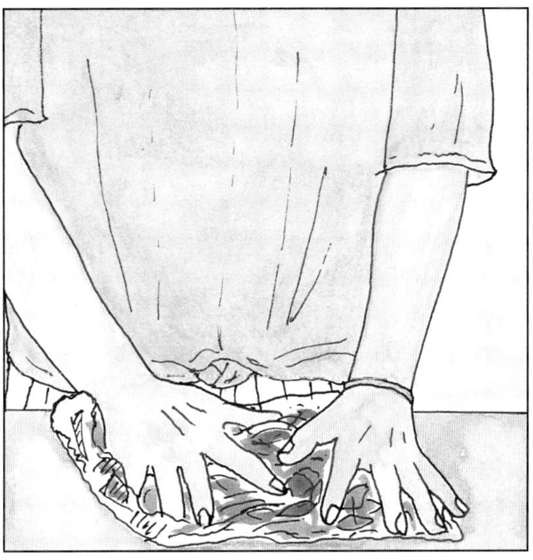

Pressing the bag of herbs flat to expel the air

you have run out of herbs. Finish with a 2½ cm (1 in) layer of salt. You can continue to add herbs to the pot as they become available.

When you need to use the herbs, simply lift out a few leaves, shake or rinse them and they are ready for use. A bonus of this method is the deliciously flavoured salt which you can use (in very small amounts) in your cooking.

Freezing Herbs

Some herbs are best frozen, and retain flavour and colour which is almost as good as fresh. The best herbs to freeze are those which don't dry well, namely basil, coriander, chives, tarragon, lemon balm, parsley and mints. Try to avoid washing herbs which you are going to freeze. You can either strip the leaves off the stems or freeze whole sprigs. Put the herbs in a freezer bag and press down flat to expel the air, seal and freeze flat. Doing it this way makes it very easy to break off the amount you need.

A nice thing to do is to put borage flowers or mint leaves in ice cube trays, fill with water and freeze. The resulting ice cubes look attractive and add delicate flavour to drinks.

The herbs are very limp after freezing so are unsuitable for garnishes. Chop the herbs while still frozen — it's very much harder to do once they have defrosted.

Recipes

Dips

Tofu and herb dip

Mayonnaise	*1 cup*	Mix all well in blender.
Yoghurt	*1 cup*	
Tofu	*250g (8 oz)*	
Dill weed	*½ teaspoon*	
Dill seed, crushed	*½ teaspoon*	
Salt or herb salt	*½ teaspoon*	
Black pepper	*to taste*	
Parsley, minced	*1 tablespoon*	Add, stir well, chill.
Chives, minced	*1 tablespoon*	

Horseradish and sesame dip

There are many brands of nutritional yeast, some of which are very bitter. I use a New Zealand brand called 'Healtheries Yeast Flakes', which is really delicious.

Ricotta cheese	*1 cup*	Mix all well together. Change quantities to suit yourself. Serve with crackers or vegetable sticks.
Toasted sesame seed, ground	*½ cup*	
Parsley, chopped finely	*1 tablespoon*	
Chives, chopped finely	*1 tablespoon*	
Coriander leaf, chopped finely	*1 teaspoon*	
Onion, finely chopped	*1 tablespoon*	
Lemon juice	*1 teaspoon*	
Brewer's yeast	*1 tablespoon*	
Yoghurt	*1 tablespoon*	
Finely grated horseradish	*to taste*	

Soups

Peanut and nasturtium — Serves 4

A good dinner party or family soup.

Peanut oil **Onion, chopped** **Celery, chopped** **Aniseed, crushed** **Garlic, crushed**	*2 tablespoons* *1 large* *1 stick* *1 teaspoon* *1 clove*	Sauté together for 5 minutes.
Peanut paste **Soya sauce, low salt** **Stock (p219)**	*1 cup* *3 tablespoons* *1 cup*	Add, mix well.
Hot milk	*1½ cups*	Stir in a little at a time until smooth. Heat but *don't boil.*
Yoghurt **Cream** **Cayenne**	*3-4 tablespoons* *3-4 tablespoons* *pinch*	Mix together, stir slowly into above.
Nasturtium leaves	*3*	Chop finely, add to above. Reheat, don't boil.

If the soup is too thick for your taste, add more stock. Serve this delicious and nourishing soup sprinkled with chopped, toasted sunflower seeds or peanuts and decorated with a whole nasturtium flower.

Peanut and nasturtium soup

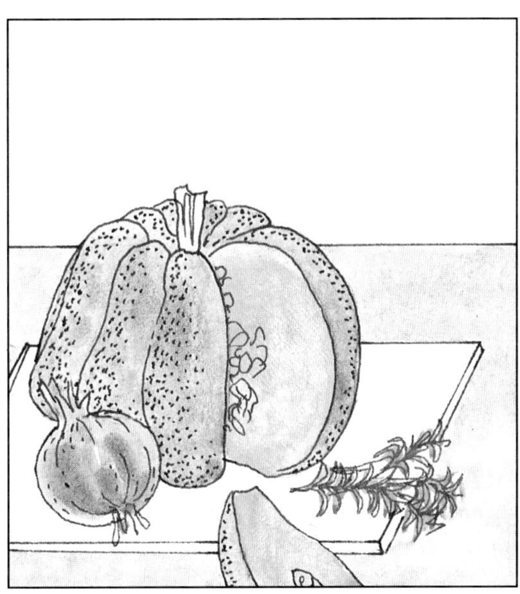

Pumpkin and rosemary soup

Golden grain soup — Serves 4-6

Don't be fooled by the seemingly boring ingredients in this soup. It's unusual, delicious and very healthy.

Onions **Oil**	*4* *3 tablespoons*	Slice in half moons. Sauté on a low heat for 8-10 minutes till golden.
Oregano **Parsley** **Rosemary** **Basil** **Boiling water** **Rolled oats**	*½ teaspoon* *4 tablespoons* *½ teaspoon* *1 teaspoon* *8 cups* *1 cup*	Chop all the herbs quite finely. Add to above. The water *must* be boiling or the oats will go 'gluggy'. Cook for 20-30 minutes, stirring occasionally.
Soya sauce, low salt **Salt and pepper**	*3 tablespoons* *to taste*	Add, garnish with chopped herbs.

Pumpkin and rosemary soup — Serves 4-6

Butternut pumpkin (squash)	*1 large*	Peel, cut in big chunks.
Onions, large, sliced **Tomatoes, canned** **Rosemary leaves** **Stock (p219)**	*2* *medium can* *14*	Put all in a pan with pumpkin and enough stock to *just* cover the vegetables. Bring to the boil, cover and simmer till soft and cooked.
Nutmeg **Salt and pepper** **Cream or yoghurt**	*½ teaspoon* *to taste* *½ cup*	Add, purée and reheat, but *don't boil.* Garnish with a few chopped rosemary leaves.

Six herb soup — Serves 4

Garlic oil (p243) **Onions, chopped** **Potatoes, medium, cubed** **Carrot, large, cubed**	*2 tablespoons* *2* *2* *1*	Sauté gently for 5 minutes.
Well flavoured stock (p219)	*6 cups*	Add, simmer till vegetables half cooked.
Parsley, finely chopped **Chives, finely chopped** **Rosemary, finely chopped** **Mint, finely chopped** **Savory, finely chopped** **Tarragon, finely chopped**	*4 teaspoons* *4 teaspoons* *2 teaspoons* *2 teaspoons* *2 teaspoons* *2 teaspoons*	Add herbs and simmer till all the vegetables are cooked.
Salt and pepper	*to taste*	

Serve with herbed croutons (p243) and garnish with a sprinkle of chopped fresh herbs. This is a tasty soup which, with the addition of croutons and grated cheese, makes a good lunch or cold night supper.

Salads

Herb salad

There is no formal recipe for this salad. I like to use two or more different types of lettuce torn into smallish pieces. I then add lots of landcress or watercress, alfalfa and red clover sprouts, chives, parsley, and very young dandelion leaves torn into about 2½ cm (1 in) bits. Then add smaller amounts of basil, dill or fennel leaves, lemon balm and nasturtium leaves. Finish with the smallest quantity of mint, oregano or marjoram and lemon thyme. Just before serving I toss the salad with a herb vinaigrette. Garnish with any of the flowers recommended for eating (Chart 16).

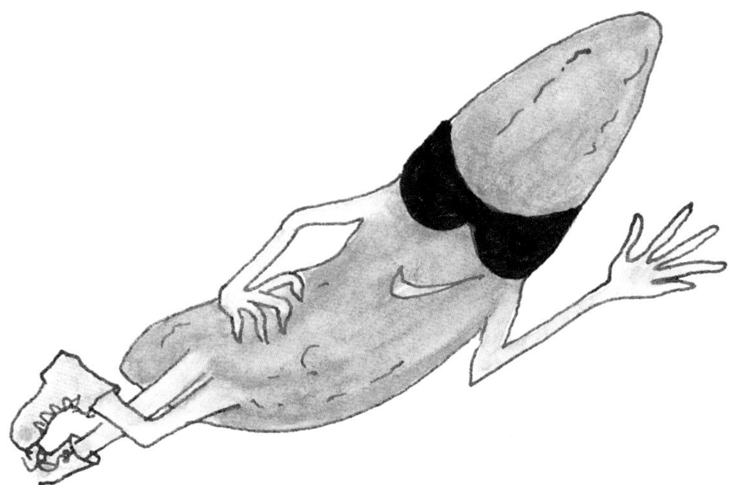

A 'cool' cucumber

Zucchini and marjoram salad — Serves 4-6

A very pretty salad which keeps for several days in the refrigerator. A delicious way to use some of the zucchini (courgette) glut!

Zucchini, medium	*2*	Cut into 1½ cm (½ in) cubes. Boil for 1 minute, strain and cool thoroughly.
Spring onion, chopped **Red pepper (capsicum), sliced** **Green pepper (capsicum), sliced** **Parsley, finely chopped** **Marjoram, finely chopped**	*5 tablespoons* *1* *1* *2 tablespoons* *1 tablespoon*	Mix all with cool zucchini.
Olive oil **Herb or cider vinegar** **Salt and black pepper** **Honey**	*½ cup* *3 tablespoons* *to taste* *2 teaspoons*	Put in a screw-top jar and shake well. Toss gently with zucchini mixture.
Olives	*optional*	To decorate.

Green and gold salad — Serves 4-6

Carrot, large **Zucchini (courgette), medium**	*1* *2*	Slice paper-thin. Blanch carrots in boiling water for 2 minutes, zucchini for one. Rinse in cold water. Drain, cool.
Spring onions **Mint, fresh** **Parsley, fresh** **Black pepper, freshly ground** **Olive oil** **Lemon juice** **Salt**	*2 tablespoons* *3 tablespoons* *2 tablespoons* *1 teaspoon* *3 tablespoons* *1 tablespoon* *to taste*	Chop onions and herbs finely. Mix all well, gently toss with vegetables. Serve well chilled.

Roast pepper salad — Serves 4-6

This is a useful salad as it can be used in sandwiches, as a side dish with hot dishes or mixed with other salads to give flavour and colour. It keeps for several days in the refrigerator.

Red peppers (capsicum) **Green peppers (capsicum)**	*2* *2*	Put in a baking dish in the oven at about 180°C (350°F). Leave until the skin is beginning to burn. Put into a plastic bag, fold the top over and leave to cool. Pull the stem and seeds out, peel the skin off and slice into strips. Arrange decoratively in a bowl.
Garlic olive oil (p243) **Lemon juice** **Salt and black pepper**	*2 teaspoons* *2 teaspoons* *to taste*	Mix together, sprinkle over peppers.

VEGETABLES

Potato pancakes — Serves 4

Potatoes	*1kg (2lb)*	Peel, steam till nearly done, chill, grate.
Oil	*3 tablespoons*	Heat in heavy frypan.
Sprouts **Spring onions** **Tarragon** **Parsley** **Chives** **Salt and pepper**	*1 handful* *4* *1 tablespoon* *4 teaspoons* *4 teaspoons* *to taste*	Chop sprouts, onions and herbs finely. Mix all gently through the potatoes. Fry in the heated oil till brown, turn and fry the other side. Cut in wedges to serve.

Cabbage or carrots with caraway

Serves 4

Caraway serves a dual purpose in this recipe. It adds a subtle and interesting flavour and protects you (by its medicinal properties) from the 'windy' discomfort experienced by many people after eating cabbage.

Carrots or cabbage, sliced	*450g (1lb)*	Steam till crisp but tender. Drain well and keep warm.
Oil **Garlic clove, minced** **Caraway seeds, lightly crushed**	*1 tablespoon* *1* *1 teaspoon*	Sauté together for 2 minutes. Mix with the vegetable.
Light sour cream (optional)	*½ cup*	Fold through, serve at once.

Dilled cucumber

Serves 4

Cucumbers **Salt**	*2 large* *1 tablespoon*	Peel, cut lengthwise, remove seeds, cut into 2.5cm (1 in) pieces. Degorge (see p216). Rinse and drain very well.
Butter **Onion**	*1 tablespoon* *1*	Finely chop the onion. Sauté in the butter till soft.
Flour	*1 tablespoon*	Add and cook, stirring till light brown.
Milk	*1½ cups*	Stir in slowly, boil 3-4 mins. Add more milk if too thick. Add cucumbers, cook till tender but firm.
Parsley **Dill, fresh** **Sour cream or yoghurt** **Salt and pepper**	*1 tablespoon* *1 tablespoon* *1 tablespoon* *to taste*	Chop the herbs very finely. Fold through gently, garnish with extra chopped herbs. Serve at once.

Bavarian red cabbage — Serves 4

Butter, melted	*2 tablespoons*	Sauté in a covered pan for 5-7 minutes.
Red cabbage, shredded	*450g (1lb)*	
Onion, sliced	*1*	
Garlic cloves, crushed	*2*	
Cooking apple, chopped	*1*	Add to above, cover and cook gently for 20 minutes. Stir often. If it's too dry you can add a little more wine.
Bay leaf	*1*	
Parsley, chopped	*1 teaspoon*	
Oregano, chopped	*1 teaspoon*	
Caraway, crushed	*1 teaspoon*	
Cinnamon	*a pinch*	
Nutmeg	*a pinch*	
Salt and black pepper	*a pinch*	
Brown sugar	*2 teaspoons*	
Red wine	*4 tablespoons*	
Orange, grated rind and juice of	*1*	

Sweet corn and pepper pancakes — Serves 4

I use lemon thyme in this recipe but either of the savories is nice as well.

Sweet corn kernels	*350g (12 oz)*	Chop half finely, place all in bowl.
Egg yolk	*1*	Finely chop the herb and green pepper. Stir all together with the corn to a soft dropping consistency.
Cornmeal (polenta)	*⅔ cup*	
Flour	*⅓ cup*	
Herb	*1 teaspoon*	
Salt and black pepper	*to taste*	
Green pepper (capsicum)	*1 cup*	
Egg white	*1*	Fold in gently. Drop a spoonful at a time into hot oil and cook both sides till golden brown.

Sauces and Dressings

Herbed vinaigrette

The herbs in this dressing can be changed to suit the dish being served. The proportion of vinegar to oil may be changed to your own taste.

Vinegar or lemon juice	*2 tablespoons*	Mix all in a jar; shake really well.
Olive oil	*4 tablespoons*	
French mustard	*2 teaspoons*	
Garlic clove, crushed	*1*	
Chives, parsley, basil	*2 teaspoons*	
Sugar	*a pinch*	

Neil's sauce

This recipe is from Neil Jackson, the chef of The Lord Forrest Hotel in Bunbury, Western Australia. He is the best chef I have ever encountered and his food presentation is a delight to the eye and the taste buds.

This is a high cholesterol dressing so it's best to reserve it for special occasions.

White wine **White wine vinegar** **Onion, chopped**	*1½ tablespoons* *1½ tablespoons* *1 tablespoon*	Simmer together unitl the liquid has almost evaporated.
Butter **Lemon juice**	*1¼ cups* *1 teaspoon*	Whisk into above.
Salt and pepper	*to taste*	Add

Variations
Add 1 teaspoon of chopped herbs to suit the dish the sauce will accompany. Red wine/ vinegar may be substituted for white to make a more robust sauce. Orange juice can be used in place of lemon.

Fresh green sauce

For serving over vegetables or pasta.

Thick sour cream **Butter** **Nutmeg** **Cayenne**	*1 cup* *¼ cup* *⅛ teaspoon* *good pinch*	Combine, simmer for 3-5 minutes.
Parmesan cheese, grated **Basil, parsley, each** **Mint, chives, each** **Tarragon, oregano, each** **Lemon thyme**	*3 tablespoons* *1 tablespoon* *1 tablespoon* *1 teaspoon* *1 teaspoon*	Finely chop the herbs. Beat into sauce, reheat, serve.

Tomato sauce (basic)

This basic sauce is the foundation for several sauces. It can be made in bulk and frozen in small amounts ready to be converted into Mexican, Italian, Indian, Spanish or herb sauce by adding appropriate herbs and spices. To make a richer sauce, substitute red wine for some of the stock. There are some variations on the next page.

Onions, chopped **Garlic cloves, crushed** **Olive oil**	*2* *2* *2 tablespoons*	Sauté till soft.
Canned tomatoes, crushed **Stock** **Tomato paste** **Salt and pepper**	*440g (15 oz)* *1 cup* *2 tablespoons* *to taste*	Add. Cook till thickened.

Some sauce variations
To 2 cups of basic sauce add the following:
Herb 3 tablespoons finely chopped herbs of your choice.
Italian 1 bay leaf, 1 tablespoon each of chopped basil and oregano.
Indian Curry powder, fried before adding to sauce.
Mexican Cummin, fresh coriander, chilli — all to taste.

Herb mayonnaise

Eggs **Herb vinegar** **French mustard, prepared** **Sugar** **Salt and black pepper**	*2* *2 tablespoons* *1 tablespoon* *pinch* *pinch*	Beat well with an electric blender or food processor.
Olive or safflower oil	*2 cups*	Still beating, dribble the oil in very slowly until really thick.
Yoghurt	*½ cup*	Stir in, adjust seasoning.

Now you can add the herbs — lots of herbs (but no more than 3 flavours). I would probably put at least one cup of very finely chopped herbs to this quantity. The herbs could be: fresh coriander; a mixture of parsley, chives and upland cress; parsley and rosemary; or basil. The choice is yours.

Green dressing

For salads, vegetables etc.

Spinach leaves	*100g (4 oz)*	Tear in small pieces. Blanch 1 minute in boiling water, drain, squeeze dry.
Garlic clove **Spring onions, chopped** **Mayonnaise** **Dill, fresh** **Tarragon** **Parsley** **Yoghurt** **Lemon juice** **Salt and black pepper**	*1* *2 tablespoons* *6 tablespoons* *1 tablespoon* *½ teaspoon* *3 tablespoons* *6 tablespoons* *2 tablespoons* *to taste*	Add to the cooled spinach. Blend all together in a food processor till very smooth.

ENTRÉES AND MAIN COURSES

Mushroom pâté — Serves 6 as an entrée

Spring onions, minced **Butter, melted**	*¾ cup* *1 tablespoon*	Sauté for 5 minutes. Take off heat.
Mushrooms **Celery** **Parsley** **Basil, oregano, each** **Sage, rosemary, each** **Eggs, lightly beaten** **Strong cheese, grated** **Breadcrumbs, dry, fine** **Salt and black pepper** **Brandy**	*450g (1lb)* *1 stalk* *3 tablespoons* *¼ teaspoon* *¼ teaspoon* *2* *1 cup* *½ cup* *to taste* *1 tablespoon*	Mince or finely chop all the herbs and vegetables. Mix all ingredients together with the sautéed spring onions. Spoon into a small greased loaf tin.
Butter, melted	*3 tablespoons*	Pour over, cover. Bake 1 hour at 180°C (350°F).

Italian fillets — Serves 3-6 depending on size of fillets

You could use basil, marjoram and parsley, or parsley, chives and a pinch of rosemary in this recipe.

Fillets of white fish	6	Arrange in a shallow ovenproof dish.
Butter, softened **Salt and pepper** **Chopped herbs**	*2 tablespoons* *to taste* *1 teaspoon*	Mix together well, spread over the fillets.
Lemon, juice of **White wine**	*1* *½ cup*	Mix and pour over. Bake in moderate oven for 10 minutes or until the fish is cooked in the middle. Lift the fillets onto a serving plate, keep warm. Pour the juice into a small pan.
Herbs (as before)	*1 teaspoon*	Add to the juice in the pan. Boil to reduce a little. Pour over the fish. Serve immediately.

Herbed Camembert parcels		Serves 4 as an entrée
Camembert	*1 whole*	Cut in 4 wedges.
Filo pastry **Butter, melted**	*4 sheets*	Brush each sheet with melted butter and fold as illustrated. Lay a wedge of cheese on each piece of pastry.
Basil, finely chopped **Paprika**	*1 teaspoon* *½ teaspoon*	Sprinkle over the cheese wedges.
Egg, beaten	*1*	Fold pastry to enclose cheese, as shown in diagram, using egg to seal edges.

Brush with egg. Place on a greased oven tray and bake at 200°C (400°F) for 15-20 minutes. Serve with slices of tomato and basil leaves to decorate.

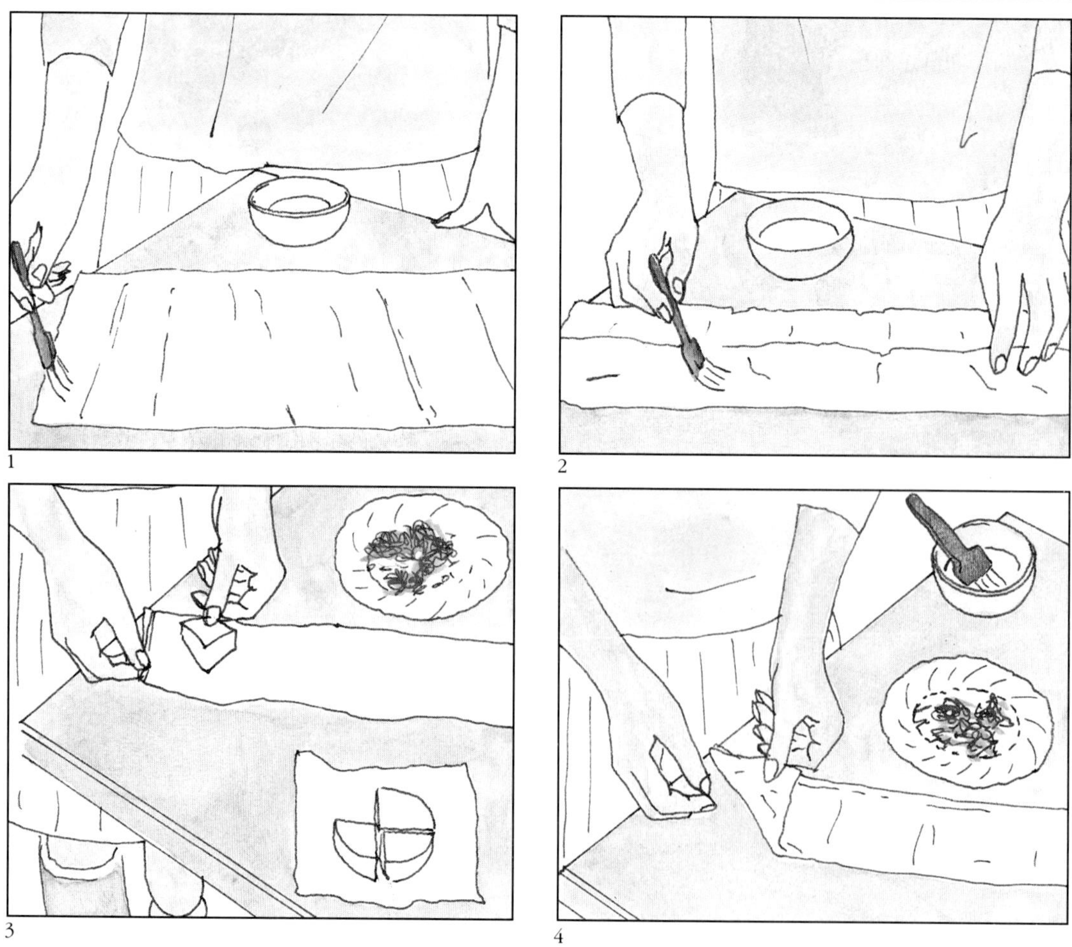

Sage and savory sausages

Serves 3-4

Egg, beaten	*2*	
Peanut paste	*2 tablespoons*	Mix all well together. The texture should be soft but 'mouldable'. You might find that you need more or less breadcrumbs. Shape into sausage shapes. Leave in the refrigerator for an hour to set.
Cottage cheese	*100g (4oz)*	
Cheddar, grated	*1 cup*	
Chopped nuts	*½ cup*	
Onion, minced	*1*	
Sage, minced	*½ teaspoon*	
Winter savory, minced	*½ teaspoon*	
Mustard, French	*1 teaspoon*	
Salt	*½ teaspoon*	
Curry powder	*1 teaspoon*	
Breadcrumbs, fresh and fine	*100g (4oz)*	
Egg white	*to coat*	Dip the sausage into beaten egg white and fine dry crumbs. Fry till golden brown.
Breadcrumbs, dried	*to coat*	

5

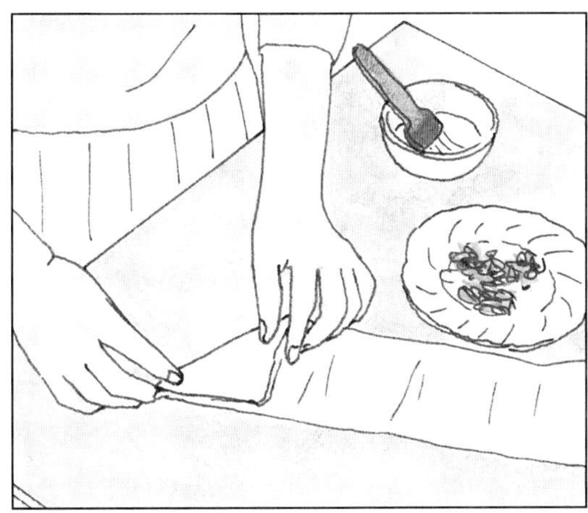

6

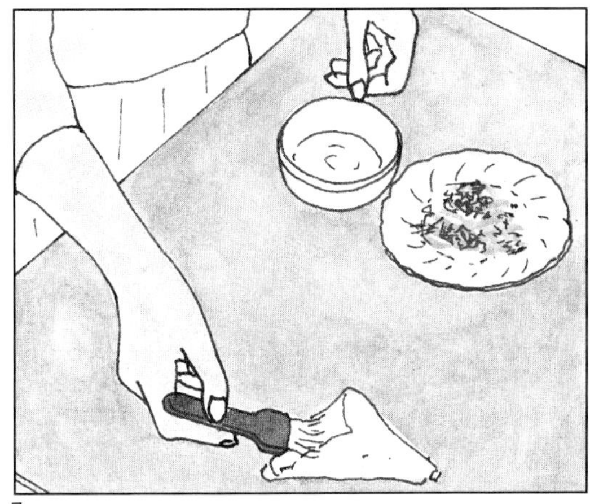

7

Herbed camembert parcels

Lemon grass and coconut chicken — Serves 4-6

I have never served this dish to anyone who hasn't loved it. It's equally good for a family meal or a dinner party and has the additional benefit of being inexpensive.

Chicken pieces **Oil**	*1½kg (3lb)* *1 tablespoon*	Fry till golden brown, remove from pan. Drain well.
Garlic cloves, crushed **Onions, chopped** **Red capsicum (pepper), chopped** **Green capsicum (pepper), chopped**	*3* *2* *½* *½*	Sauté in the chicken pan, remove, drain well.
Turmeric **Tomatoes, canned** **Garlic cloves, crushed** **Coriander, fresh** **Fennel seed, ground** **Cummin** **Coconut milk** **Cornflour** **Root ginger, grated** **Chilli powder**	*2 teaspoons* *225g (8oz)* *2* *3 tablespoons* *½ teaspoon* *1 teaspoon* *2 cups* *1 tablespoon* *1 teaspoon* *½ teaspoon*	Put all in a blender, process till fine.

Place chicken in baking/serving dish, arrange vegetables on top.

Bay leaves **Coconut, toasted** **Lemon grass stalks** **Cinnamon stick**	*2* *1 teaspoon* *2* *1*	Arrange over chicken and vegetables, pour sauce over. Cook at 180°C (350°F) for 45-60 minutes. Remove cinnamon, bay and lemon grass. Serve.

Italian chicken and spaghetti — Serves 4-6

Olive oil **Onion, finely chopped** **Garlic cloves, crushed**	*3 tablespoons* *1* *2*	Sauté until onion is transparent.
Chicken pieces	*1½kg (3lb)*	Add, brown all over.
Italian flavoured sauce (see p230)	*2½ cups*	Pour over the chicken. Cover, simmer until the chicken is tender, about 30-40 minutes. Add stock if needed. Remove the chicken to a warm dish.
Parsley, finely chopped	*3 tablespoons*	Add half to the sauce.

Boil enough spaghetti for four to six people and put in a hot dish. Arrange the chicken pieces on the pasta, pour the sauce over and decorate with the remaining parsley.

Nasturtium kebabs		Serves 4
Marinade		
Herb vinegar	*4 tablespoons*	Marinate the cubes of meat overnight. Use marinade to brush over kebabs as they are being grilled or barbecued.
Garlic oil	*4 tablespoons*	
Soya sauce	*1 tablespoon*	
Ginger root, crushed	*1 teaspoon*	
Sherry	*1 tablespoon*	
Chicken, cubed	*450g (1lb)*	
Button mushrooms	*24*	Cut the peppers in small pieces. Allowing two skewers per person, alternately thread the vegetables and meat. Grill or barbecue.
Cherry tomatoes	*24*	
Green/red peppers (capsicum)	*1 of each*	
Baby onions	*12*	
Dressing		
Chives	*2 tablespoons*	Chop the herbs, flowers and seeds. Mix with yoghurt. Push meat and vegetables onto nasturtium leaves, top with dressing, roll up and eat.
Nasturtium flowers	*8*	
Nasturtium seeds, pickled	*to taste*	
Yoghurt	*¾ cup*	
Salt and pepper	*to taste*	

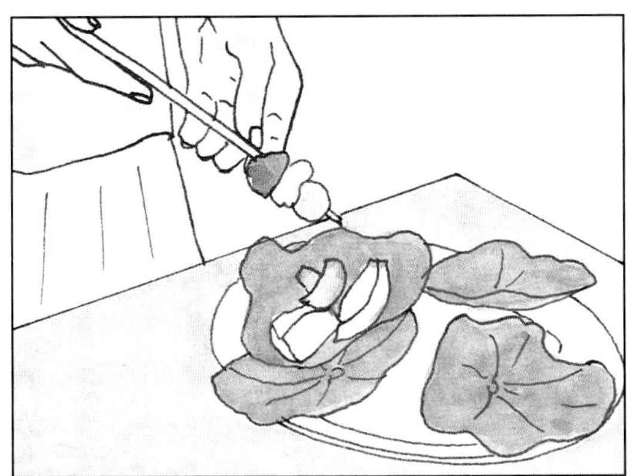

Nasturtium kebabs

Herbed eggplant (aubergine)		Serves 4 as a side dish
Eggplant, medium	*1*	Cube, degorge for 1 hour (see p216).
Garlic olive oil (see p243) **Ginger root, crushed** **Garlic clove, crushed**	*2 tablespoons* *1 tablespoon* *1*	Sauté with eggplant for 6 minutes.
Chives, chopped **Onion, minced** **Parsley, chopped** **Mint, chopped** **Lemon, juice of** **Sour cream** **Yoghurt**	*2 tablespoons* *1 tablespoon* *1 tablespoon* *2 teaspoons* *1* *½ cup* *2 tablespoons*	Mix all together, fold into eggplant. Serve hot or well chilled.

Cheese and eggplant (aubergine) balls — Serves 4

If a Mexican flavour is desired, use coriander in both the balls and the sauce. Oregano in both will give an Italian-style dish.

Eggplant, medium size	*1*	Grate and degorge (see p216). Squeeze really dry.
Eggs, beaten **Cheddar cheese, grated** **Parsley, chopped finely** **Ground almonds** **Coriander or oregano, chopped finely**	*2* *3 tablespoons* *2 tablespoons* *2 tablespoons* *1 tablespoon*	Mix all with the eggplant. Shape into small balls. Fry in wok or frypan till golden.
Sauce		
Sauce (see p230) **Salt and pepper**	*3 cups* *optional*	Pour half into an ovenproof dish. Add balls, cover with remaining sauce. Heat at 180°C (350°F) for 30 minutes.

Desserts

Lemon balm and mint fruit salad

Choose enough fruit for the amount of salad you want to make, paying attention to colour combinations and texture. It's pleasing to the tongue and teeth to have a mixture of soft and crunchy. Eye appeal is most important to start the saliva flowing. I like green and gold combinations with just a touch of red. This salad could be made from pineapple, kiwi fruit, apples and a small amount of red plums. Another good-looking mixture is melon, kiwi fruit and strawberries.

If you are using fresh fruit you can make juice by mixing 1 part fresh orange juice with

1/2 part fresh lemon juice and sweetening to taste with honey or sugar. To this or any fruit salad add finely chopped lemon balm and mint leaves for a really zippy flavour.

Mango magic — Serves 4

I substitute ginger honey (see p217) for the honey and ginger root in this recipe as it saves the bother of grating the ginger.

Mangoes, large and ripe	*3*	Peel and cube. Put in dish.
Honey **Ginger root, finely grated**	*2 tablespoons* *1 teaspoon*	Warm honey till runny.
Lemon, juice of **Lemon balm, finely chopped** **Mint, finely chopped**	*1* *1 tablespoon* *1 teaspoon*	Add to honey and ginger root. Pour over mangoes, chill for 30 minutes.

Angel custard — Serves 4

Angelica stalk	*3 tablespoons*	Peel and cut into *very thin* rings.
Milk **Ginger honey**	*2¾ cups* *3 tablespoons*	Mix and bring to the boil, add the angelica. Take off heat, cover and stand for at least 2 hours. Reheat to blood temperature.
Eggs, beaten	*4*	Stir into above.
Butter, melted	*1 tablespoon*	Add, stir well. Pour into a baking dish. Bake in the centre of the oven at 120°C (240°F) until set. Don't overcook. Serve hot or cold.

Mint sorbet — Serves 4-6

Sugar **Water**	*1½ cups* *2 cups*	Stir together over a low heat until the sugar has melted. Simmer for 5 minutes.
Mint, crushed to a pulp **Lemon balm, crushed to a pulp** **Lemon thyme, crushed to a pulp**	*2 teaspoons* *1 teaspoon* *1 teaspoon*	Add to above, cool.
Lemons, juice of	*3*	Strain and add. Freeze in shallow container until setting around the edges. Scrape into a bowl, whisk.
Egg white	*1*	Beat till stiff but not dry. Fold in gently, re-freeze. Scrape into small, chilled glass dishes. Decorate with herb leaves.

Mint sorbet

Caramel oranges

Caramel herb oranges — Serves 4-6

I usually use mint and lemon thyme for this recipe.

Oranges	*6 large*	Peel, remove all white pith and pips, cut into thin slices, arrange in a dish.
Herbs, finely chopped **Caster sugar** **Cointreau (optional)**	*2 teaspoons* *1 teaspoon* *1 tablespoon*	Sprinkle over the oranges.
Sugar **Water**	*½ cup* *4 tablespoons*	Heat gently until melted. Simmer until golden brown. Don't overcook. Pour over the oranges. Refrigerate to cool.

Angelic pie — Serves 4-6

Cooking apples, medium size **Raw brown sugar**	5 *5 tablespoons*	Peel, core, slice thinly. Mix with apple slices.
Angelica stalk, chopped finely **Lemon thyme, chopped finely**	*1 tablespoon* *½ teaspoon*	Layer in an ovenproof dish with the apple mixture.
White wine	*⅔ cup*	Pour over, cover and cook in a slow oven for 1-2 hours. Cool thoroughly.
Plain flour	*2 tablespoons*	Fold through apple mixture.

Pour the apple mixture into a large pie dish lined with shortcrust pastry which has been pre-cooked for 15 minutes. Cover with cream, yoghurt or a mixture of both. Bake at 190°C (375°F) for 40 minutes.

Pickles, Sauces and Things

Dill pickles

Cider vinegar **Water** **Salt**	*4 cups* *2 cups* *½ cup*	Bring to the boil, allow to cool.
Gherkins or small cucumbers **Garlic** **Bay** **Dill seeds** **Mixed pickling spice**	 *3 cloves* *3 leaves* *3 tablespoons* *1 tablespoon*	Layer all in a jar or crock with a wide mouth. Pour brine over. Cover. Leave one week before using. The crock can have more gherkins added as they are used.

Horseradish sauce

Store this sauce in a covered jar in the refrigerator.

Horseradish root	60g *(2oz)*	Grate finely.
Mustard, dry **Sugar**	*½ teaspoon* *2 teaspoons*	Add to above, mix well.
Cider vinegar	*to cover*	Pour over, leave overnight.
Thick cream	*½-1 cup*	Fold in, adjust seasoning.

Coriander, mint and coconut chutney/spread/dip

I don't know what to call this recipe because it can be used in any of the ways suggested in the title. If you like fresh coriander and peanuts you will love this dish. It could be used over rice, and with curry dishes, baked fish or curry patties.

Dessicated coconut **Peanuts, raw, unsalted** **Coriander, fresh, chopped** **Mint leaves, chopped** **Chilli powder** **Ginger root, grated** **Lemon juice** **Yoghurt** **Sugar** **Salt**	*1 cup* *¾ cup* *4 tablespoons* *5 sprigs* *⅛ teaspoon* *1 tablespoon* *2 tablespoons* *1 cup* *1 teaspoon* *to taste*	Blend all together, leaving the nuts 'crunchy'. Add more yoghurt if the mixture is too dry.

Pickled nasturtium seeds

Soak the seeds in a brine made from 1 heaped tablespoon of salt dissolved in 1½ cups of water — this should just cover the seeds. Increase or decrease these quantities depending on the number of seeds you have. Change the brine every day for three days. Rinse seeds well, put in a jar and cover with either white wine or cider vinegar. Leave 5-6 weeks before using. These can be used in place of capers; I find them much tastier and better textured.

Pickled nasturtium seeds

The very best tomato ketchup

Very ripe tomatoes, peeled	*2kg (4lb)*	Chop, put in a non-aluminium pan.
Allspice **Mustard seed**	*3 teaspoons* *2 tablespoons*	Tie in a muslin bag, add to above.
Onions, medium, minced **Garlic, minced**	*3* *3 cloves*	Add, simmer till thickened and reduced — about 30 minutes. Stir often.
Sugar **Basil, finely chopped** **Oregano, finely chopped** **Lemon thyme, finely chopped** **Cider vinegar** **Black pepper, ground**	*1 packed cup* *3 tablespoons* *1 tablespoon* *1 tablespoon* *2 cups* *½ teaspoon*	Add all to above, continue to simmer until mixture reaches sauce consistency. Pour into hot sterilised bottles and cover well.

Mustard, grainy and gorgeous

This is a mild, coarse mustard which is really tasty. The green peppercorns give a milder flavour than black. All mustards need to be matured for about two weeks before use as they taste acrid until the flavours have blended.

Mustard seeds, mixed **Green or black peppercorns**	*4 tablespoons* *1 tablespoon*	Blend to a coarse texture.
Red wine **Red wine vinegar** **Garlic cloves, minced** **Bay leaf, minced** **Worcestershire sauce** **Honey** **Water**	*2 tablespoons* *⅔ cup* *3* *1* *½ teaspoon* *1 teaspoon* *3 tablespoons*	Mix all with above. Soak for 2 hours. Put into a small pan, cook, stirring continuously, 5-10 minutes. Add more vinegar if too dry. Spoon into a jar. Seal well. Keep refrigerated.

Herb Vinegars

It's important to use only a very good quality vinegar. Cheap vinegars are harsh and they completely overpower the flavour of the herbs. The method is the same for all types: Heat the vinegar but don't boil. Pour over the whole herbs (don't chop them), leave for one week, strain and bottle. You can top up with fresh herbs and vinegar as needed.

Here are some good combinations:

Basil garlic vinegar
4 tablespoons basil
3 garlic cloves, cut in 4
2 cups cider vinegar

Ginger coconut
1 tablespoon ginger root
1 cup coconut vinegar

Mixed herb
10 stalks chives
10 leaves tarragon
1 teaspoon lemon thyme leaves
6 leaves oregano
1½ cups cider vinegar

Orange or lemon mint vinegar
2 x 2½cm (1 in) strips orange or lemon rind (no pith)
12 peppermint or apple mint leaves
2 cups white wine vinegar

Raspberry vinegar		
Raspberries	*500g (1lb)*	Mash, put in a large jar.
Honey	*2 tablespoons*	Mix in well.
White wine vinegar	*2 cups*	Heat, pour over, cover and stand for two days. Strain through double cheesecloth and then through a coffee filter. Bottle.

Gourmet vinegar		
White wine vinegar	*3 cups*	Heat, don't boil.
Horseradish root, grated	*1 tablespoon*	
Spring onions, finely chopped	*2*	Mix all in jar, pour vinegar over,
Winter savory, basil, of each	*1 teaspoon*	cover. Leave one week.
Marjoram, thyme, of each	*1 teaspoon*	Strain well.
Tarragon	*2 teaspoons*	Bottle.
Lemon, rind and juice of	*1*	

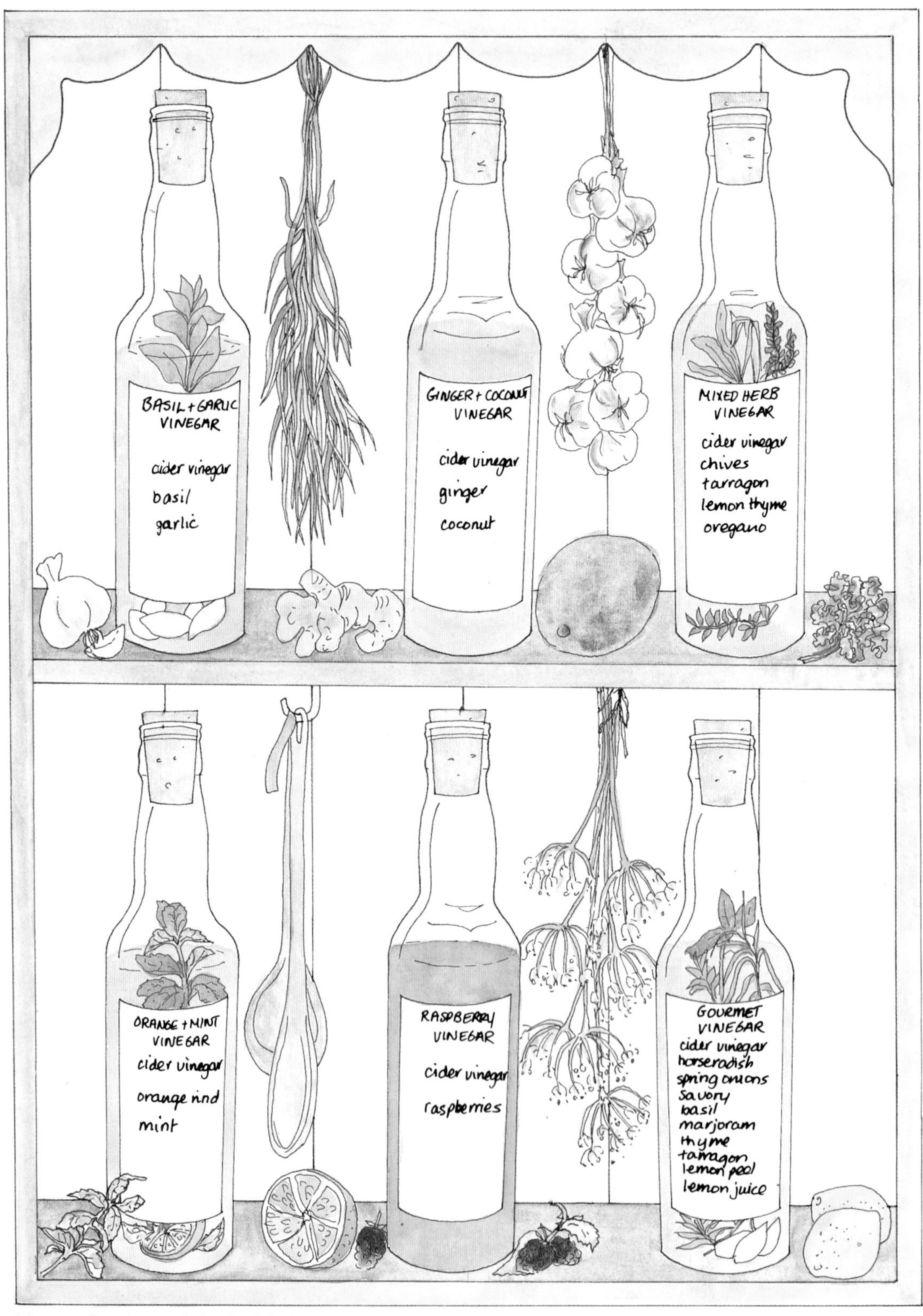

Vinegar bottles with herbs labelled

Garlic or Herb Oils

These take only minutes to prepare, taste delicious and will save you a lot of time if you use garlic often.

Three-quarters fill a reasonably wide-necked bottle with gently warmed, best quality virgin olive oil. Into this put 3-8 cloves of garlic cut in half. The number of cloves depends on the size of your bottle and how strong you want the oil to be. The oil will be ready to use the next day but will become stronger as the days pass. Keep topping up the bottle as needed. After about four weeks I remove the cloves and add fresh ones. This method can also be used for herbs such as basil, tarragon and oregano and the oil used for dressing or for cooking. Crush the herbs *lightly* before adding to the oil.

Sundries

To preserve angelica stem (an old recipe)

I have tried lots of recipes and find this to be the best — it's a bit of a bother but worth it in the end.

Cut young angelica stems into 5 cm (2 in) lengths and boil until tender. Remove from the water and peel. Return to the water and simmer gently until very green. Drain and cool, then weigh. Allow an equal amount of sugar to angelica. Sprinkle the sugar over the stems, leave for 2-3 days. Bring to the boil, simmer for 10 minutes, drain, spread in a cool oven to dry.

Frosted leaves and flowers

This method can be used for any leaves or flowers you would like to use as garnishes. They will store for a short time between layers of greaseproof paper in an airtight tin.

Beat an egg white with a pinch of salt. Don't overbeat, it should be just broken down. Brush (don't dip) the leaves and flowers very lightly with the egg white, using a fairly fine paint brush. Sprinkle with caster sugar and place on greaseproof paper. Set your oven to its lowest heat and dry the herbs on the bottom shelf, with the door open, for 20-30 minutes.

Herb croutons

These are great in salads, soups and stews. Make a pile and store them in an airtight container. They will keep for a month or two.

Cut cubes of bread from an unsliced wholemeal loaf. Drizzle with garlic oil (see p243). Chop a heap of mixed herbs and mix through the bread cubes. Add salt and pepper if you like. Put in a single layer on baking trays and bake in a medium oven (180°C/350°F) until very crunchy. Children will enjoy them as munchies.

Preserved ginger root

Ginger root, fresh	*1kg (2lb)*	Wash, scrape and cut into ½cm (¼ in) cubes. Cover with water in a non-aluminium pan. Bring to the boil and simmer for 10 minutes. Drain.
Soda bicarbonate	*1 rounded teaspoon*	Put in the pan with the ginger, cover with water, boil for 20 minutes. Drain. Re-boil the ginger until it is tender, about 30-45 minutes.
White sugar **Water**	*2 cups* *1 cup*	Stir in a pan over a low heat until the sugar dissolves. Cook gently for 5 minutes. Add the ginger, cover, simmer for 10 minutes. Pour into a dish, cover and leave for 2-3 days. Strain, return syrup to the pan.
White sugar	*1 cup*	Add to the syrup, stir over low heat until dissolved, cook gently for 5 minutes. Pour over ginger, leave for 24 hours. Strain.
White sugar	*1 cup*	Add to the syrup and repeat previous stage.

Cheese and herb biscuits

Choose one or two herbs from the chart — I like basil and chives best.

Tasty cheese, grated **Flour, self-raising** **Butter, melted** **Herbs, finely chopped** **Salt and cayenne**	*4 tablespoons* *4 tablespoons* *4 tablespoons* *1-2 teaspoons* *a pinch*	Combine all and mix thoroughly. Roll into small balls.
Dessicated coconut, toasted		Roll the balls in the coconut, flatten slightly. Bake at 180°C (350°F) for 15-20 minutes.

Cottage cheese with herbs

You can add finely chopped capsicums (peppers), gherkins, spring onions or anything you like to this cheese. It's very easy to make but be *gentle* with it or it might be tough. Make in a non-aluminium pan.

Lemon juice or vinegar **Warm water**	*2 tablespoons* *2 tablespoons*	Mix together in a cup.

Skim or whole milk	*4 cups*	Heat to boiling point. Turn heat off. Drizzle the lemon mixture slowly into the milk, stirring very gently. Stop stirring and adding when the curds separate and the whey is yellowish and clear. Leave for 1 hour. With a slotted spoon gently lift the curds into a bowl.

Curds and whey separating

Herbs, very finely chopped	*1-2 tablespoons*	Fold gently into the cheese; add salt and black pepper to taste. Put into a cheesecloth-lined sieve/colander/anything with holes in. Leave to drain for 1-2 hours.

Savoury pikelets

Summer savory, chives and parsley go well in this recipe but you can choose any herbs you like. These pikelets are very tasty served with the cottage cheese recipe which follows.

Milk **Yoghurt** **Egg**	*½ cup* *½ cup* *1*	Put all in a blender, mix well. Stand for 5-10 minutes.
Flour, self-raising **Bicarbonate of soda** **Herbs, chopped finely** **Parmesan cheese, grated** **Paprika and salt**	*½ cup* *pinch* *1 tablespoon* *2 tablespoons* *pinch*	Add, blend to a thick cream adding more milk if needed. Cook tablespoonfuls in an oiled frypan or griddle till brown both sides and cooked through.

Herb stuffing for roast chicken

Parsley, chopped **Lemon thyme, chopped** **Lemon rind, grated** **Salt and pepper**	*2 tablespoons* *2 teaspoons* *1 teaspoon* *to taste*	Mix together. Leave for about 1 hour for flavours to mature.
Egg, beaten	*1*	Mix in.
Breadcrumbs, fresh, fine	*½ cup*	Add enough to make a soft but firm consistency.

Dried or Fresh Herb Mixtures

Herb 'salt'

Sesame seed, roast, ground	1½ cups
Celery tops, dried, ground	½ cup
Garlic, dried, ground	2 teaspoons
Dill seed, dried, ground	1 teaspoon
Parsley, dried, ground	4 cups
Oregano, dried, ground	2 teaspoons
Lemon thyme, dried, ground	2 teaspoons
Coriander, dried, ground	2 teaspoons
Paprika, ground	2 teaspoons

Mix well, pass through a fine sieve. Store most of the mix in the freezer. Keep out enough for table and cooking use. I add 10 parts of mild brewer's yeast flakes to this recipe to boost the vitamin B content. Some yeasts are very bitter but the 'Healtheries' brand which I use is really tasty.

Most of the herbs in the following combinations are either dried and crumbled (not powdered) or fresh. Add the combinations of herbs towards the end of cooking time. Add a small pinch and keep tasting until the flavour is to your liking. Don't overlook the fact that the flavours will intensify with time. If you intend to freeze the dish it's better to leave the addition of herbs until the reheating stage.

Fine herbs

Parsley	1 part
Chives	2 parts
Celery tops	½ part
Thyme	½ part

Omelettes

Parsley	3 parts
Chives	2 parts
Dill	1 part
Tarragon	1 part

Tomato dishes

Oregano	1 part
Basil	2 parts
Lemon thyme	½ part
Garlic	¼ part

Soups and stews

Parsley	1 part
Chives	1 part
Bay	½ part
Thyme	½ part
Lemon thyme	¼ part
Garlic	½ part

Roast chicken rub

Garlic	1 clove crushed
Thyme	½ teaspoon powdered
Salt	½ teaspoon
Pepper	to taste
Paprika	2 teaspoons
Tarragon	½ teaspoon, powdered
Oil	2 tablespoons

Mix. Rub into flesh. Stand 30 minutes before baking.

Meat casseroles/stews

Parsley	1 part
Chives	2 parts
Marjoram	1 part
Thyme	½ part
Celery tops	½ part
Garlic	½ part

Fish

Parsley	2 parts
Hyssop	½ part
Fennel	½ part
Oregano	¼ part
Lemon thyme	¼ part

General bouquet

Parsley	1 part
Chives	2 parts
Oregano	½ part
Tarragon	½ part
Thyme	½ part
Sage	½ part

Salads

Borage	2 parts
Chives	1 part
Dill	1 part
Mint	1 part
Lemon thyme	½ part

Poultry casseroles

Parsley	1 part
Chives	2 parts
Tarragon	½ part
Celery tops	1 part

Desserts

Lemon balm	1 part
Lemon thyme	½ part
Angelica leaf	½

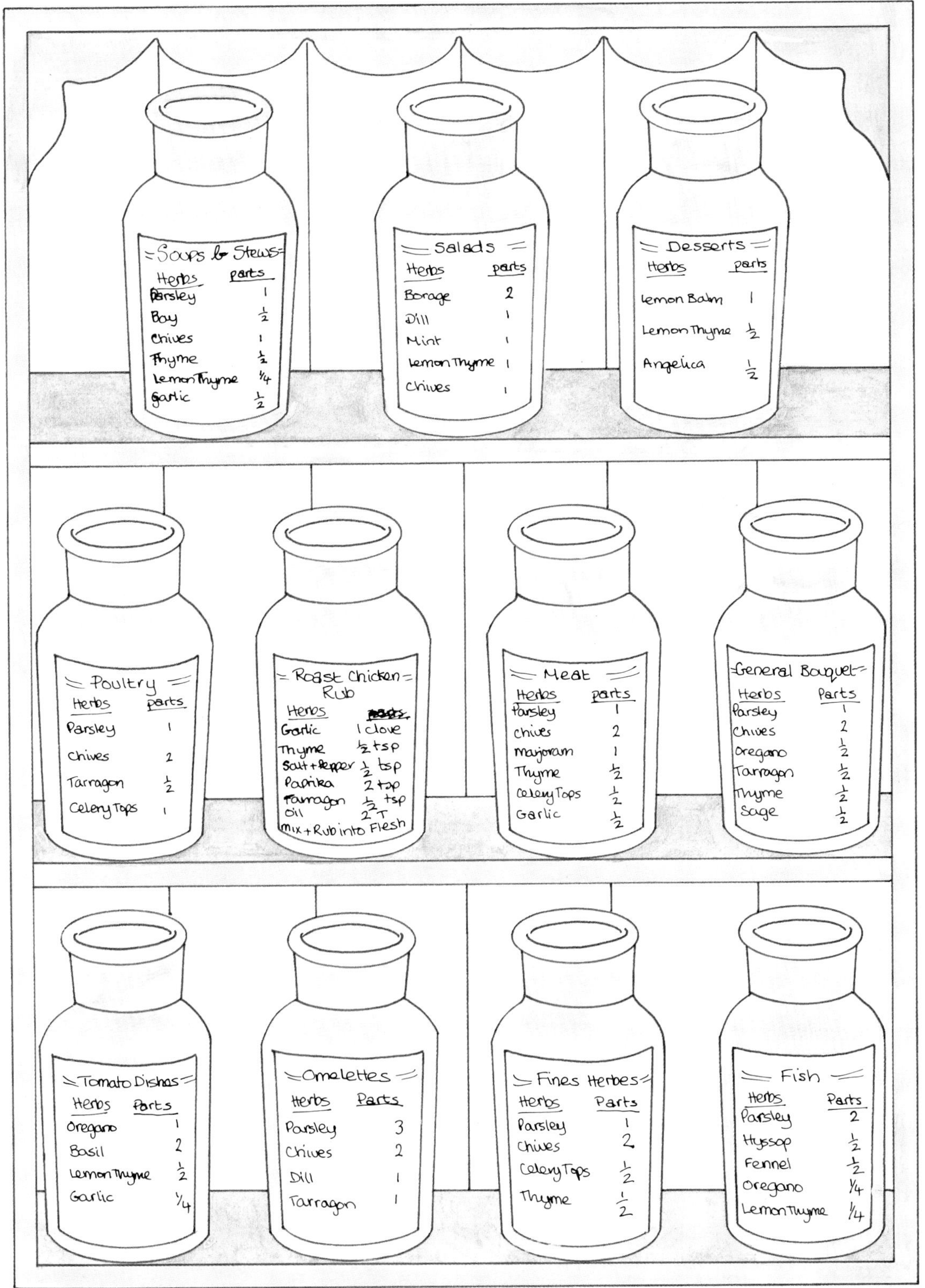

Jars with herb mixtures labelled

Herbal wines

It is possible to make delicious medicated wines which act as tonics, digestive aids, sedatives and breath sweeteners as well as tasting good. In fact, by using Chart 5, you can devise wines for many different complaints. Be adventurous!

If you want a really mellow wine then let it mature for a month or so after straining. Store in a cool, dark place. If you want your wine to last a long time, it's best to choose a full-bodied wine. For tonics I use a good Muscat as I find the flavour seems to blend well with herbs.

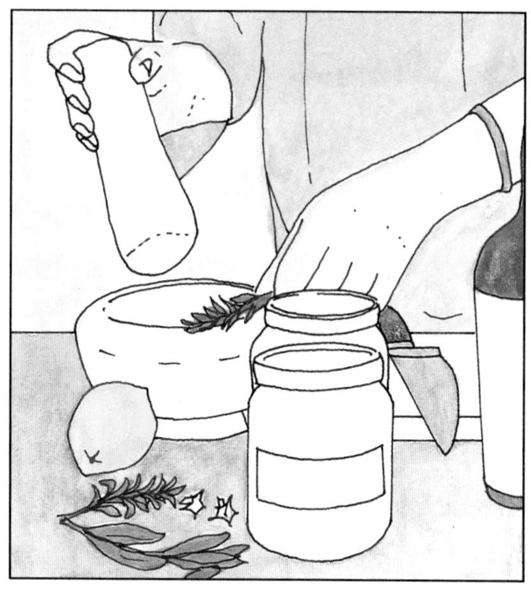

Bruising the herbs lightly using a mortar and pestle

Tonic wine

Bruise the herbs one at a time by putting them into a mortar and pounding gently two or three times with the pestle. The herbs shouldn't be crushed. All the herbs should be fresh if possible.

Muscat	*2 cups*	Pour the wine into a very clean jug.
Wormwood **Rosemary** **Thyme** **Sage** **Ginger root** **Cinnamon bark** **Cloves** **Lemon peel, pared thinly and sliced** **Aniseed**	*1 teaspoon* *1 teaspoon* *1 teaspoon* *1 teaspoon* *2 cm* *2 cm* *3 whole* *1 lemon* *2 teaspoons*	Put the herbs and spices in the bottle, top up with the wine. Cork and store in a cool, dark place for two weeks. Strain, filter and pour back into the bottle. Leave in a cool dark place for one month before use.

This wine is great any time you feel 'under the weather' or 'down in the mouth'! It is a good 'pick-me-up' after illness to stimulate the appetite, or can be drunk just because you like it.

Nerve calming and digestive wine

This simple, effective recipe has been around since the turn of the century. Sip a wineglassful after a stressful day, to calm you down.

Dry white wine	*1 bottle*	Pour into a clean jug.
Rosemary leaves, chopped **Cloves** **Honey** **Cinnamon stick**	*1 tablespoon* *4* *1 tablespoon* *2½cm (1 in)*	Put into the bottle, top up with the wine. Shake daily until the honey is dissolved. Strain well. Drink after one week.

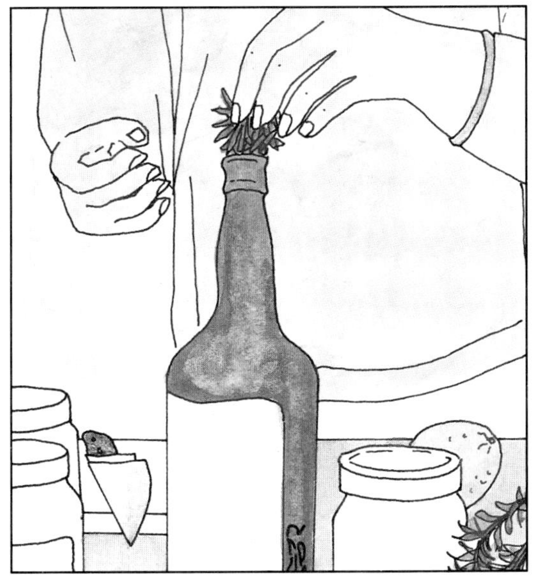

Putting the herbs into the wine bottle

Pouring the wine over the herbs in the bottle

Digestive liqueur

Caraway seed, crushed	*1 tablespoon*	Mix together and stand in a cool place for 3-4 weeks. Strain and filter. Stand 3 months in a cool, dark place before drinking.
Fennel seed, crushed	*1 tablespoon*	
Ginger root, crushed	*2cm (1 in)*	
Peppermint leaves, chopped	*1 tablespoon*	
Lemon peel, 5cm (2 in) strips	*2*	
Brandy	*2 cups*	
Honey syrup (see p249)	*½ cup*	

Mint liqueur

Peppermint leaves, bruised	*2 tablespoons*	Put all in a large jar. Shake daily for 2 weeks. Strain and filter
Spearmint leaves, bruised	*2 tablespoons*	
Orange peel, 5cm (2 in) strips	*4*	
Lemon peel 5cm (2 in) strips	*4*	
Brandy	*2½ cups*	
Honey syrup (see p249)	*½ cup*	Add, bottle, store in a dark, cool place for 2-3 months.

Honey syrup

Mix together equal quantities of water and honey. Bring slowly to the boil. Remove from the heat and stir until the honey is dissolved; cool.

Honey syrup is suitable for adding to any drink which has a spirit base such as whisky, brandy or vodka. If you add honey syrup, then the 'liqueur' needs to be matured for a further 2-3 months at room temperature.

Booklist

This is by no means a comprehensive list but it does include some of the books which have given me pleasure and information and whose authors I trust.

Bach E. *The Twelve Healers.* Daniel and Co Ltd 1964

Bem R. *Everyone's Guide to Home Composting.* Van Nostrand Reinhold

Cacton C. *The Incredible Heap.* Pelham 1982

Christopher, Dr J. *School of Natural Healing.* BiWorld 1976

Davies J. *Garden of Miracles.* Muller

Grieve M. *A Modern Herbal.* Hafner Publishing 1959

Hemphill R. *Herbs for all Seasons.* Angus and Robertson 1972

Hylton W.H. *The Rodale Herb Book.* Rodale Press Book 1974

Levy J. de Bairacli. *The Illustrated Herbal Handbook.* Faber 1974

Leyel, Mrs C.F. *The Truth About Herbs.* Culpeper Press 1954

Mervyn L. *The Dictionary of Minerals.* Lothian 1985

Mervyn L. *The Dictionary of Vitamins.* Lothian 1984

Mills S. *The Dictionary of Modern Herbalism.* Lothian 1985

Mindell E. *The Vitamin Bible.* Arlington Books 1979

Philbrick H. & Greg R. *Companion Plants.* Stuart and Watkins 1967

Rohde E.S. *A Garden of Herbs.* Medici Society, London

Rose J. *The Herbal Body Book.* Grosset and Dunlap 1976

Tisserand R. *Aromatherapy.* Mayflower, Granada Publishing 1979

Valnet, Dr. J. *The Practice of Aromatherapy.* C.W. Daniel Co Ltd 1980

Wren R. *Potter's New Cyclopaedia.* Harper Colophon Books 1972

INDEX OF RECIPES

General Index

Italic numerals refer to an illustration. See Index of Recipes for names of individual recipes.